Celebrating

Stories of Humor & Humanity in Everyday Life

the Underdog

Celebrating

Stories of Humor & Humanity in Everyday Life

the Underdog

Tom Sieg

compiled by Elva Sieg

Celebrating the Underdog by Tom Sieg (compiled by Elva Sieg)

First Edition, August 2002.

Grateful acknowledgment is made to the following for permission to reprint previously published material:

Tom Sieg's columns are copyrighted by the *Winston-Salem Journal* and are used with its permission. Copyright ©2002.

Photographs from the *Winston-Salem Journal* and *The Sentinel* (formerly named) are copyrighted by the *Winston-Salem Journal* and are used with its permission. Copyright ©2002.

Photographs by Hugh Morton, owner and president of Grandfather Mountain in North Carolina, are copyrighted by Hugh Morton and are used with his permission. Copyright ©2002.

Cover photo of turtle hatchling by Frans Lanting/Minden Pictures.

Printed in China.

Book design by Whitline Ink Incorporated   bookdesign@yadtel.net

To schedule book events, contact:
Elva Sieg—311 Salisbury Street, #30, Kernersville, NC 27284

To order additional copies, check your local bookstore or contact:

Carolina Avenue ™   114 Carolina Avenue South, Box 668
PRESS   Boonville, North Carolina 27011

Applied for Library of Congress Cataloging-in-Publication Data
ISBN 0-9718231-0-3

Acknowledgments

Many thanks to journalists R.C. Smith of Jamestown, N.C., and Larry Queen of Greensboro, N.C., for their hard work, time, advice and support. Hugh Morton, owner of Grandfather Mountain, and Jon Witherspoon, publisher of the *Winston-Salem Journal,* helped enormously. Special thanks to Ed Friedenberg, my family and friends for their support; to the staff of the Winston-Salem Public Library, especially those in the North Carolina Room, for their patience and helpfulness, and to Virginia Hauswald, *Winston-Salem Journal* news library manager, and Craig Rhyne, library staff member, for their time and effort.

Photographs owned by the *Winston-Salem Journal* that are included in this book were taken by: Allen Aycock, Allie Brown, Charlie Buchanan, David Rolfe, Christine Rucker, Cookie Snyder and Tom Sieg.

In his newspaper retirement column, Jan. 5, 1992, Tom made this dedication for all his work:

"To those kind folk who allowed me to enter their lives for so many years, and to share their stories with readers...[and to] the readers themselves, so many of whom [were] so supportive for so long."

Photographs

Table of Contents

Preface

My late husband, Tom Sieg, a writer of humanity above all else, summed up his work:

"The stories I have written…are of, for and about people who live and breathe and work and loaf and love and grieve and exult and despair, as we all do; and they were written in the hope that readers could laugh or cry or smile or scowl along with the writer or his subjects—and sympathize, maybe even really *share* in some of the human experiences…"

In his newspaper retirement column, Jan. 5, 1992, Tom made a dedication for all his work: "To those kind folk who allowed me to enter their lives for so many years, and to share their stories with readers…[and to] the readers themselves, so many of whom [were] so supportive for so long."

That was my husband Tom.

Browsing through my late husband's columns and features has been sad, amusing and informative. I reminisced over tales of our mountain travels, laughed about the antics of the news staff and found answers to questions that had plagued me after my husband died. I found out where my father-in-law's boyhood home was located; the dates when my husband graduated from high school, entered the Air Force and left the military; and even the brand of coffee he had been buying as the family's major food purchaser. Early in our marriage he had become the main shopper because I didn't know how to drive. He became quite skilled at ferreting out the best bargains and, I think, enjoyed the challenge.

His columns have been labeled according to the newspaper in which they ran. For the epilogues, I have either interviewed the appropriate persons or used *Journal* or *Sentinel* clippings.

Near the end of his career, Tom wrote:

"I am, in short, not very important, although I sometimes write about important things. The reader is important; he must be informed, but if he wants and needs more than information alone, if he needs some humanity or humor toward the end of his day, why not give it to him?"

Foreword

We will always be indebted to the late Grover Robbins Jr., for founding the Land of Oz at Beech Mountain, and for bringing the all-star cast of creative people that included Tom Sieg to the mountains to make sure the enterprise thrived. Of course, Tom Sieg already knew about the mountains, but being here full-time, while he reaped tons of favorable press for Oz, gave him an even keener insight into the charm of the mountain area and its people. Tom Sieg never forgot the mountains even after he left Oz, and some of his marvelous human interest tales of the mountains cropped up in his columns for *The Sentinel* and the *Winston-Salem Journal.*

Tom Sieg's loving wife Elva has done us all a great favor by collecting in this book many of Tom's most interesting, most humorous columns. Because these columns cover a vast variety of subject matter, it is hard to say that they follow a theme or pattern, except that all of them are extremely well written. The title chosen for the book, *Celebrating the Underdog*, does come close to revealing what Tom Sieg was about. Tom was invariably for the underdog, always ready to do what he could to call attention to struggles with adversity, ever eager to correct wrongs that should be righted. No one but The Good Lord will be likely to know the magnitude of Tom Sieg's beneficial influence in assuring that right prevailed over wrong. Tom did not crow about the good deeds he did.

My closest working relationship with Tom Sieg came when Tom wrote the script, and I was executive producer, for the PBS hour-long coast-to-coast special, titled "The Search for Clean Air." The highly respected newsman Walter Cronkite narrated the program, and he was well pleased, as was I, with the job Tom Sieg did writing the script. The program won the CINE Golden Eagle Award, and thus became part of the United States entry in foreign film festivals. Today it is quite fashionable to be concerned with the damage air pollution is doing to forests, streams, agriculture and human health. It was entirely different in the early 1990s, and most government and business leaders would not give the time of day to the worries spotlighted by "The Search for Clean Air" when it was broadcast for the first time. As best we know, nobody since has done a more comprehensive program on the subject, and schools and universities still use it extensively as a teaching tool. Tom Sieg has died, but his words in a widespread manner are living on.

–Hugh Morton, owner of Grandfather Mountain

Introduction

When I first met Tom Sieg in the 1970s, he was the stereotypical newspaperman—tough and hard-nosed, driven to find stories anywhere they were hiding. And he liked to have a good time—a good time that always seemed to find him.

But more than a reporter, an editor or a columnist or *bon vivant,* Tom was a people person. He loved to observe people through their trials and their triumphs, their pride and their prejudice, the good and the bad, and then he told their stories with objectivity, sensitivity and a writing style that brought the reader into the story.

Along the way, life had taught Tom many lessons. He grew up in Minnesota during the Depression in a loving family where at times there was a struggle to put food on the table. He joined the Air Force after high school, and then went on to the University of Missouri for a degree in journalism. He worked for awhile at newspapers in Charlotte and then did public-relations work at the Land of Oz, an amusement park in the North Carolina mountains. He came to the *Winston-Salem Journal* and *Sentinel* in 1972 and retired in 1991 (officially) when he and many others were offered "early buyouts."

Retirement left Tom free to do other things, and as usual he tackled them with gusto. He teamed up with Hugh Morton and others to do an award-winning public broadcast documentary on clean air; he did volunteer work with youth groups and with older adults. He worked on a never-published book with a psychologist friend, and he took some time to relax and enjoy life a little…

Then cancer struck Tom in 1995, and he began a fight that sapped his strength, claiming his life on Sept. 30, 1996.

The columns that you'll find in this book reflect Tom's love of life. He writes of the experiences of people, great and small. You'll notice his superb use of the English language, his disdain of cliches, his dry wit and his passion for people, a passion that will make the characters and events that Tom describes a part of your life, too. Enjoy.

–Jon Witherspoon
President and Publisher, Winston-Salem Journal

In Memoriam
Tom Sieg 1933–1996

The Loving Parent Never Really Leaves

Dear Nick:

Your mom, Kathy, showed me your letter to Santa, telling him that you lost your father Nov. 26.

In the letter, you say that your only Christmas wish is for Santa to "please ask Jesus to ask my father to write me a letter."

I know it's hard for you to understand why, but that can't be done. If you were 30 years old instead of 10, it would still be difficult to understand. Losing someone we love deeply leaves any of us, at any age, feeling lost, cheated, even fearful—especially at a time like Christmas.

Because your mother knew you felt that way, and knew how much you adored your father and how much you wanted that letter from him, she considered writing the letter herself and pretending it was from your father.

In a way, that wouldn't have been difficult for her to do. She had talked with your father about some of the things that he had intended to say in a tape recording he planned to leave behind for you. He would have said them, too, except that his disease moved so fast at the end that it didn't give him time.

Your mom showed me the letter that she had in mind.

The words in it rang true.

Because nobody knows better what your father wanted to say, and because your father has no other way of saying it to you, the *Journal* offered to publish the letter—for you, and for all the others like you who have suffered the painful loss of a loved one in recent months.

This is your letter from your dad, Bennie, as written for him by your mom:

My dear son:

I wanted to let you know I am fine.

I am not alone. You are always with me, for you would not have been born without me, and I would not have known true love, joy and happiness without you.

These feelings of love will never die in me, nor will they in you. So, you see, you will never be without me.

Don't worry for me. Be a child when you are young. Don't grow up too fast. Choose the right path through adulthood....Tell your children about me. Show them the love I gave to you.

Listen to your mother, for she loves you as much as I do....

Talk to Jesus often. I will be listening. And always celebrate Christmas, for without the birth of Jesus I would not be safe. My son, I love you. Have a merry Christmas.

As someone who has been a son and lost a father, and as a father who will one day leave his own son and daughter behind, I see in the letter some of the kinds of things every loving parent wishes for his or her children.

I see something else, too, something that will likely be important to you, Nick, as your burden of grief begins to lighten.

Your dad was trying to tell you that a loving parent never truly leaves you. That's true.

You're a lot like your dad already, I'm told. Chances are, in later years, you'll be amused when you look at traits within yourself and recognize your father. And you'll think loving thoughts as you recognize those traits.

In the end, that's as much as any loving parent ever hopes for.

It's as close to immortality as any of us can ever come on earth—and it's enough.

(12/25/89 WSJ)

CHAPTER 1

God's Country (The Mountains)

Returning to the mountains always refreshed Tom Sieg, physically and mentally. Sometimes our family (including our two children, our parents, siblings and various assorted relatives) was fortunate enough to accompany him. One of our favorite pastimes was guiding friends from other states through the wonders of the mountains in all seasons. We all delighted in the fine scenery, friendly folk and occasional glimpses of blossoms or wildlife. For 35 years, we drove many times to Beech Mountain, Grandfather Mountain, Linville Falls and the Blue Ridge Parkway (north and south). We might stop awhile, perhaps at Mount Mitchell for a short hike or venture on to the Great Smoky Mountains National Park. Our happiest times were spent in the mountains.

During Sieg's journalism career, he traveled through the Appalachians from Murphy to Lansing and on into Virginia on many assignments.

Tom and Elva Sieg in 1988. –RICHARD SIEG

As Sieg wrote: "When a story needs to be done in the mountains, it's very easy for an editor to find volunteers.

"It's partly because of the beauty of the area, the freedom of getting away.

"Mostly, though, it's because of the people.

"Pause, during your hectic day, to consider this: Four consecutive times when I either needed help finding my way around those mountains or couldn't drive because of road conditions, I have ended up with a volunteer chauffeur."

The journey begins…

Rhododendron beautify North Carolina mountainsides in June. –HUGH MORTON

Senses Reel in God's Country

Gib Church was wielding the barbecue-sauce mop on the "half a 700-pound cow" that sat over the coals in the open pit.

"Get yourself a piece of that meat," said Roscoe Wingler, handing me a razor-sharp hunting knife.

"It ain't done yet," said Herb Garner. "Cut into one o' them smaller pieces and see what you can get."

The beef had been on only eight hours, but "done" or not didn't matter. The double assault on the senses of sight and smell had completed the seduction.

It was a delicious beginning, enhanced by a kind of isolation that is all but impossible to find within 65 miles of Winston-Salem unless you're a hardy hiker, which I am not.

Across from and above us was a 100-foot waterfall. Over beside the "campground" was a narrow dirt road whose challenges have kept the area all but undiscovered except by the local folk of Wilkes County.

The 100 or so who were there had crossed Reddies River four times without benefit of bridges, leaving the last dwelling a couple of miles behind and the next one several times that far ahead.

"Today, you're going up into God's country," Judena Bulis had said as we prepared to hop into Bud Moore's wagon for the ride up.

She was right.

If anything, the atmosphere was even easier and more relaxed than on the Blue Ridge Wagon Train, where I had met most of these people.

And it became clearer, perhaps, why almost-total relaxation is possible when you are with such people. They, or most of them, are truly able to do what the rest of us only talk about: Live one day at a time, concentrating on the moment's pleasures, keeping yesterday's and tomorrow's problems in the past and future.

On the way up, I enrolled in the Bud Moore School of Wagon Driving.

Bud's horse, Goldy, is almost as good as its name except for the habits of biting and kicking other horses. It is necessary, therefore, to keep Goldy positioned so that she can do neither.

I had already emphatically declined another offer to drive a wagon, not knowing that Bud had developed a greatly simplified method of teaching.

"Do you know how to drive one of these?" he asked as we made our way up the mountain road.

"No," I said.

"Aw, you can do it," he said, handing me the reins. Then he jumped out and got in another wagon.

From the start, there was concern about our floorless tent.

"If I slept in something like that," said one woman, "I'd be sleeping with snakes."

Snake talk is common on such outings, and usually meaningless. I paid no heed.

I did not know, of course, that the weekend traffic up and down the mountain would leave a timber rattler and a copperhead dead in the road.

Does anybody accept trade-ins on tents?

Herb Garner got the tall tales going with one he swears is the truth.

Experienced wagon-trainer Bud Moore knows to rest when he gets a chance. –CHARLIE BUCHANAN

Seems Herb—who is the chef for many backwoods outings—had been up about two days straight and decided to stay in camp when the others in a group of bear hunters left with a guide for what was to be a futile day's effort.

Some of the dogs that were around camp later took off running. Herb followed for a short distance and found that the dogs had treed a bear.

"I had no choice," he said, "but to shoot that bear out of the tree."

Oddly enough, it turned out that a lot of other people sitting around the fire had either had similar experiences or knew of folks who had.

After the truly fine feast, the group broke up into knots, some wandering, others sitting at their campsites talking to those who wandered in and out.

As usual, there was some telling of unprintable jokes—and a whole lot of outrageous ribbing.

At one point, Rob Grimes allowed as how a friend who was acting a bit of the fool gets "a day older and a week dumber every day."

And Rob Miller—whose horse had seemed intent on destroying wagon and driver during the Blue Ridge Wagon Train and showed again over the weekend that service to mankind isn't his bag—wandered around talking about the horse, flirting with the girls and insulting the men.

"You any kin to Roscoe Wingler?" Rob asked Wade Wingler.

"Wouldn't be surprised," said Wade.

"Both of you ought to be ashamed," said Rob.

So it went, on through early-morning bedtime and again during break-fast and preparations for the ride back down the mountain.

In fact, it didn't end. It is to be continued this weekend at Triplette. Much of the cast will be the same, except that one of the stars—barbecued beef—will be replaced by real country ham.

No wonder wagon-training is habit-forming.   *(8/30/77 The Sentinel)*

Ruby Days
Oz Magic Gone

When young David Nelson called from Appalachian State University to tell me that he was producing a videotape on the old Land of Oz, I was pleased.

"We're going to interview Jack Pentes, the designer," Nelson said. "And we want to interview you."

No problem. Oz, atop Beech Mountain at Banner Elk, occupies a special niche in my memory. I was its public-relations man in 1970, when it opened late and incomplete and proceeded to break Tweetsie Railroad's state record for attendance at a tourist attraction.

It was magic, pure and simple and unsullied.

A video on Oz? Sure.

"Just one thing," I said. "There's a man who works here in Winston-Salem—Ernie Rhymer, at Quality Oil. You need to talk to him. He was general manager at Oz. He and Pentes are the key characters."

Thus, I set into motion my own undoing as a video star. In the end, the video, which arrived in the mail recently, featured Rhymer, Pentes—and no Sieg.

No matter. It brought three old friends together and produced a telling video for the Appalachian Cultural Museum at Appalachian State University in Boone.

On screen, Dorothy, the Cowardly Lion, the Tin Man and the Scarecrow cavort through Oz to Emerald City as the four-octave presence of the late Mary Mayo commands the mountaintop.

"The sky is a blue-and-white marble today, and a tangerine sun wants to stay out and play…Would you believe every day looks this way, in the Wonderful Land of Oz?"[1]

It was a dynamite beginning in 1970; it still is.

As the Oz scenes fade, Dr. Charles Watkins, the museum's director, talks about the days when the park was created. The first push was to create resort homesites in mountain areas where, for too long, young people had to move away to find good jobs.

With the homesites on Beech Mountain, which were being developed by the late Grover Robbins and his Carolina Caribbean Corp., came ski slopes. Those helped provide jobs during the winter.

Watkins and the scenes of Oz fade out and Pentes, the Charlotte design genius, speaks about his first trip to the mountain with Robbins. Robbins wanted to round out the work year, to create year-round jobs, Pentes says. "He wanted to know…if there was anything that could be done there to provide summer employment without destroying the top of the mountain."

The scenes of Oz, of Auntie Em's house and Munchkinland and the witch's castle and Emerald City, are interspersed with the principals themselves as the video switches from Pentes to Watkins to Rhymer, who adds: "Anything that Grover put his name on, he wanted it to be first class…something that someone would remember."

People remember Oz. They remember how it captivated them and their children and sent their imaginations soaring above the 5,506-foot mountaintop.

Pentes could see it almost from the moment he saw the mountaintop: "I was just absolutely amazed at the beauty…The trees reminded me of the trees in a film I had seen when I was nine years old about the Wizard of Oz.

"I just knew that that piece of magic that had affected me so deeply would visit my life again."

It did. Pentes looked out through the eyes of imagination at Munchkinland, the Scarecrow's and Tin Man's houses, the lion's den—a natural cave—as he walked among the twisted, wind-battered beech trees, some with limbs twisted around themselves as if in embrace.

Dorothy and her companions follow the Yellow Brick Road in the Land of Oz. –HUGH MORTON

15

In time, after Grover Robbins died and the parent company incurred financial woes, Oz was overcommercialized, its revenues diverted to other operations. But while the magic was allowed to live…

"There really was a Yellow Brick Road that you could walk on," says Pentes. "You really did see those trees with the faces on them. You met the Tin Man and the Scarecrow and the lion. You actually *saw* the Wicked Witch. You *went* to Emerald City…It was an adventure."

Now, "Over the Rainbow" rings out, over the mountaintop and through the television sound system, reminding again of the brief time when pure magic lived on the mountaintop.

That was before Oz became just another tourist attraction.

"There was a sense of loss," Pentes says of the cheapening of Oz.

"It started off as a magical kind of undertaking—a place where designers and decorators and actors and dancers came together to produce something that was unique."

But it did become just another attraction, and one that, in its perch atop a mile-high mountain, was difficult to reach. It faltered and died, and with that, something in Pentes died, too:

"It was the love of my life. I will never get over it. And [it was] the sadness of my life, that it's not there anymore.

"I've learned to live with that, I guess through being grateful for the joy that it did create in the time that it was here."

For people who remember Oz, and for some who don't, the video is well worth seeing.

(6/21/91 WSJ)

The Appalachian Cultural Museum at Appalachian State University is located on University Hall Drive, just off U.S. 321, Blowing Rock Road in Boone, N.C. Besides Land of Oz memorabilia, it also includes exhibits of looms, spinning wheels, tools from early mountain life, crafts, mountain music, mountain Jack tales, American Indian artifacts, fossils, the skiing industry, the Blue Ridge Parkway and Winston-Cup racing.

Go to the Mountain and Hang Loose

GRANDFATHER MOUNTAIN—If you come to this big two-headed mountain that soars to almost 6,000 feet near the town of Linville, expect the unexpected.

That way, you will seldom be disappointed.

Most places you go, for example, you expect sooner or later to see someone out walking his dog. That's too mundane for people like Hugh Morton, the owner of the mountain.

This Sunday, Morton had John McNeely, a young hang-glider from Connecticut, out flying his pet red-tailed hawk.

McNeely and the hawk took off from the rocks above the mile-high swinging bridge and were partners in flight until the final descent to the clubhouse in the valley below.

All the while, because the mountain belongs to a quiet but consummate promoter, the cameras of ABC television were whirring, preserving the occasion for a July "Good Morning America" segment. (NBC had already done its filming, for its July 5 "Prime Time Saturday.")

And much of the while, McNeely was talking to his bird.

"They had me fixed up with a microphone and everything," the young man said, showing us where the mike had been sewn into his jacket.

Then he introduced members of our group to his bird.

I recalled the time I brought a group of very important visitors to Grandfather Mountain as part of the routine I followed when such personages needed impressing.

Coming down the mountain, we got stopped in a line of traffic. Suddenly there was a bear—or at least a bear's head—in the car with us.

As my friends trembled, shouted and asked the Lord's forgiveness, I explained that it was only Mildred, who was perfectly tame. For some reason, however, they continued to cower as I coaxed, cajoled, beat on and pushed and pulled the bear until she got down and I was able to close the window.

When we got a bit farther down the road, we rounded a curve, and there was Morton, holding a session for photographers. With him was Mildred. The real Mildred.

Aside from the young man and his bird, and the fact that there was practically no wind on the mountaintop, there was nothing terribly unusual happening Sunday.

Oh, Morton offered to let us meet Mildred up close and personal, as they say, but it was time for the hang-gliding, and that was mostly what my friend, Charlie Brown, had come to see.

A cougar, in an animal habitat, surveys its mountain domain. –HUGH MORTON

Later, we went down to the animal habitat, to see the bears and the deer and the cougar, which turned out to be the biggest, fattest, laziest cat I have seen in some time.

"I wouldn't even have seen him," said Charlie, "if he hadn't moved his eye."

We talked to the thing like a tabby, trying to coax some movement from him besides the occasional yawning and stretching. But it did no good, and my wife inquired why the cougar would be so lazy.

"Because he's a cat," I said.

"I expected a wild animal, not a house cat," she said.

Mildred watches over her cub on Grandfather Mountain. –HUGH MORTON

John McNeely and his pet red-tailed hawk try out the winds on Grandfather Mountain. –HUGH MORTON

Finally, we left, having seen and done what we came to the mountain for. And later, of course, the cougar got up, gave himself a running start, cleared a 10-foot wall in a single leap, picked out his dinner and quickly dispatched one of his neighbors to deer heaven.

We should have stayed.

I should have known that the mountain had not finished the act it often puts on for me when I'm there.

(6/3/80 The Sentinel)

Resisting Change in a Special Place

LINVILLE FALLS—A sign along the Blue Ridge Parkway tells travelers that this community exists, but relatively few venture off the scenic road to learn more.

To them, Linville Falls is just that—a scenic waterfall to be reached in a short walk from a National Park Service visitor center. Then it's time to motor on, north to Grandfather Mountain or south toward Asheville by way of Mount Mitchell and Craggy Gardens, with its blazing rhododendron.

They're missing a lot.

For one thing, they won't see Wiseman's View.

If you don't know about that view, you might want to stop along the dirt road above both falls and village. There, in a rustic Forest Service cabin, you may be greeted by Elizabeth Runyon, who is employed under the Older Americans program.

She may say, as she did to tourists one recent day, "Have you been to Wiseman's View yet?"

And then, if the answer is no, "Forget the falls. You'll have to come back on the same road (past the falls) anyway."

On a clear day, it's good advice, although the road is—well, call it exciting. The Wiseman's overlook juts over Linville Gorge, the most rugged American wilderness east of the Rockies, exposing a panoramic view that is truly both breathtaking and unique. And you *can* stop later at the parking area on the edge of the town, and walk as little as four-tenths of a mile to the falls.

Then, if you choose, you can turn right and head out for N.C. 181 to head north for Boone or south for Morganton. Or you can turn left and look over the peaceful village. Operators of the charming restaurants and motels, which are rather informally run, would appreciate that.

Here, the church is in a little-red-schoolhouse kind of building; a restaurant and other buildings are built of native rock; the impressive array of flowers includes rhododendron and azaleas flaming together; and you might get lucky and learn some history from older natives.

The only hitch is that the natives may have mixed feelings about seeing you.

Albert Dean Franklin, the town's postmaster, said: "We don't want it to become *too* commercial. I'm just so tickled that the Park Service got the falls so that can't be commercial."

Franklin is a sprightly, energetic man who behaves like the 39-year-old he laughingly claims to be. He talks as if the acquisition of the falls property occurred yesterday—it was 35 years ago, actually—because he comes from the area's oldest stock and takes a historical view.

"My great-great granddaddy was the first settler," Franklin said during a chat in the tiny stone building that is his post office. "He was Samuel Franklin. Samuel's daddy, John, got a grant because of his service in the Revolutionary War.

"I live in the same house I was born in....It [the property] never belonged to anybody but us. My daddy gave it to my sister, and I mortgaged everything and my wife and I bought it from my sister in 1961.

"It's never going to be out of my family in my lifetime—and I hope in my son's."

The old Franklin homeplace, just around the corner off U.S. 221, is a lovely white-frame house in a farm setting where, like so many other people in Avery County, Franklin grows Christmas trees.

Inside, the home has aged gracefully, its hardwoods and old furnishings lending a serenity that matches its surroundings. There, Franklin's wife, Emma, was using modern technology to help her preserve the past that fascinates her.

She had just plugged in a brand-new computer, which will ease her work in recording the history of the family and the area that she has already shared with so many people—in the *Avery Journal*, which features her weekly column, and elsewhere.

Mrs. Franklin is a preservationist, well-known for her work with the park service and others. Like her husband, she welcomes well-meaning visitors but worries about overdevelopment. "Surely you've heard of 'our' condominium," she said. "A 10-story concrete matchbox [on Little Sugar Mountain]— a monument to the death of the mountains!

"The kind of people that bother us is the kind that come up here and build a cheap house and sell it, and then they build another cheap house... cheap and gaudy."

Some of the history Mrs. Franklin has written says much about why she and others are skittish about outsiders. After the Civil War, David Franklin bought the falls property for $31.50 in back taxes and then traded it for a suit of clothes because it was "not suitable for farming."

Then came three hotels and the Morganton Development Co., with an early idea that has never died in the mountains: Perch a model white-frame home over the falls and use it as an office to sell land for similar second homes. The only ingredient missing was the word "chalet." Fortunately, the development company went broke in 1897.

Enter Niagara Falls Light & Power Co., out of New York. "They were going to dam up the gorge in seven different places," Mrs. Franklin said.

Fortunately, the man in charge of what then passed for a feasibility study, one Frank Bicknell, fell in love with a local girl and married her, and they moved into the house overlooking the falls and became permanent residents.

Linville Falls beckons to hikers, photographers and other nature enthusiasts. —HUGH MORTON

He apparently recommended against the idea, and the land, having been shown to be too poor for farming and too risky for development, passed through several owners before John D. Rockefeller Jr. bought it and donated it as park land in 1952.

Nowadays, Mrs. Franklin said, most of the people who live in and around the town itself care about the land and their neighbors. She doesn't foresee any serious—or even seriously gaudy—threat to the village.

"I honestly think Linville Falls will stay pretty much the same," she said. "Basically, the people that build here are in tune with the mountains."

Her husband hopes she's right.

"I hope Linville Falls is the same the next time you come," he said. "I hope it hasn't changed a bit!"

(6/14/87 WSJ)

Hello in There...

BOONE—"There's a story about one of these old farmers way back in the boonies during the worst of this weather (in 1960) when they were dropping supplies to farmers.

"There was a 20- to 30-foot snowdrift between him and civilization.

"He hadn't been heard from in a week or 10 days, and they got worried. They hacked a trail in through to his cabin, and the snow was level with the roof of his house.

"They were looking down the chimney, and they yelled down the chimney, 'Hello in there, this is the Red Cross. Is anybody there?'

"There was a pause, and this voice came back and said, 'Well, we've been having a rough winter, and I don't believe we can give any this year.'"

–Tom Corbitt, Appalachian State University

(2/7/79 The Sentinel)

"Couldn't Be No Other Way"
Grandson Thinks Siamese Twins Were Individuals

Eng Bunker came down from Surry County the other day "just to spend a few days."

He didn't stir the kind of commotion that his grandfather and namesake did in his 19th-century travels. *That* Eng Bunker and his brother Chang were the original Siamese Twins.

Eng and Chang were brought to the United States from what was then Siam (it's Thailand now) when they were young boys. They traveled with Barnum & Bailey, as well as on their own, made their fortunes, married Sarah and Adelaide Yates and settled in Surry County, raising 21 children between them.

"I'll tell you," said the 20th-century Eng—who goes by the assumed name Woo E. Bunker—"I don't know too much about them. My father never did tell too much."

But it became obvious that Bunker, 74, had picked up some knowledge of the twins while growing up and farming near Mount Airy.

"I understand that when they died—when they retired that night, one of them [Chang] had pneumonia, a fever," Bunker said. "He died in the night. The other one woke up, looked over and saw his brother dead and said something like, 'Oh Lord, my brother is dead; have mercy on my soul.'"

Eng died a short time later the same day, and Bunker's account seems to lend credence to the conclusion of an attending physician that Eng had died of fright. It has been reported that an autopsy showed that the twins shared a common liver in the six-inch tube that connected them at their stomachs. If so, this could account for Eng's death shortly after Chang's, but that's not the way Bunker heard it, or believes it.

"I think that's wrong," he said. "I think...they had two normal bodies, except one was an inch or so shorter and had to wear inch-high soles on his shoes."

Being linked together for all of their 62-plus years had little effect on the twins' ability to function individually or together, to hear Bunker tell it.

"They went all over the world," he said. "They used to travel with the 'Greatest Show on Earth.'

"I've heard my uncle say that when they'd make a trip on a train, one of them would buy a ticket for himself. The conductor would ask about the other one, and the one would say, 'I paid for my ticket—you can put him off if you want to....'

"They were expert rifle shots. They hunted some, I believe...

"They could carry up a corner of a tobacco barn (lift a log into place, a two-man job) as good as anyone.

"They used to play chess. They said they didn't enjoy playing each other. Both of them would play another person, and they were pretty much liable to beat the other person. They were shrewd and smart."

Eng and Chang were said to have quarreled, sometimes violently, but Bunker isn't sure how much truth there is to that.

"I've heard it both ways," he said.

"I think one of them (Chang) liked the dram pretty well and the other one didn't drink much.

"On different subjects…certain things, their opinions would be far apart. But I think in general they got along pretty good and agreed pretty well."

When the twins died in 1874, they were buried near Eng's house. Later they were disinterred for reburial at White Plains Baptist Church, to which they had given land.

"I saw them take up the bodies," Bunker said. "There were just the bones left, is all."

Then he added:

"I guess you knew how they lived. They had two homes, one on one side of Stewart's Creek and one on the other. One of them would go live with his wife for a week, and then the other would go and live with his wife a week."

That, of course, brought up the touchy and much-speculated-upon subject of just how Eng managed to father 11 children and Chang 10, when they never could part from each other's company.

"Well," said Bunker, "my estimate is, the twins and the women just had to get together and agree to certain things. Couldn't be no other way."

(5/10/76 The Sentinel)

EPILOGUE: *The bridges over Stewart's Creek on U.S. 601 in Surry County have been named the Eng and Chang Bunker Memorial Bridge. These bridges connect farmland that used to belong to the original Siamese twins.*

"The bridge is a connecting link as was their ligament," Kester Sink said on Dec. 1, 2000. Sink, whose late wife, Adelaide, was Chang's granddaughter, wrote a letter to state officials in July 2000, asking for the designation.

Sink lives in Chang Bunker's house, which was built in 1845.

(12/2/00, 7/28/01 WSJ)

"You Know God Made the World..."

Sylva—As clouds tumbled below, lining every mountain pocket with soft white fleece, a Mississippi woman approached the edge of an overlook south of Newfound Gap and stopped to stare, open-mouthed, at the spectacle.

Finally, she shook her head and said, softly and slowly:

"This must be how the angels feel."

The words captured our feelings—mine, my wife's and our son's—as we began a rare early November vacation that was about to open new perspectives on one of our favorite havens: the Great Smoky Mountains…

We have yet to have an unhappy visit to these mountains. Changes in weather and seasons merely put new faces on the beauty of the Smokies and surrounding ranges.

The face we began to see more clearly the second morning, as skies above the clouds turned a sparkling blue, was indeed new. Oddly, more than two weeks after the traditional "peak of autumn color," the leaves remaining on the trees were still vividly hued in red, maroon, copper, yellow and burnt-orange.

"I like it better with leaves on the ground." Richard said. "It's like the leaves are lighting the place up, because they're the brightest things in here."

He was right. The fallen leaves let the sun do double duty, creating spaces to let the rays intensify the brilliance of the leaves on the trees while creating colorful reflections from the leaves lining the forest floor.

There were to be many new discoveries in our old haunts, including Grotto and Flat Creek Falls.

These were reachable because, two full years after laying my cigarettes down and 18 months after starting an almost-daily walking regimen, I was no longer intimidated by three- and five-mile mountain hikes.

In both instances, the falls and the rugged terrain around them were well worth the hike, although I did complain once to Elva and Richard, whose eagerness and superior conditioning left me struggling at times to bring up the rear respectably.

"The guide book calls this an easy trail," I noted of the path to Grotto. "But it also calls it a 2 and 1/2-hour round trip. We just did it in less than 50 minutes. That *ain't* easy!"

Among our other discoveries was a huge scar on the mountainside below Newfound Gap on the Tennessee side of the national park. On earlier trips, the full spring and summer foliage had blocked any view of the scar and another beside it. Surely, I said, they were too big to have resulted from any landslide.

I should have kept my mouth shut.

"Those happened on Aug. 10, 1984," said Margie Steigerwald, a park public-information specialist. "We had two different landslides in the park after heavy rains.…

"They were within a few minutes of each other and trapped 35 vehicles and 113 people.…It was six days before the road was opened."

Oh. *Those* landslides. Of course.

Somehow, during our entire stay, the sun remained out for us. When it did retreat again, it was to accommodate a three-inch snowfall that came, regrettably, hours after we left.

For me, as I reflected on a trip full of new highlights, the bears kept coming to mind. We had seen bears often in the Smokies, but these—a very young mother and cubs that were at least half her own size—were different. These were November bears, fat, sleek and shiny, with long heavy coats, ready for the long winter's sleep that will begin very soon.

Richard agreed, but threw in the Cades Cove deer as well: "You know what I like best. Any time I see bears and deer, I like that best."

For Elva, however, the blossoming ladies' tresses, a delicate-looking fall flower, and the witch hazel and new varieties of gentians topped the list.

"In early November," she said, "I just never expected to find anything new. I expected that to wait till next spring."

It didn't have to wait. Newness is the Smokies' oldest charm, and we find it every time we visit.

As we left, to head for home largely via the Blue Ridge Parkway, the Mississippi woman's "how the angels feel" observation still summed up our own impressions.

That and another remark, by another woman at another vantage point—the Carlos C. Campbell Overlook, where the autumn colors shone in their greatest glory on that crystal-clear second day:

"You know God made the world when you see this."

That's the kind of inspiration you come to expect of the Great Smoky Mountains, whatever the season.

We have yet to be disappointed.

(11/8/88 WSJ)

The Winter Outlook—Once and Fur All

As everyone who reads newspapers knows, the Chinese have become expert in predicting natural phenomena.

The most publicized example has been the forecasting of earthquakes. Nevertheless, the more significant advances seem to have been in predicting weather.

One Chinese scientist, in fact, was said to have forecast average winter snowfall and temperature to within one percent accuracy for the past 15 years. Naturally, when I discovered that he is living in the North Carolina mountains for a year in an effort to duplicate his feat there, I looked him up.

"I am looking for Wo Lee-wurm," I said to the man I found in the woods near Tater Mountain.

"Wo is me," he said, bowing slightly.

I then introduced myself and proceeded to the interview.

"Why are you living in North Carolina?" I asked.

"I have been highly honored," he said. "Appalachian State University, which is engaged in a serious study of winter weather, invited me. When I learned that the university has established a Center for Wo Lee-wurm Studies, I could not refuse."

"Dr. Wo," I said, "I understand that in your country you are a national hero because of your brilliance in forecasting weather. Have you really predicted winter weather correctly for 15 consecutive years?"

"Many more years than that," he said. "Yet if it hadn't been for Mao, I might still be unknown today."

"Oh, you knew Mao?"

"We were friends. When he was planning to flee from Ching-kangshan to Yenan in 1935 he asked me about the weather. I told him it would be a hard winter, particularly during March. He then asked if I could think of a catchy slogan for the 8,000-mile walk to Yenan. 'No,' I said. 'I am not good at words. But heed what I say: It will be cold; especially it will be a long March.' He said, 'Hey, I like that,' and we were very close from that time."

"I see," I said. "To what do you attribute your powers?"

"Poverty."

"I'm not sure I understand," I said. "By the looks of that swell fur coat, you're not poor now, but you're still hitting the target." I reached out and tugged playfully at the fur.

"Ouch," said Wo. "Please, you are not pulling the fur on a coat. You are pulling the fur on Wo Lee-wurm."

"Oh, golly," I said. "I'm so sorry."

"No need. Forgive my outburst. You see, in my youth we were too poor to afford clothing or houses. This led to my first great scientific discovery: If man lives with nature, without building barriers against it, his system responds by giving him a coat of fur like those of many animals. And you will notice that my fur is not particularly thick and is rather light in color?"

"Yes," I said. "But what does that mean?"

"This means it will be a mild winter. See, my fur is very light down here, a little light in the middle and very light up here. In normal years it would be fairly light on top and bottom and rather dark in the middle. Last year it was dark at the top and bottom and very dark in the middle. You *know* what happened then."

"Brrr," I said. "But tell me, why hasn't anybody else ever discovered any of the things you have discovered?"

"To some extent, they have," said Wo, "although they may not have refined their powers as well. Right here in Cherokee, N.C., you have one of the top people in the field, but nobody in your country listens to him."

"What's his name?" I asked.

"Chief Black Bear," he said.

It appeared that time was running out. Wo was restless.

"Just one more question," I said. "Living in the open like an animal, do you ever sort of get to *feel* like an animal? And don't you get sick a lot? I mean, you look a little peaked right now."

"Nonsense," said Wo. "Of course, I don't feel like an animal, and I almost never get sick. But you look like you do not believe."

"Well…" I said.

"See for yourself," he said. "Here—feel my nose!" *(7/29/77 The Sentinel)*

Eyes of Insight Guide a "Good News" Preacher

GLADESBORO, VA.—The Rev. Duane Steele is something of a rarity in Virginia's rural Carroll County, where even the Blue Ridge breezes seem to sing Baptist hymns.

He is, first, a Lutheran minister, a self-professed "liberation theologian" who shuns hellfire and brimstone and would rather love Jesus into the hearts of his congregation than try to scare the devil out.

"I'm a good-news kind of preacher," Steele said during a visit at Gladesboro Lutheran Church, where he is the pastor. "I preach freedom—freedom from your guilt and your sin and your shame."

There is another unusual facet to Steele, as mountain minister and optimist: He is blind, robbed of vision just after birth in 1947 by a hospital incubator that gave him too much oxygen.

"There are a lot of blind people my age," he said with a shrug. "It was a common screw-up back then."

He spoke with a lilt, and a mischievous-looking smile lit his face. Minutes earlier, he had ushered guests into his church office, navigating by memory and hardly using his collapsible white cane. He sat behind a wooden desk that could be described as cluttered, except that clutter is a visual effect.

Behind him, two large bookcases held 58 giant Braille volumes. They made up only three books: the Bible, Standard and King James versions; and the Evangelical Lutheran *Book of Concord*.

"If I want to read books that are current, I have to do it on tape," Steele said. "I read a lot of stuff on cassettes and discs. In fact, I'm into reading Andrew Greeley's books (*Ascent Into Hell, Virgin & Martyr* and others) right now." The mischief flashed in his smile again: "He's a priest. I don't know how he knows so much about sex."

As a telephone call came in, Steele reached for a piece of his special paper, nearly covered on his desk, and fluidly inserted it into his Brailler—a typewriter for the blind—and began typing.

Moments later, he came back to the conversation without losing track of a syllable.

He was reared in the Catskills of New York state, where only the tourists have money—the second of six children and "the least likely to succeed."

"Being visually impaired meant I wouldn't amount to much," he said. "That was the concept…If I was going to make it, I had to be a survivor."

When his grandmother learned of the New York Institute for the Blind—a free school in New York City—he got his chance for a quality education.

There he learned to read and write, made lifelong friends, took piano lessons that led to a steadfast love affair with music, got his first Braille Bible—and attended a Lutheran church.

"I always looked up to the pastor," he said. "I wanted to be up there in the pulpit."

He has been in the pulpit in Gladesboro for 10 years. Getting there was a struggle, however. After graduation from the institute in 1967, he attended Hartwick College in Oneonta, N.Y., where he met and married his wife, Jane, with whom he shares two sons and two daughters.

He attended the Shenandoah Conservatory of Music in Winchester, Va., graduating in just over two years. In 1974, he entered Lutheran Theological Seminary in Gettysburg, Pa., after overcoming some resistance to his candidacy.

"When you're a boy and you say you want to be a minister, that's OK," he said. "But when you grow up and you're sightless and you tell people you want to go to seminary, they look at you differently."

He had similar problems when he graduated and became a blind shepherd in search of a flock. Luckily, the church here was without a pastor at the time. "They wanted a pastor who would be willing to try to be the best," he said. "Most of the people around here had never dealt with a sightless person before, [but] they were willing to take me on my value as a person."

Today, the church has changed. Its bright red double doors open now to new liturgy, new music—even new hymnals. And during tourist season, they also open, for some parishioners, on a pastor who was the previous evening's pianist at the nearby Shenandoah Restaurant.

"I play anything from cocktail to gospel to jazz to classical," he said of his music, adding that his blindness helped fine-tune his musical ear during the years he and schoolmates sat in a special box at the New York Philharmonic orchestra's Young People's Concerts in Carnegie Hall.

"It's kind of like when I watch football with the guys," he said. "I know more about what's going on than they do. I *listen*." He talks that way routinely—saying he "watches" behavior or "sees" friends. And in a sense, he said, he does: "It's all insight. Insight and hindsight."

Steele writes his own sermons and types his own church bulletins, first in Braille and then on a regular typewriter. He walks to church from his nearby home, and parishioners—mostly older ones—volunteer to drive him on his visitation and counseling rounds.

Members of his congregation joke that he is the only one in the community who can still get around when the fog hangs heavy on the hills—because he can't see where he's walking whether it's foggy or not. And he jokes that they can't tell when he's reading his sermon—unless they crane their necks and get a good look at his fingers.

It is here, at least for the foreseeable future, that he will continue to practice a theology of life that was best described in his own words about a 90-minute "program sermon" of music and message he has carried up and down the East Coast:

"It's all kind of buoyed up by the concept that God cares about us—no matter who we are, where we are and what we are." *(2/28/88 WSJ)*

EPILOGUE: *The Rev. Duane Steele is still a "Good News" kind of preacher and a musician and singer who plays and produces contemporary Christian music. He and his wife are also the grandparents of six.* *(9/4/00, 8/7/01 Interview)*

Dear Aunt Zuzu, Please Send My...

BURNSVILLE—One nice thing about being a columnist is that it lets you get word back home without spending a lot of money on telephone calls.

Since this is essentially a letter to the family and will contain some rather personal information, I would like to ask everyone else not to read any further.

There is much good news to report.

First of all, the helicopter did not crash. And, although I forgot to take my airsick bag, I did not make a complete fool of myself.

As you know, in the past my fear of heights has caused me to decline all helicopter rides. This one was not too bad, however. It was a very big helicopter, and I sat over in the middle where I felt somewhat closed in, except when they opened one of the doors from time to time, which is something I think Allie put them up to.

You won't believe this, but by the second time we had landed and taken off again, I was able to keep my eyes open most of the time. And I think my stomach will recover in time for Thanksgiving.

I was also happy that the bulls did not charge the helicopter.

There was this one huge one that kind of kept his distance when we landed in his field. You know how scared I am of bulls and things, so I was relieved that he stayed away.

Later, however, after some of us got back to the helicopter, the big bull called a couple of others and a whole bunch of cows and came and *surrounded* us. He stood there, looking mean, his ears lowered, grunting and sniffing, occasionally consulting with the others.

"This looks like a horror movie," I said. "We could call it 'The Bulls.'"

"How about 'Gone With the Bulls'?" said the helicopter crewmen.

I was about to suggest that we leave Allie and Gary and a Pentagon man named Clanahan behind when all three returned and somehow got past the animals without injury.

It turned out to be a good experience, though. For the first time, I was eager to get into the air. Me—who won't get on a ski lift.

But the best news is that my back must be better, because today I jumped higher than I ever have and didn't even feel a twinge when I came down.

The way it happened was, I was walking around the boondocks with the sheriff, talking to people who are still stranded by the floods. Somehow in our wanderings we got on the other side of the fence from the pasture where the big olive-drab bird had sat down.

The sheriff did one of those little hand-assisted leaps over the fence, but I didn't feel up to that.

"Is that thing live?" I asked, nodding toward the electric fence.

"I don't know," he said. "Here, I'll hold it down for you with my foot."

As he held it down, I carefully put my left foot over it, straddling the fence.

Well, we'd been walking in the mud and a lot of other stuff, and about that time his foot slipped.

"Holy mother of pearl," I said as I made like the helicopter and went straight up.

"It's live," said the sheriff.

I think I'll be walking normally again by the time I get home.

Well, that's about all the news. I believe we'll wait until we get back to tell the boss about Allie's broken camera.   *(1/22/77 The Sentinel)*

Mabry Mill
Selling of Mill Was Part of Passage of Old Ways

Charles Edward Mabry has pleasant memories of youth in Patrick County, Va., where he and his brothers worked their father's fields and their great-uncle Ed ran a mill.

"My father owned a farm and worked for the highway department," Mabry said. "With five boys, he let us do the farming mostly. I worked hard on that farm….My great-uncle, he made a living by the old grist mill. He ground buckwheat flour, cornmeal, wheat. And he also did blacksmith work and all that stuff.

"That was back years ago, when I was a real young kid. I heard my daddy talk about what Uncle Ed made—cane syrup and all that.

"The old cane mills are still there, and his old copper whiskey still is still up there. He made a little drinkin'…The cabin's just like it was. His bed's still there. I was up there last year."

"Up there" is Mabry Mill, the popular scenery-and-nostalgia stop along the Blue Ridge Parkway—one of the most photographed spots in the United States.

The mill has been out of family hands for half a century and more, but Mabry still loves it and the Virginia mountains. And he still takes pride in the old wooden bridges in that area of the Parkway—bridges he helped his father build back before World War II.

He made $14.40 a week building those bridges and others with his father, James Mabry, he said. That was more than double the $6.71 a week the government had paid him to help build the Parkway after he quit school at age 15.

It was in those years that Mabry Mill passed to the government by an odd route. Ed Mabry died, but nobody told Charles' father, James, that the mill had been left to him.

"My father didn't know this was willed to him until he got a letter from the parkway people in Salem, Va.," said Mabry. "They was a-comin' right through it. The way they was routing that road, they wanted the old historic buildings and things."

He never knew what his father got for the mill, but he's sure it wasn't enough. "Back then," he said, "one hundred dollars was one hundred dollars. He never did tell me. He said he got little or nothing for it."

The selling of the mill was just part of the passage of old ways in the Blue Ridge, and the mill itself was soon to become a symbol both of and for a generation that had to leave to make a living and then could not go home again.

Like other young people, Charles Mabry left. He served in the Army in

World War II and in the Korean War. He remained in uniform until 1961, when he was retired on disability because of a heart problem.

He later was a deputy for the Patrick County Sheriff's Department for two-and-a-half years, he said, and then owned a 24-hour service station in Ridgeland, S.C. He had married in 1952, and when his wife became sick and disabled, he sold the station and took her to Hilton Head, where he worked in security. In 1982, he retired, and his wife died.

Through the years of a marriage that he said was very happy, family members kept in touch with one another and their past.

"Before my mother and father passed away," he said, "we used to get the whole family up there to the mill to eat breakfast. There'd be seven of us, and five wives would make 12…

"We all enjoyed going up there. Oh, we'd talk about what it could have been worth and all that. But my daddy always said, 'That's water under the bridge'…"

In Charleston in 1984, Mabry said, "The doctors lost me twice" during quadruple-bypass surgery for that heart problem.

He made it through that, and he has made it through other health problems. He is staying at the Winston-Salem Rescue Mission now because of one of them: a sporadic battle with alcohol.

"I drank," said Mabry. "I'll be honest with you, I drank heavy. I'd take it in spells—a month, two months at a time. And then I might be sober for years."

He's sober now, and hopes he'll stay that way the rest of his life. He plans to stay awhile, with the mission as his base. He enjoys its Christian atmosphere and fellowship, he said.

Mabry wants to visit the mill again. His parents and all but one of his brothers are gone now, so he won't be going with an old gang. But he says he'll go. "It brings back memories," he said. "I like it because—it's the name, for one thing. It's sentimental things. I can look back and say, 'Well, my daddy did own it one time.'"

If he has a regret, it's that his life became too complicated. As he looks back on his 67 years, he finds much to recommend the simplicity of old mountain ways, when life was hard but there was little of the uncertainty that plagues people today.

"It was a good life," he said. "We knew what we were going to do every day, and we did it…We pulled those logs with horses and mules, right out of those mountains.

"Today, we're in too big a hurry, I think. A lot of people don't seem to enjoy life." *(6/23/87 WSJ)*

Homecoming in the Hills
A Taste of the Genuine

LAUREL FORK, VA.—If you've traveled toward Dogwood Mountain or Mabry Mill along the Blue Ridge Parkway, you've passed this place.

It is one of those pockets of humanity in the hills above Mount Airy that most of us never seem to explore, perhaps partly because we think the people will resent our intruding and poking around.

But they don't really mind at all; not if you're halfway civil.

Especially on a day like Sunday, which was homecoming at Crooked Oak Baptist Church.

Before the service, the people were warmly welcoming their guests—and rejoicing. After all, in a community where springs and wells are beginning to run dry and the streams are lower than any living person can remember them, there was good cause: rain.

"We've had three inches of rain this week," said one woman, raising three fingers high, as if in triumph.

"We need it," said a man, shaking his head. "The water's been low. I've been living here 43 years, and this is the lowest I've ever seen it."

Inside the tiny white building, with room for only two rows of short, solidly crafted pews that did not look factory-made, almost everything seemed to be solid, shiny knotty white pine.

The feeling of closeness was partly a matter of space, but it also came from the warm welcome by people who were truly glad to have visitors from the flatlands.

The service itself may have been the day's biggest surprise.

It was brief, which you somehow don't expect in a back-country Baptist church even if you know that these are people who seldom waste anything, including words.

There was, of course, the singing—where else would you find babes in arms and other little ones among the choir?—and it was strong and joyous and with a faster beat and less sophistication than in the city. It was, basically, country gospel, and if I felt a little foolish finding myself tapping my foot, well, the pastor was doing the same thing.

As for the message, delivered by the self-described "uneducated" guest preacher, Norman Goad, it was a lesson in economy of words. Watch out for imitations, he said. First, margarine imitated real butter—which brought one of the day's strongest "amens"—and now there are even imitation margarines; and if those imitations of the good and real things in life are disappointments, the real danger lies in evil imitating good. We live in a world where Satan is imitating God, where faith healing can become fake healing, where religious cults pose as religious cultures.

So beware. And be genuine.

Later, as two long and wide tables were heavily laden with from-scratch foods of all kinds that would have done the entire Dixie Classic Fair proud, there was time for a talk, some of it about the families that peopled these hills.

"We're all Nesters in one way or another," said a woman who was also a Goad, with maybe a bit of Webb lurking somewhere in the background. There are other names in the area, some of them quite common, but when the conversation goes back over a period of years, those seem to dominate.

It was necessary, of course, being visitors, to start at the front of the eating line. Necessary, and near-fatal.

From salads to casseroles to beans and potatoes and homemade desserts of all kinds, irresistibility overwhelmed good intentions. If church homecomings represent the homecoming we will share at the Lord's return—well, it certainly seemed close enough to heaven.

And there was, again, the chatter and camaraderie.

"I wouldn't tell him which one was my cake for the world," said Ruth Hall, speaking with mock gruffness of a friend who, at an earlier homecoming, had made a big show of "disliking" her pie.

"Y'all go on and get yourselves some plates to take back home with you," said Joe Hall and several others, just as the minister's wife and a couple of her friends made sure that nobody but their visitors got that last precious piece of homemade cheesecake. (We took only one take-home plate, but it looked like a foil-covered pyramid.)

Crystal Stringer talked about school in Winston-Salem, about being a nurse on the seventh floor at Forsyth Memorial Hospital, about her husband John's starting out in banking at Wachovia. She spoke of the big city with some fondness as she held her tiny baby; but she and her husband are back living in the hill country, and there seemed no doubt that it's where they want to be.

It had come as something of a surprise to learn that Mrs. Stringer had been a nurse. It was more so, for some reason, to find that Mrs. Hall, a tall, 60-ish woman, had a degree from Radford. They didn't act or feel superior to anybody else, and they had listened as intently as anyone to a preacher who hadn't made it through the fifth grade.

There followed the better part of an afternoon exploring the creeks and hollows of this mountain country, scaring up a gray fox in the process, and looking over the cascading waters where the mill where people took their corn to be ground stood before a long-ago flood. The hiking was intended partly to walk off the effects of the food, but it didn't work.

Toward the end of the day, we found ourselves on the front porch at the

Halls' house, where we were to pick up a huge sack of yellow mountain tomatoes, and where somehow the talk turned to "skeletons" in the hill-country closet.

It seems that one General Webb became the last man to be hanged in Carroll County, for shooting his father-in-law, who had hired some people to kill Webb. General's wife had poisoned a Nester and her own son-in-law, who died as a result. Webb's brother had repaid a dinner invitation by shooting his host…

"You think you'll be coming back?" asked Hall. "I'll tell you, folks used to be *mean* up here."

Yes, Mr. Hall, we'll be back.

And if there has been meanness in these hills—well, you got that "used to be" part right.

(9/8/81 The Sentinel)

Old Ways Are Gone, But Life's Still Sweet

SHOALS—Reaching the now-lifeless heart of the old Shoals community requires effort—or being lost.

Only a chimney stands along the Yadkin River now, reminding old-timers of old ways and old days, where there once was a village clustered around a railroad station and post office. The station is gone, and the chimney is all that's left of the post office.

Today, when someone says he is from here, he might live on the slope of Pilot Mountain—or down on the river, where he can wade to islands of 45 and 15 acres. The entire township, bordered by Stokes County on the east and Yadkin to the south, is now Shoals community.

The rails still run along the water, but the ferry has been gone from its moorings, 200 yards east of the post office, for over 40 years (since about 1945). These days hardly anybody fords the shoals, at the edge of what is now the Yadkin River section of Pilot Mountain State Park.

The settlers came about the time of the Civil War, O.W. Hauser says.

"They were people who came in from various parts of North Carolina and Virginia, Scotch-Irish," he said. "Most of 'em came to farm, and the place was named because of the shallow, rocky part of the river."

Hauser is only 54, but he's something of a legend. People only a few years younger talk of him as a man who has "always" been an anchor for young people and a help to all. He was born in a frame house that is now a park ranger's home, and he's moved only 250 yards, to a brick home across the road.

He was baptized in the Ararat River, near where it enters the Yadkin. He attended Shoals High School, where he taught and became principal before it became an elementary school in 1961, and where he has remained as principal. He had to leave the area as a young man, to go off to High Point College, Appalachian State University and the U.S. Army. He came back as soon as he could.

Hauser's great-grandfather John was among the original settlers of Bean's Shoals, as it was first known. John Hauser buried his first wife in the old cemetery in 1864. At least one church, Missionary Baptist, had been organized by 1867, and others soon followed. The original Shoals Public School was built in 1880.

The site of the village of those years is at the end of a bumpy, rutted, narrow dirt road that remains inhospitable to most modern vehicles. It is the road people used, until the 1930s and beyond, to get to the post office, railroad and ferry.

"Back then," said Hauser, "most people settled along a waterway because it provided easy transportation. The ferry went across the river. It's just a couple-three miles from there to East Bend. That's how most people traveled in those days.

"And, of course, the railroad ran along the waterway. The community just grew out from those."

He remembers his father cutting ice out of the river in the winter and packing it in sawdust inside a cave, to keep it all summer. And he recalls the horse-and-buggy days that lasted, here, until after World War II.

"Most people in this area still worked horses and mules," he said. "They didn't have any tractors when I was growing up. Cars were few...

"They hauled all the tobacco to Winston-Salem by wagon. They went on down to Donnaha. You didn't have to cross the river that way. My father used to make a lot of trips. Most of the time, they stayed overnight."

It was a life of "work, work, work," Hauser said, but it was also a time of pleasures that are all but lost today.

"Back then, people got together for more social events like hog killings and barn raisings...Lots of times they had corn shuckings. All the neighbors would come and they'd tear the husks off the corn. Then after the shucking was finished, they had time for games.

"It all was connected with work because most everybody farmed. They grew tobacco, corn and vegetables. They believed in going to church and working hard and saving money. All the children had chores to do, like milking the cows and feeding the hogs and the horses and the mules.

"But you know, people used to get together on Saturday afternoon and make ice cream and things of that nature. They just seemed to enjoy life more. For example, people who walked to church would come an hour before time and sit under the tree and talk....Today, people can't get to church on time."

Now that most everyone has cars and there are paved roads to drive them on, he said, many people have quit tending crops. Where there once were three-and four-acre tobacco farms, there are 50- and 60-acre operations worked largely by migrant labor, and many natives work in surrounding towns and cities.

But churches and schools have remained the bedrock. The Extension Homemakers and Ruritan clubs have also been important, working together to build an attractive brick community center.

From north to south in Shoals Township, from above the old house that was once the Pinnacle Hotel down to the Yadkin River, people flock to the center, bringing cakes and pies and appetites for the reunions and other gatherings.

When motorists pass the state "Shoals" village-limit sign on their way to the lower part of the state park, they don't know that it is not the Shoals that is, but the Shoals that was. They see the old Trulove store, rotting and fallen in, and cluttered with old one-horse turning plows and cultivator blades and harness and even a rusting iron stove.

If they look closely, travelers may even see the "wallpaper" inside the century-old building, with its cardboard Kellogg's Corn Flakes motif. But that won't tell them about the days when youngsters hid eggs to take to the store to trade for all-day suckers.

They won't see the Shoals that has kept O.W. Hauser and his family—and a host of Marions and Smiths and Browns and Allens—right here in south Surry County.

There are so many Marions that when Hauser took a basketball team to a Mount Airy tournament in the 1950s, all five members of the starting team were Marions. And there were two more on the bench. Today, some Marions— four brothers and three sisters, their parents and others—see each other every day, because they're neighbors.

So don't tell Hauser about the joys of city life. He has seen the metropolises. He's even seen Paris, the "Paree" whose temptations are such, an old song says, that people don't go back home once they've been exposed.

"I was stationed at Orleans," he said. "We used to go up to Paris on weekends…

"I came back down on the farm. I like this country. I like country life."

(4/14/85 WSJ, newsfeature)

Nearby are Horne Creek Living Historical Farm, a project demonstrating family farm life from a century ago, and Pilot Mountain State Park, including the Yadkin River section. To get to the farm, take the Pinnacle exit off U.S. 52, Pinnacle, and follow the signs. Admission is free.

Something to Chew Over

A local gentleman of some repute, who hates to see his name in the newspaper, recently discovered that R.J. Gold, a relatively new hometown product, can be almost worth its weight in the real thing.

But I'm ahead of the story.

The man was visited by friends from central Florida, passing through on their way to the Grand Ole Opry in Nashville. Naturally, he wanted his visitors to enjoy as many of the delights of our area as possible during their brief stay.

"So," he said, "after a bountiful meal at Bell Brothers, we went over to the Whitaker Park plant. Nobody in the crowd smoked, so they got chewing tobacco—the R.J. Gold. See, my friend operates a large service station (where smoking isn't a good idea), so he chews tobacco now and then."

The next morning, he took them to a favorite mountain spot owned by an elderly gentleman of his acquaintance.

"They're not mountain people, now," the man said of his friends. "The only thing they know is that they look beautiful—like looking at a rose bush without seeing the thorns.

"The first thing that startled them after they got used to the place up there was a huge black snake that was cooling himself in a mountain stream, right under their noses, practically. The woman in the group yelled, 'It's a water moccasin. Get back! It's a water moccasin!'

"The owner of the property explained to them that it was just Clyde. He explained that Clyde's been there in that spot off and on for five or six years. Clyde didn't pay any attention."

By then, the lady probably was as worried about the old mountain man as she was the snake, since one was keeping about as cool as the other in a situation that obviously called for panic. At any rate, the group, including three youngsters, continued to climb and hike around very impressed with what they were seeing.

"They wanted to capture this on film," said the gentleman, "because it was about the prettiest place they've ever seen. And I went out to a very precarious spot, because of the jagged rocks and sharp dropoff and so forth, to see if I could find a solid place for the kids to stand so I could get a picture of a large cave in the background."

By this time, though he is an experienced mountaineer himself, the man had also started looking at the roses without keeping his eyes out for the thorns. He found them soon enough, while stomping around to make sure the ground was solid enough for the youngsters.

"My left foot went into a crevice which contained a large yellow jackets' nest," he said.

And then nature and the yellow jackets (wasps) took their normal course.

"The yellow jackets concentrated on my left ankle," the man said, "and from there proceeded up my britches' leg as far as possible. The kids, seeing my predicament, took off, but not without some stings of their own.

"Anyway, they made it down to the house before I did, because I was still trying to get 'em [the yellow jackets] off me. I was taking off my shirt and everything else I could. There wasn't a thing I didn't have stings on.

"The host—the owner of the property—said that the best thing for stings was just plain old tobacco juice."

Enter, with fanfare, the hero of the piece—the R.J. Gold picked up as free samples the night before.

"Our host brought a saucer of water and we soaked it [the tobacco] in there and began to apply it on all the yellow jacket stings. I had 27 on me— 19 on my ankle and several in [other] places..."

Did the old country remedy really work?

"It was fantastic," said the man. "It's the best remedy there is. Somebody ought to market it."

Are you paying attention, RJR?

Who knows—it might even work for chigger bites.

(8/15/81 The Sentinel)

Serendipity
Nature Feasts the Traveler With Radiant Surprises

ALMOND—You can't go wrong enjoying nature from a base in this surviving fragment of a community that was washed away by the rising waters of TVA's Fontana Lake during World War II.

Here, whether wind and rain blow or the sun bursts through Smoky Mountain clouds to warm your day, you simply find different ways to go right.

From our first rainy outing, discovering Joanna Bald and her Catesby's trillium high above the grave of Chief Junaluska, to our fifth day of intense sun, visiting Shining Rock Wilderness for the first time, there was a sense of discovery.

The glow of triumph came first at Bear Lake, whose existence seems to have eluded mapmakers. There, on the dirt road called N.C. 281, Richard explored a spillway bank.

"Mom," he shouted, "there's a flower here I've never seen before."

He suspected what it was, but he didn't dare suggest its identity lest he raise false hope.

It was, indeed, a pink lady's-slipper in full glory. We had seen a field full of the yellow variety in Canada in 1981, but this was our first hardy and certifiably wild pink one.

"I've been looking for that for 20 years," said Elva.

The road yielded another lady's-slipper and the loveliest flame azalea we had ever seen, as well as new mountain vistas. We were to see one yellow and 50 pink lady's-slippers before our travels ended, but that first blossom had etched Bear Lake and N.C. 281 in our travel memories forever.

In what has become an annual rite, with our only departure being the foregoing of our tent for the comforts of a lake cabin, we have found again that mountain highlights come unannounced on side roads.

For me, one came as we left Cades Cove, in Great Smoky Mountains National Park, on the narrow one-way road called Parsons Branch. Nothing is as rare as a wild turkey in May, and there is escape in a forest-tunnel of a road that asks a driver to ford a stream every half-mile.

Along Fontana and Cheoah Lake and in the TVA country to the northwest, we could have snapped pictures and passed them off as portraits from Upper Michigan's Copper Country, which has been my favorite place at least since I learned to walk.

If there was regret at turning away from the lakes, however, it quickly changed to happy surprise. The Foothills Parkway, north of the park in Tennessee, is as spectacular as most of the Blue Ridge Parkway, and its frequent overlooks and trails offer clearer views. From a viewing tower, half a dozen 6,000-foot mountains were visible at once.

And Connemara, forced upon us by a need to escape rain and fog to the northwest, was incredible. There, Carl and Paula Sandburg spent 22 years, he writing his prose and poetry, she raising champion goats.

Elva said it best: "It's not just visiting a place. It's more like visiting a life."

There was satisfaction, too, in just riding along U.S. 441 in the national park. The renewal of spring had arrived full-force, with green-layered mountainsides dappled by the whites of pincherry, black cherry and serviceberry blossoms—and even full-blooming dogwoods lingering late in the high country.

Who would expect one trip to offer up not only dozens of lady's-slippers and flame azalea, but also the rare Clinton's lily, Dutchman's pipe, massed pinxter flowers, squaw root, jacks-in-the-pulpit, mountain laurel, three kinds of phacelia, six varieties of trillium and countless other blossoms—all in one area, at one time?

And where else would you see a hawk dining on a mouse, watch herds of deer graze, discover black mice and salamanders that defy identification, see and hear a mother woodchuck shrilly lecture her young on the perils of impetuousness, and find a bear spying on a picnic area from behind a tree on a hill?

And such words as "stunning" and "breathtaking" are too weak to describe the views from the Blue Ridge Parkway between Balsam and Mount Pisgah, our route home only because Richard insistently chose Shining Rock over the Biltmore House.

"This," I confessed, "is the most beautiful section of the parkway we've seen. You know, when you find a favorite area, you keep going back. You miss places like this because you quit exploring."

"Yup," Richard said, mercifully omitting further comment.

We stowed our cameras and lenses. The pastrami and corned beef and kraut and cheesecake at Catherine's Cheese House in Hickory, our traditional finale, would be a fitting complement to our five-day mountain feast.

(5/24/85 WSJ)

Work of Love Attracts Thousands

GLENDALE SPRINGS—A love story continues to unfold in this small, somewhat remote village in mountainous Ashe County, and now the story is being shared by thousands.

There is a painting in Holy Trinity Church here that has drawn 100,000 visitors so far this year and may well attract a total of 150,000 before the year's end. The artwork depicts the Last Supper.

"This is the event in which Jesus gave us the new commandment that we love one another, and that's what we are called to do," the Rev. J. Faulton Hodge said recently.

"The thrust of what has happened here since the frescoes have been completed," he said, "is that people have come from all walks of life and from all over the United States and many countries of the world to be inspired and uplifted with the message of love that they are able to see and share through a magnificent painting.

"The artist left a vacant stool at the table, at the very center of the fresco, symbolic that there is a place at the table of love for everyone. That stool is there for the rich, the poor, the educated and the fool, and for the prostitute, because love always forgives.

"Love never rejects. Love never turns away. Love says, 'Come unto me, all ye that travail and are heavy-laden, and I'll give you rest.'

"This fresco helps us to better understand that we are called to a life of service. We are to break bread, share the cup, wash one another's feet and go into the world to take good news. And the good news is that we live, and we live forever."

Hodge was discussing a 17-by-19½-foot painting done by North Carolina artist Ben Long, who has been living in Europe for a number of years. Since meeting Hodge nine years ago, Long has done three smaller frescoes at nearby St. Mary's Church. "The Last Supper," completed in 1980, is the most recent. That year, Long was named Italy's most promising young artist.

In creating a fresco, the artist mixes sand, lime and water and applies the mixture to a wall. He then paints directly into the fresh plaster, and the work becomes an integral part of the wall.

When Long started work on the Holy Trinity project, he was named an art professor at Wilkes Community College and had the help of 20 students—plus the people of Ashe County, who "adopted" the entire group and saw that none of its members went without a meal through the entire summer.

At that time, nobody was thinking in terms of visitors by the hundred-thousand. But during a recent visit by a reporter and photographer, the church filled and refilled with people as quickly as the fresco's story could be told by a hostess.

Hodge doesn't seem terribly surprised by the lure of the fresco, which was featured recently on ABC Television News, and is bringing people in from many nations.

But the frescoes, impressive as they may be, are just a part of Hodge's mountain ministry.

Hodge, an Episcopal priest, conducts services frequently; at a recent late-evening service, he asked the 12 worshippers—the same number as are in the Last Supper fresco—to reach out and embrace each other, and he then reached out to warmly embrace a woman who had recently lost her mother.

The church had been closed and abandoned for almost 40 years when Hodge, and then Long, happened onto it.

Even as the first fresco was being finished, the windows rattled in the wind, and the door banged.

"It was a trash dump for the community," said Hodge. "We took out 11 truckloads of broken glass and trash…Then we took a bulldozer and made holes and buried much more."

And if the church's growing fame is threatening to turn Glendale Springs into a major tourist attraction—two new restaurants have already opened here—well, that wasn't Father Hodge's purpose, but he is glad the spirit and beauty of the church and its frescoes have proved so attractive to the public.

"I believe the church should offer opportunity to people to be expressive and to express what they feel that is inside them, the gift of God to them," he said.

"That may be in the form of a painting or a sculpture or a dance…or helping children who are physically handicapped. Or it may be tending a garden.

"We try to provide that atmosphere here."

And they succeed.

(8/19/82 The Sentinel)

EPILOGUE: *The Rev. Stephen A. Miller is now the rector of Holy Trinity Episcopal Church, Glendale Springs, and St. Mary's Episcopal Church, Beaver Creek, both belonging to the Parish of the Holy Communion.*

Ben Long, a Statesville native, finished a fresco at the Statesville Civic Center in 2001 called "Images at the Crossroads." In 2002, Long planned to paint religious frescoes in St. Paul's Episcopal Church in Wilkesboro, N.C.

(1/9/01, 12/26/01 WSJ; 10/15/00 Interview)

Blooms to Mellow a Recluse

"**We**'ll get along just fine," said Alex (Alec) Wilder, "as long as you understand that I don't like newspapermen, I don't like television people, and I don't like public-relations men who try to get me to do things."

I had been warned that Wilder, who had written more than 400 popular songs and was known as "Frank Sinatra's composer," was—well, odd.

"Don't ever expect anything from Alec," said Loonis McGlohon, the Charlotte orchestra leader and composer. "He's totally unpredictable: He may be laughing with you one minute and telling you he doesn't want to talk to you the next."

Alec lived up to that billing.

When he arrived at his mountain motel, he made it plain that he would come and go as he pleased; no plans were to be made for him.

At times, he was an affable raconteur; at other times, a recluse.

One morning, he walked through the breakfast buffet line with the whole Land of Oz crowd, then declined to sit with us, retreating instead to a corner table. He was scribbling in a notebook—and he kept it up all day, ignoring the rest of us.

As it turned out, this crusty old gentleman had decided that the Oz music lacked a little something, and he had written two songs for us in one day—with no charge.

Toward the end of his visit, Mary Mayo and her husband, Al Ham, who also had much to do with the music of Oz, talked Alec into going along on a sightseeing trip.

He grumbled and said there wasn't much time and we'd have to keep it short, but he came along.

The season was right, so I drove them to Roan Mountain. By the time we were halfway up the road, Alec was grumbling that we were running late, it was already time to head back.

I don't remember the exact adjective he used when he saw an entire mountainside laced with wild rhododendron, but it was on the order of "fantastic" or "unbelievable."

I do remember, though, what he kept repeating as he walked up and down the mountainside insisting that we actually had more time than he originally had thought: "This knocks me out—it just knocks me out."

We missed out on dinner at Hound Ears Lodge and Club—an experience I would normally have hated to miss—but it was more than worth it.

All of which is a very long way of leading into this: It's May, a time when the mountain wildflowers are blooming and the tourists aren't.

You won't see the rhododendron, which doesn't peak until about three weeks into June in the higher elevations, but during this relatively traffic-free month, there should be quite a show.

There will be the flame azalea and a wild pink azalea whose technical name I don't know. Also—and always depending on the elevation—you'll be able to see the fire pink, dwarf iris, wild geranium, Solomon's seal, the false Solomon's seal, little brown jugs, galax (yes, it does have flowers in addition to its attractive leaves), trillium of various types, bloodroot, mountain violets, bluets, jack-in-the-pulpit, May apple, white foamflower, dog hobble and the umbrella magnolia, to mention a few.

You won't see all of these on one trip, of course, but as the TV people might say, it's a spectacular.

And what better way to give someone flowers for Mother's Day? As long as you just look, and don't succumb to the temptation to pick.

(5/9/74 The Sentinel)

She's Mountain Smart...

NEWLAND—Mountain people can get along with most anybody, as long as they aren't gawked at or otherwise treated as oddities.

Miss Betty, whose boss sometimes made her the somewhat-unwilling guide for flatlanders, could usually get along, period.

She often wore rather unstylish dresses with flowery prints, so that she could tell tourists she made them out of flour sacks, if that became necessary.

If she'd been made of chocolate, she'd have been bittersweet; but she was pure mountain honey—sourwood, of course, the kind that bites back but is nevertheless a rare treat.

One day Miss Betty had to show some flatlanders around the hills.

When they came to a mountain that particularly impressed the couple from out-of-state, she found herself being pressed for a "legend" from the mountain. She had never heard a thing about the place except that there were berries and snakes on it, which there are on just about every mountain.

That, of course, didn't stop her.

"Wayell," she said, adopting her finest drawl and forgetting her normally-impeccable grammar, "there was this young couple fall in love, and they used to meet at night there by the creek.

"Now, their families was a-feudin', had been for a long time, and they wasn't of legal age to get married."

She paused. For effect, of course.

By this time the tourists were breathing hard and aching for more.

"He went to her paw," said Miss Betty. "He told him he knew his paw had busted up her paw's still and that there'd been bad blood between them for a long time—there was always one or another of 'em shootin' each other up or stealin' things.

"He said if he'd just let them get married, he'd fix things up between them.

"But her paw just said that if they tried to get married, he'd shoot her lover *and* his father. You know, there's a lot of folks around here are still like that; you get bad blood goin' and there just isn't ary thing that'll change it. They're just set in their ways.

"So anyway, it got so that they just couldn't see each other at all, because every time they'd try to, somebody'd be watchin' and there'd just be more trouble.

"By this time, though, they just figured life wasn't worth livin' if they couldn't live it together. So one day in church when no one was lookin', he passed her a note askin' her to meet him by the creek at 3 o' clock in the morning."

Fog blankets peak—a familiar sight in the mountains. –HUGH MORTON

Another pause. Same effect.

"Well," said the visiting woman, "what happened then?"

"They jest took each other's hand and walked all the way up to the cliff rocks way up there on top, and nobody in town ever saw 'em again."

By this time, the visitors were almost desperate for the chance to take their very own legend back home with them.

"Did anyone ever find out what became of them?" asked the woman.

"The way I heard tell," Miss Betty said with her best mountain-girl smile, "they went down the other side."

The sophisticated city people had been country-slickered, but they loved it. In fact, they bought a piece of land in the area for a second home.

Miss Betty could do that sort of thing to you. I wonder what she's up to now, since she's moved to the city.

(8/25/81 The Sentinel)

CHAPTER 2

Celebrating the Underdog

Tom Sieg talked to those who had a difficult time in life, and he told their stories. He felt an affinity for those who had to struggle; his parents had suffered during the Depression. His sister Carol told him that although the children never went hungry, their mother and father sometimes did. When Sieg could help those in need, he would, often in his off hours.

In chapter two, we deal with people who faced great challenges:

- young Joel Stafford, who struggled with a severe debilitating bone disease, but who lived to enter college—his life, more than most, an example of triumph over adversity...
- the woman who supported her retarded son part of the time by performing wonders with hair pieces. (From the time she was six, she said that she was dreaming about a world in many colors, and she lived accordingly.)...
- the infant Pearce who was the definition of tiny—he weighed one pound, 13 ounces, at birth — but who grew to be a happy, healthy, active youngster...
- a humble woman who led a hard-scrabble life; yet, she provided solace to one who became her benefactor...
- the black brick-maker who was interviewed by TV reporter Charles Kuralt and traveled to Africa to teach brick-making...
- the couple who had a difficult decision to make regarding their family member, Luke, a cocker spaniel...
- the lifelong alcoholic who finally succeeded in overcoming his addiction...
- the woman who could not prove to the government that she was alive because her mother had declared her stillborn at birth...
- the man who lived under a bridge...and many other colorful characters.

Miracle

He Heard a Joyful Noise

Ask Benjamin C. Williams why he sings with the Christmas carolers at Forsyth Memorial Hospital each December, and he'll tell you that he has been where the patients are and knows how important the caroling can be to them.

We talked about that recently, and about his own experience in the hospital eight Decembers ago—his personal Christmas miracle.

"When you're laid up in the hospital," he said, "and you're looking at all those walls, and the room seems so cold and nobody comes to see you for what seems to you like a long time—you work on yourself and Satan works on you, and it's good for people to come through and cheer up other people.

"The best way I know of to cheer up people is to sing, and to get them to sing with you if you can."

In 1982, when the carolers came to his room at Forsyth Memorial Hospital, Williams, then 20 years old, was laid up in a way that seemed to bar any hope of help or cheer.

The month before, on Nov. 14, he had lost control of his automobile on a tricky curve and crashed into a culvert.

An emergency tracheotomy allowed him to breathe, and he was taken to Forsyth Memorial Hospital. There, a brain scan produced a virtually hopeless picture.

"He was in a coma," said his mother, Joyce Williams. "He knew nothing. His head was swollen up about three times normal—and I'm not exaggerating....He was moved into the intensive-care unit, and he stayed there for 12 days.

"One doctor told us there was no possibility that he could make it—and even if he somehow did, he would vegetate the rest of his life."

Benjamin was moved from intensive care to a fourth-floor bed on his 13th day in the hospital. There, he hemorrhaged and went into convulsions and cardiac arrest. A quick response and emergency stomach surgery saved him again. It didn't bring him out of the coma, however.

"He had gone from 182 pounds to 120 pounds in 13 days," said his mother.

"Then he began to improve, but he was in a deep coma. He did not react to any stimuli. There were therapists coming into the room and working to prevent atrophy. They were trying to put ice into his mouth and do things to stimulate him."

At that point, another doctor told her there was no realistic hope.

The family didn't give up. Benjamin's mother; his father, George "Bernie"

Williams; his brother David; and other family members, including his maternal grandfather, did everything they could think of to stimulate a response.

"We read to him and showed him pictures, and his eyes focused on nothing. We touched him. You know, it's really hard, because you get no response whatever. Every day, religiously, my husband did all kinds of therapy."

Through it all, Mrs. Williams said, the family appreciated the care—and the caring—of the hospital staff.

Despite all the care, however, nothing happened for Benjamin. He remained comatose.

And then, on one of those December nights eight years ago, the carolers came singing down the hall.

Wally Carroll, a retired employee of Western Electric and devoted hospital volunteer, was acting as guide, as he does every year.

"I heard the carolers singing," said Mrs. Williams, "and Benjamin began to sort of twitch. I thought, 'Well, he *loves* Christmas carols.' I went out into the hall and Wally Carroll and the group were there.

"I said, 'My son is in a coma, and I would really appreciate it if you would come in his room and stand at the foot of the bed and sing.' So they came in, and they began to sing."

The singers finished "O Little Town of Bethlehem" and began "Silent Night."

"Now, this is a person whose eyes look as if they have cellophane over them," Mrs. Williams said of Benjamin.

"His body doesn't move, except in convulsions. And tears started to run down his eyes!

"The nurse said to me, '*Did you see that?*' I thought she was talking about the tears, of course. I said yes. She said, 'There's just a glow in this room.' And there was. It was a feeling I just can't explain."

"God Rest Ye Merry Gentlemen" was followed by "Joy to the World."

"Benjamin's tongue had been clinched [between his teeth] for a month.... His mouth opened, and he began to mouth the words of a carol they were singing. No sound came. He could not force the air through his diaphragm."

Like Mrs. Williams, Carroll was excited—and deeply touched.

"Normally," he said, "if we are asked into a room, we stay three to four minutes. We sing one carol, because we're short on time. But we were so excited about him, we probably stayed at least 20, maybe 30 minutes.

"By the time we left, he had given us a weak little wave and had his eyes open, and he was moving his lips. You can rest assured, there wasn't a dry eye in the house. Everybody was just totally overwhelmed."

The next day, Benjamin spoke, telling his brother David that he needed to go to the bathroom. David immediately called their mother, who rushed over with assorted other relatives.

"When I came in, my son David was so happy that he threw me up in the air—and broke two of my ribs," Mrs. Williams said.

With the help of speech therapist George Dicola and others, Benjamin started bouncing back with surprising speed.

"It was like people came out of the woodwork to help me," he said. "A network of people. For instance, when I first started walking and getting out with people my own age, those who initiated it were people I hadn't seen since grade school or high school at Parkland."

The carolers, who had returned to the hospital to visit him, became friends. Later, he added his tenor voice to theirs. He also went back to Forsyth Technical Community College—his father enrolled right along with him—and then got a job with Sears.

Today, a hesitation remains in his speech, but when he does speak, it is obvious that he is an intelligent—and lucky—young man.

He *feels* lucky. That's one reason he sings with the carolers—because he hopes that, in some small way, he can help people as he was helped, eight years ago.

"There are a bunch of people in this world," Benjamin said. "If we can't help each other, we're a dying race."

(12/23/90 WSJ)

EPILOGUE: *Benjamin Williams recently lost his job as a machinist at BE (Aerospace Inc.). He's job-hunting, and he said, "Machines don't talk to you. People do. I want to get out among people and participate in life more." He sang for about five years with the Christmas carolers at Forsyth Memorial Hospital. At Oaklawn Baptist Church, he teaches a class of young boys about Christian living, Christian ideals and Christian missions all over the world. He said, "Children are a special gift." He occasionally sings in the church choir, and he said, "I feel blessed."*

(9/00, 7/01 Interview)

"It Ain't No Time for Makin' Bricks Now..."

About 11 years ago this winter, CBS-TV newsman Charles Kuralt came to Winston-Salem to do an "On the Road" story about George Black, the brickmaker. Members of Black's family were impressed and thrilled.

"Oh, Papa," one of them told the old man, "this is a national television reporter wants a story."

"I can't help that," replied Black. "It ain't no time for makin' bricks now." Kuralt and CBS would have to wait until it could be done right.

Celebrity came late to George Black, who died here...(10/9/80) at age 103.

Hard work came first—as it always had. He had walked to Winston-Salem with his father and brother from the town of Liberty in 1889 to get a job that paid $1 a day, and he was to make bricks by hand for the next 86 years.

Over the years, Black was interviewed many times about his craft. In one of the interviews, two years ago when he was 101, Black talked about the beginnings.

"My daddy fed the mud mill," he said, "and me and my brother off-bore [carried away the molded brick]."

Soon his father died, and Black—the son of a former slave—began thinking about what he and his brother were getting out of their jobs in the brickyard.

"Me and my brother was discussing it," he said, "and I said, 'Will, how come we can't put us up a mill? We'd get everything Mr. [R.W.] Hedgecock gets for selling the bricks and everything we get for molding 'em.'

"By us being colored, he [the brother] said they wouldn't buy them from us."

But Black started his own mill anyway. And people did buy the bricks, which were delivered by mule. Soon Black had four people running the operation, and he could turn out 4,000 bricks a day.

And when mechanization came in, Black pretended not to notice, and his business thrived.

Wachovia Bank & Trust Co. still wanted his bricks. So did R.J. Reynolds and Old Salem and Colonial Williamsburg. The product, after all, had that instant-old look—and in addition to that, it was good.

So George Black just kept on making his bricks, and by 1978 he could say with a satisfied smile, "I've got bricks scattered all over the world."

After Kuralt was finally able to do his story on Black, he slipped off to a mountain retreat where he relaxed, ate good food and, in the middle of the night, played pool in the basement game room of a chalet.

"Let me tell you about this old man in Winston-Salem," he said.

And Kuralt talked on and on about George Black, the craftsman, the black man who had earned dignity in the turn-of-the-century South, who cared about every brick he made.

Kuralt's visits brought Black to the attention of the governor and the president of the United States. The old man was honored by Gov. Bob Scott; he was triply honored by President Richard M. Nixon. He was invited to the White House and sent to the underdeveloped nation of Guyana to teach people how to make bricks.

"I enjoyed it, all right," Black said of his months-long 1971 visit to Guyana. "I had a good time with the white people. They wanted to learn how to make brick, and I taught them, and they treated me much like they did white men."

By then, Black was something of a folk hero. He'd had his picture taken several times with the president; the national press had been making a big fuss over him; and in 1972 Nixon used Black's picture in one of his re-election advertisements.

And when asked what his greatest pleasure had been in his 100-plus years of life, he replied: "Our church used to have a picnic, and I enjoyed that."

As recently as two years ago, Black was demonstrating brickmaking at Carolina Street Scene. "Some of them wanted me to show 'em how to do it," he said. "I can show them, all right."

But Black wanted to talk more about another of his great pleasures, one he had lived through for about 90 years—the change in relationships between the races. "It's been a wonderful change," he said, sitting on the porch of the well built, well kept home he was proud of. "It used to be so that a colored man, he didn't have a chance.

"Now, if a colored man does right, he'll have as good a chance as anybody."

In 1972, Kuralt spoke in an interview in the Columbia Journalism Review.

"In the past year," he said, "I expect my own favorite story has been the one we did with George Black, a 92-year-old brickmaker in North Carolina, a black man who started in his trade in 1889 and has hand-made the bricks that were used to build many of the buildings in his home town...

"He is quite a remarkable man. It is rare that a newsman gets to see positive results from his work, so when something like this happens and a man who has worked long and honorably receives some credit in his last years as a result of one's own work, that is very satisfying."

In addition to the uncounted bricks seen around town today, Black left behind a son and daughter, 26 grandchildren, eight great-grandchildren and five great-great-grandchildren.   *(10/10/80 The Sentinel)*

EPILOGUE: *The George Black house on Dellabrook Road has been added to the National Register of Historic Places. Black's granddaughter Mrs. Evelyn Terry said that Grace Napper, sculptor/student of Earline King, is working on a bust of Black to be placed in downtown Winston-Salem.*   *(9/00, 7/01 Interview)*

Here Is "The Gift"

As usual, Dr. B. was running hard and late.

He had to hurry, to get back on schedule.

The doctor couldn't know, then, that there could be no rushing this day because Mrs. R. would arrive bringing him what he now calls The Gift.

Mrs. R., a chubby, uneducated child of poverty and the rolling hills of Piedmont North Carolina, wobbled uncertainly into the office.

As a youngster she had staved off hunger by eating grass and weeds as she worked in the fields. Later she lived her life doing for others while doing without, and things never got much better.

Now she was in her 50s and her bright eyes and country-stout body could no longer tell the lie of robustness. She was worn to the depths of muscle and nerve tissue too long deprived and depleted.

She was so weak that she couldn't stand during the examination, but she had somehow summoned the stamina to earn money for the visit by priming tobacco.

Dr. B. quickly dismissed any idea of payment for himself, but he worried about the money other treatment would cost.

He also wondered about her own worries, which he was certain must be many.

"Mrs. R.," he said, "tell me: Do you worry a lot?"

She looked up, shaking her head no, her eyes widening and chasing away the creases that had come with age.

"Dr. B.," she said, "God answers every prayer in His own time."

She paused, then added:

"What prayer won't, worry can't."

And so, as usual, Dr. B. continued to run late. When he finally went home, he kept thinking, "'What prayer won't, worry can't.' What a beautiful gift."

Little did he know that The Gift would be severely tested the very next morning.

Mr. A. was a successful man who wanted for little but peace of mind. He had been through psychological counseling, neurological evaluation and more, and still the weight of his worries was too heavy to bear at times.

The doctor knew his patient had been given everything that higher education and training and specialization could give him.

He decided to share The Gift of a totally "uneducated" woman of the fields.

The effect was stunning. If there are revelations, this must have been one.

"Dr. B," said Mr. A., "I've tried almost everything. I just didn't know what to do next. And now—well, that woman doesn't have to worry about any medical expenses. I'll take care of them.

"She has given me the greatest gift that can be given."

The Gift has lasted. Mr. A.'s new found emotional ease and optimism have remained.

What prayer won't, worry can't.

If the words aren't "sophisticated" enough, change them.

But keep The Gift. It will still be giving a dozen birthdays or Christmases from now.

(10/27/81 The Sentinel)

Joel Likes Doing Things Himself

"**I**'m going to buy me an electric wheelchair," said Joel Stafford. "I'm going to take it to school so I can roll myself around."

Joel likes doing things himself, and he wants the money for the chair—perhaps $1,500—to come largely from his own efforts.

You have to believe he'll reach his goal. Joel is a bright, quick-minded little boy who at age nine is already doing well in fifth grade; he is also a little charmer whose wide eyes and happy smile make you want to cuddle him.

But you don't dare cuddle Joel. You might just add to the uncounted number of broken bones he has suffered during his brief life.

Joel was born with osteogenesis imperfecta ("I can't say that"), a condition that robs the system of the calcium needed for bones to harden and develop. There are steel rods in his small legs where most of us have bones, and his arms have not developed enough even to allow bone-replacing surgery.

And how is a little boy who can't get around by himself going to raise all that money for a wheelchair?

"I've cut a record," said Joel.

He explained that he sings regularly at Beck's Baptist Church, where his parents—Wayne and Linda Stafford—are members, and has been invited to sing at other area churches. And since he has a cousin who plays with a band called The Starlighters—well, the next step seemed logical.

"I talked to my cousin," Joel said, "and he talked to the guy over the band. They played for me."

Since then, the record—"God Is So Good" and "Because He Lives"—has sold about 1,000 copies.

Joel is still a fragile boy, but he hasn't had a bone break since February—a big improvement from earlier days when simply moving the wrong way could cause a break.

"When we brought him home from the hospital, we had to carry him on a pillow," said Mrs. Stafford. "He had break after break…You couldn't even rub him with a cloth…He could roll over in bed and break a bone."

The Staffords have been lucky. Their moderate income was too high to allow treatment of Joel in a state hospital, but with the help of a good insurance program—Stafford is a postal clerk—and acceptance at the Shrine Hospital in Greenville, S.C., Joel has gotten the best of care.

"He's been down there three different times for operations," Stafford said, "and once for therapy. He's stayed as much as eight weeks at a time. Since 1970, he's spent about six months there."

"I don't keep count of that," said Joel. "Daddy keeps it."

Joel goes to school at the Children's Center, and when asked what he does there he replied: "Work, mostly."

But as he talked about that "work," it was obvious that he likes it. Reading, for example, is an enjoyable part of his school and home life:

"I read books and I have a workbook. After I read stories I have some work pages. I have to answer some questions about the story.

"I like to read about animals. I read library books, and then I've got a... take-home reader."

Joel goes to ball games and other events, as well as church, with his parents. And, like almost all nine-year-olds, he likes to play and watch television.

Because he is not strong and can't get around, Joel has to stay with play-things he can handle. He plays cards and enjoys matchbook cars, and he has just about all the Fisher-Price miniatures that are on the market:

"I've got a gas station, a Holiday Inn, a house, camper...schoolhouse—oh, yeah, the farmyard...

"I play with Lori and Darin [his sister and brother] and my two friends named Cindy....

"Oh, yeah—I've got one dog, a Pomeranian."

Having provided what he considered the last bit of necessary information, Joel broke into one of those wide grins, looking as happy as he sounds when he sings on that record:

"God is so good...He's so good to me."   *(9/14/76 The Sentinel)*

EPILOGUE: *Joel got his coveted wheelchair in 1978, but it was stolen. When people heard of his misfortune, they sent him money to buy a new one.*

"This one I had only went five miles an hour," he said. "The next one will go nine miles an hour. Plus the wheels will be twice as wide."

Young Stafford wheeled his way through North Forsyth High School, where he graduated with honors in 1984. He attended Wake Forest University, planning a business career, and had intended to go back after dropping out temporarily. He died Nov. 28, 1985, of injuries suffered when his wheelchair tipped over. Sieg wrote... "Stafford was not quite 19 and severely disabled, a winner in life despite cruel adversity."

(12/01/85 WSJ)

Lurl Tyson, a Class Act

The lady with the elegant little-white-lie hairdo was all smile and sparkle as she welcomed a visitor to her home on East 22nd Street and put him at ease.

This was Lurline "Lurl" Tyson, a near-legendary figure in East Winston, whose claims to fame included wearing her hair in 58 different colors over the years.

And by previous standards, this day's hair could hardly qualify as even a fib.

"This is my natural hair," she said.

"My whole family, their hair turns white when they get old."

Then, smiling, she added:

"I use a peroxide rinse. You know, white hair can get dingy and yellowish. I don't like that yellowish."

There is nothing dingy about Lurl Tyson.

Never has been.

She was a class act even before she went into business 40 years ago as the state's only maker of human-hair chignons—add-ons for someone's own hair—and wigs.

She still is, although she's toned down both hair color and lifestyle—which may be why old acquaintances have been asking SAM (news column) and others about her of late.

Although she may no longer be the livest wire in town, she still seems to run on high voltage. At 70, recovered from cancer, she still makes hair products in her home, where she cares for her 52-year-old retarded son, Leon Wendell Pate, who has lived with her since his birth. Her flower paintings also have brought her a first-place prize this year.

During a recent visit, Mrs. Tyson seemed pleased to recount some of what made her such a fixture here from the 1940s through the 1960s. "All of my jobs were centered around being able to care for my son," she said, adding that Wendell used to be a rather well-known man-about-town himself before inner-city development and drugs made it too dangerous for him to walk the streets.

Mrs. Tyson's 1947–1959 marriage, her second, was Wendell's doing in a way. As a youngster, he needed surgery that was offered by a state institution in Virginia.

To get the surgery for him, she needed to establish Virginia residency. That part was no problem; she simply moved. But she also needed to be married.

"I told my boyfriend, 'I need a husband,'" she said. "He knew my son. He loved my son. He was happy to help me." In Virginia, she had made straight

A's at Hicks Beauty School in Richmond, where she studied hair manufacturing. She took an advanced wig-and-styling course in Chicago.

In 1948, with $8 worth of hair, she set up shop as Lurl's Tresses House at 11th Street and Gray Avenue in Winston-Salem.

"I made a chignon," she said. "I made several. And my business grew from that…North Carolina didn't have any handmade hair whatsoever."

She began weaving real-hair pieces into people's own hair, as well as making chignons, wigs and other pieces. Her business also operated as a regular beauty shop.

Soon she had several employees and a larger shop and mail-order business. The good times had arrived.

Then, however, something else also arrived.

"These two big fine-looking white fellows came in with some briefcases. One of them said, 'I'm looking for Mrs. Tyson.' I said: 'Well, she's not in right now. Could I take a message?'

"He said: 'I'm from the IRS. We want to check her books. So tell her to have her books straight when we come back.'…When he got back, I had my hair a different color. I was Mrs. Tyson that day."

She ended up owing $300 in back taxes—and going off to business college so that she could be sure to keep straight with the IRS. It was one of many trips back to school.

The Tresses House moved several times, twice because of fires. Finally, with real handmade hair fading in an assault by cheap competition, she closed down except for a small in-home shop. She went to work first for the Robert E. Lee Hotel and then for the Children's Home.

Mrs. Tyson and the business had become famous for at least two things in those years, however.

One was the beehive—that cone of hair that women by the millions set on top of their own to give them a "regal" look.

"I invented that," she said. "I went to a convention in Washington, D.C., in 1954, and I needed something to show."

She told a friend she wanted something unusual, she said, and he pointed to a hornet's nest above her head, and said, "There's your piece of hair."

"I've seen in the paper several times where they wonder who invented the beehive," she said. "I don't have any proof [records were lost in a fire]. But that's how the beehive was born."

Another claim to fame came when she rode as parade queen for the Winston-Salem State Teachers College (now University) homecoming through the 1950s—and in the city's merchants' parade in 1956 and 1970, when she entered three floats.

"I was the first blonde colored lady in Winston-Salem—in North Carolina, they said," Mrs. Tyson said with a hearty laugh.

"And then I always had convertibles, and my clothes and my hair matched. One year I had a long black and white Impala convertible, and I had on a black stole and a white satin dress. My hair was two-tone, black and white.

"In the merchants' parade in 1970, I rode in a pumpkin…as Cinderella." Wendell rode in the parades, too.

Today, as always, he is at the core of Lurl Tyson's life. Even in 1975, when she learned that she might die of cancer, her fear was for him. She gladly accepted an experimental treatment, she said—and it worked.

And as he began to require more time, she spent more time at home.

"You know," she said, "my hobbies are raising flowers, painting and reading the Bible. That's my favorite book."

Recently, she won first place in an art show at the Sawtooth Center. That pleased her, but not as much as another prize—Wendell's.

"He paints," she said. "I teach him. I've just taught him to do a little bit of everything I've done….He won a prize at the fair last year in a special program for the retarded."

That's Lurl Tyson, update 1988.

She's still very much around.

And still a class act.

(5/22/88 WSJ)

EPILOGUE: *Today, Wendell, 65, entertains passers-by with his harmonica playing, said Mrs. Tyson, 82.* *(7/13/00 WSJ)*

Ahead of her time, Mrs. Tyson has worked over the years to get help for the handicapped and spoken up for better education for everyone. She brought the same attitude to her work, where she created colorful hairdos at a time when they were unique. Today, tinted hair in various combinations is popular. Asked how her ideas grew, she said:

"Mama said to be independent, to be a woman who could take care of herself and use her own mind." Mrs. Tyson said her accomplishments came from "believing in myself and knowing I needed to take care of my son."

(9/4/00 Interview)

He Faced Himself and Found Himself

Johnny B. didn't make it.

Or did he?

Johnny died last week at age 49, a victim of lung cancer that had been diagnosed less than four months earlier.

But if death were defeat, we would all be losers in the end. What matters, I suppose, is the victories we win for ourselves or others during our lifetimes.

If life had been a football game, the bookies would have stopped taking bets on Johnny years ago. As a homeless street alcoholic, he was too big an underdog, fated not only to lose, but to lose dramatically.

He bounced from the streets to jail to local hospitals and to Butner, where he was treated for alcoholism so many times that he seemed to develop an immunity—to the treatment, not the disease.

Once, as he stood before A. Lincoln Sherk, then a District Court judge, Sherk looked down at Johnny's records and said in his most solemn court-room voice, "Johnny B., acute alcoholic."

Johnny smiled. "Thank you, your honor," he said.

Years later, he would explain: "I thought he meant I was pretty—you know, a cute alcoholic."

Sherk, who now practices law here, remembers Johnny well.

"He was a regular," said Sherk. "It was a revolving door....I offered Johnny a deal: If he'd stay sober, I'd find him a job. He never would. He couldn't do it."

David Abernethy, who now directs substance-abuse programs for the Forsyth/Stokes Mental Health Authority, also remembers.

"He was one of the first patients I encountered in 1970, when I came to work," Abernethy said. "He had been classified as a chronic homeless street alcoholic. A number of times, since we were located on the eighth floor of the O'Hanlon Building, I had to physically help him into the elevator after a taxi dropped him off outside."

Often, Johnny's home was the Buzzard's Roost, the old Eighth Street hang-out and watering hole for street drunks. His living room was a stone wall and concrete sidewalk; his bed was the ground, his cover a bush.

But then, 10 years ago, something happened to Johnny. He started to face the truth about himself and his life.

I first talked to him in 1976, when he was staying at the Winston-Salem Rescue Mission and working on a mission truck, picking up donated goods. He'd been sober awhile, and he liked the feeling.

"It's a terrible problem," he said then. "I am an acute and chronic alco-holic. I've been to Reynolds [Health Center] a few times. I've been in Butner [alcoholic-rehabilitation center] a few times….I've been out at Union Cross. It's messed my life up."

Amazingly, Johnny stayed sober, with the help of his church and his wife, who had lost everything because of his drinking but had never divorced him. But he did it by withdrawing from much of life, sheltering himself from challenge and disappointment rather than meeting the world on its terms.

Once more, briefly but near-lethally, he went on a binge. And then, after years of trying to blame other people and circumstances, he told a doctor: "I am the problem." It was his way of hoisting the white flag of surrender.

From that moment on, Johnny lived to help himself and other alcoholics. He joined Alcoholics Anonymous, and soon he was speaking at meetings, telling his story and giving hope and faith to others who thought they had none. He began sponsoring other alcoholics, counseling them and staying close to them as they struggled to follow him and others in recovery.

Now, he felt, he was really living.

"This program is my life," he told me in 1983. "The next time I drink, I'll either die or go crazy as hell….This is the only way I know how to live now—one day at a time."

The news of his lung cancer was not easy to take.

"I started aching in my chest," he said, but he delayed going to the doctor. Finally, he listened to his friends who urged him to get medical help.

His chest was X-rayed, and he was immediately referred to a specialist…. In a letter reporting on the condition, the doctor wrote, "Specifically, he is felt to be suffering from a small-cell carcinoma, a tumor of the lung that is generally rapidly fatal…."

"I had an emotional crisis to start with," said Johnny. "I was just so sick and wore out. I was dead tired and didn't know which way to turn. I felt despair."

But, later, a month before he died, he felt differently.

Then, Johnny said, "I'm not depressed about life whatsoever. I'm wanting very much to live and try to help other people…."

During his illness, Johnny's A.A. friends saw that he and his wife lacked nothing. After his death, they donated money to help with expenses. One woman, who is not an alcoholic, was moved to remark: "If all us Christian people supported one another the way A.A.'s do, what wondrous works we could do."

In his later years, Johnny did some wondrous works. He did them by being decent, caring and sober, and by demonstrating through example that the road back was indeed open.

"I don't think you could get no lower than he was and come back," said George, who was sponsored by Johnny. "He helped me a lot. I got close to him, just like a brother."

For Jim, the personal relationship wasn't that close, but both the sponsorship and the example were important.

"He was about the first one I ran into in the treatment center," said Jim. "I was dragged in, kicking and screaming. I didn't think I needed to be there. He was a big help....I could relate to him. I knew if he could do it, I could do it."

That was precisely the point Johnny was trying to make. Jim and others understood it and used it to help rebuild their own lives. In turn, they are helping others rebuild theirs.

Did Johnny B. make it in life?

You bet he did.

I think it's important that we understand that.

(8/17/86, 9/30/86 WSJ)

City Is in Dire Need of Compassion Clause

When a sewer line backed up and pumped its foul flood ankle-deep through 90-year-old Effie Fox's home Sunday, the city was quick to demonstrate an apparent lack of compassion.

The furnace was flooded, and everything on or near the floor was tainted by the reeking, unsanitary effluent. A city clean-up crew worked on the house and was to have continued working yesterday.

The city's immediate concern, however, seemed to be for its liability, or lack thereof. It would pay no more than its established $1,000 limit in such cases, a spokesman said, adding: "Legally, we are not liable for any of the damage....If any citizen thinks that their home is not healthy, it is their responsibility to take care of it."

Legally? What about ethically? What about morally?

It seemed obvious from the sheer quantity of sewage pumped into the woman's home—an estimated 1,000 gallons—that the flow came from one of the city mains, and not from the line from Mrs. Fox's house to the main line.

Why, then, should it be her "responsibility to take care of" the fecal and bacterial contamination?

One person questioning the city's stance Tuesday, after the situation had been reported by the *Journal* and by WXII-TV, was Clyde Dula, a 65-year-old manufacturer's representative who called the newspaper.

"It was almost like— 'Are you really dumb enough to believe this?'" Dula said. "The description of what happened here is a backup in a main, not her own sewage.

"I just feel that the explanation smells as bad as the sewage. It's a blow at our intelligence....

"I was just wondering if someone couldn't say, 'Come on. Let's get with the real world. Water doesn't run uphill.' And so on."

Dula's call came as I was leaving the office to talk to people around town and ask their thoughts.

If responses of 17 people in and around the Parkway Kitchen and Dunkin' Donuts restaurants were any indication, the city's $1,000-and-no-more position would be thrown out in any court of public opinion.

"I think the city should pay, 100 percent," said Phil Froelich, a retired Cadillac dealer. "It was the city's sewage system that caused the problem, wasn't it? That's how I read it....

"When I say 100 percent, they should replace everything that's ruined: carpet, clothing, everything. I don't think $1,000 is going to cover it....

"If it happened to my mother, I'd take 'em to court. I wouldn't hesitate, if I had to borrow the money. I just think they have a responsibility. Let them stand up to it."

Verlie P. Cox, a retired R.J. Reynolds employee, said almost the same thing that several others said:

"The city should pay for all of it. The sewer line—doesn't it belong to them? If it was mine that did that, I'd think they ought to pay for it….They got money for everything else. Why not pay her for this?"

Only Greg Proctor, who works for a seafood restaurant, was even slightly hesitant, saying that he knows that people often try to get out of paying when the responsibility actually is theirs.

"First," he said, "I think they should find the problem. If it's the city's fault, I think the city should pay for it."

By then, although neither Proctor nor the interviewer knew it, the city had acknowledged that the problem indeed seemed to have been with a stoppage in a main line.

But others who were interviewed had already come to that logical conclusion.

Shirley Bradley, a lab technician for a health-screening service, recoiled at the very thought of such a backup.

"I think they ought to buy her a new house, with furnishings," she said.

"I wouldn't want to live in it, unless I was sure it was sanitary."

Mrs. Bradley's co-worker, Pat Burchell, agreed: "I certainly wouldn't want to live in such an unsanitary atmosphere….It's the worst kind of bacteria."

Her husband, the Rev. Harry Burchell, the pastor of Mount Carmel Church of the Living God, said: "I see more than a legal liability. I feel like they've got a moral responsibility to this lady."

The views from construction workers, an insurance agent and a homemaker were similar to others: The city did it; the city should be liable for whatever it takes to put everything back the way it was before the backup left the house awash in feces.

And Paul Williams, retired from AT&T engineering and teaching now at Forsyth Technical College, wondered aloud about Mrs. Fox's advanced age, about her financial ability to cope with the situation without the kind of help he thought she was owed.

"I guess what they say is that anywhere in the house that it backs up, the homeowner should pay," said Williams. "But even if it had been backed up, it would have been only what had been flushed in the commode.

"It must have been some back pressure somewhere. I think the city should be responsible for it."

That made it 18 for Mrs. Fox, none for the city.

I suspect that views would have been less harsh had the city merely seemed to possess that missing compassion.

This, after all, is a 90-year-old human being in a terrible spot, with serious and possibly health-threatening problems.

The city should be concerned, first and last, with her well being.

It's a simple matter of that "civilization" our fair city urges visitors to rediscover.

(11/24/88 WSJ)

EPILOGUE: *"It was the worst thing that I've been through in my life, but I've pulled through. I've been across Jordan's River, and it's good to be back home," Mrs. Effie Fox said of her experience.*

After publicity from the Winston-Salem Journal *and WXII-TV, the city spent about $3,000 to get Mrs. Fox's home back in livable shape, and many volunteers also helped.*

(12/3/88, 12/7/88 WSJ)

Mrs. Fox died Nov. 18, 1993.

The Utilities Commission kept its established $1,000 payment limit on sewage backups until recently, when it raised the cap to $5,000, according to Thomas W. Griffin, assistant city manager of public works. A property owner would receive the money if the backup was the first occurrence, and the owner agreed to pay for installation of a stop valve, which, hopefully, would prevent future backups.

(2/14/01 Interview)

Leukemia Patient Likes Being a Student

Marvin Cobb spoke slowly, but distinctly and without hesitation, as he read from a book held in front of him: "THIS IS A GIRL....THE GIRL HAS A BIRD....THE GIRL HAS A BIRD IN HER HAND...."

Cobb, who is 59, is known across the state and beyond for his craftsmanship in shoeing thoroughbred horses. But he had never learned to read, never paused long enough, until illness slowed his pace last fall.

"I just didn't think about it," he said recently as he waited for a checkup at Baptist Hospital.

"I had a job I made a good livin' on. I didn't think I needed any education. When I worked, I always found plenty to do without reading. I ain't lazy."

Cobb, who lives in Gibsonville, near Burlington, learned in November that he has leukemia. Since then, he has spent much of his time in Baptist Hospital. There, he met Sadie Blevins, a retired local elementary-school teacher who works as a volunteer five afternoons each week in three departments.

Mrs. Blevins had taught other patients to read, although that isn't part of any of her volunteer duties. She'd had some marked successes, using materials from Forsyth Technical College, but she found Cobb hesitant at first.

He said: "They told me they wanted to send somebody up to the room.... I said, 'I'm pretty well satisfied with the way Marvin Cobb is right now.'

"Anything you ain't ever been used to, you're not going to miss too much. But I didn't know I was going to be in the hospital so much."

It was difficult for Cobb to accept the help. Through his work with thoroughbreds, he had become respected not only among his peers but in the wealthiest and most powerful circles in the state. He wasn't rich, but everything he and his wife owned—including their comfortable brick home—was paid for. He was, and is, a proud man.

But he was going to need help and support in other ways. Confident of what had seemed robust good health, he had carried almost no medical insurance. When medical bills soared toward $100,000, his home folks quickly organized a benefit horse show to help pay them.

"I've got more friends," Cobb said. "A woman told me at the horse show that if I had as much money as I've got friends, I'd be worth a million dollars."

He accepted those friends' help. He also accepted Mrs. Blevins', and both of them are glad he did. And his wife, Vallie, is as happy as either of them.

"I've always been a reader," Mrs. Cobb said. "I go to the library....I've tried to tell him, but somebody who's never read can't understand the enjoyment. A lot of your troubles disappear when you open a good book."

Cobb laughed.

"I don't think I'd like the same books she would," he said. "She reads about haunted houses and things."

Mrs. Cobb said, "I like Gothic novels."

It will be some time before Cobb can read novels or other books, of course. He's not ready for those yet. But he's been a good student, Mrs. Blevins said, paying close attention during lessons and doing homework at other times.

"The other day," she said, "he read four full sentences. When he realized he had read everything he's been given, he was deeply touched....That's worth a lot."

Cobb agreed. "It's nice to see Miss Sadie here again," he said. "She's one more fine lady....

"I feel good about it now. The studying has been easy. I've enjoyed it. I'd like to be able to pick up the newspaper and read it. I don't know what all I'll do with it [being able to read], but I'm going to read the paper, for one thing. I don't care about television anymore. It's all the same old stuff."

He probably won't be able to go back to work, but Cobb intends to have a lot of time for his new pastime.

"I'm going to lick this stuff," he said of his leukemia. "If I ain't gonna be able to work, I need something to pass the time off."

That kind of outlook is one of the rewards that makes the work worthwhile for Mrs. Blevins.

"It gives me a sense of accomplishment, in a way, to see another person begin to learn to read and to see the doors it begins to open," she said.

All of the efforts are about hope, of course: hope for a good life after recovery and for new pleasure to replace the old one that came with hard work.

"If we didn't have hope," Mrs. Blevins said, "we wouldn't have much, would we?"

(5/7/87 WSJ)

EPILOGUE: *Marvin Cobb died Dec. 30, 1987. Mrs. Cobb said, "He was very sick, and our time together was very precious to us."*

She is still reading her Gothic novels. "I still love to read," she said. "It's a godsend...when you're alone in a house to get lost in a book."

(12/6/00 Interview)

Brenner Gives Life to Young Boy

Call this a thank-you card.

The thanks, to the staff of Brenner Children's Hospital, are for a young life that might have lasted only hours or days without the expertise and technology available at places like Brenner.

The life belongs to Pearce Shoaf Dougan, a happy, energetic youngster who turns a full year old next week.

The people at the hospital might not recognize Pearce today. When they first saw him almost a year ago, he weighed one pound, 13 ounces. A photo, taken then, shows him to be little more than the size of a nurse's hand.

"He was born 13 weeks early at Forsyth Memorial Hospital on Easter Sunday, April 15, 1990," said his mother, Linda Shoaf Dougan. "About five hours after he was born, he was transferred to Brenner."

Mrs. Dougan and her husband, Kent, had more reason than some parents might have for concern. A year earlier, she had given birth to a girl, Kendra, who arrived even earlier than Pearce.

Kendra didn't make it. Her lungs weren't well enough developed.

"So when you're there with this tiny new baby [Pearce], all these things are running through your mind: things that happened a year ago," said Mrs. Dougan.

Unbeknownst to the Dougans, the year since Kendra's birth and death had made a great deal of difference, to them and to Pearce.

"They told us that if Pearce had been born six months earlier, he would not have had the advantage that he had," Mrs. Dougan said. "That's because of a new drug that they give to the child with his first breath."

There were other differences, as well. Kendra was never able to be moved to Brenner.

As it was, Pearce faced unfavorable odds.

"Once they got him to Brenner, they told us the next three days would be critical," Mrs. Dougan said. "At that stage, their organs are not completely developed."

The baby was put on a ventilator, she said, and his heart and other organs were constantly monitored. "He required a lot of attention at first, but mostly what they said he needed to do after the first couple of weeks was just to lie there and get bigger."

The Dougans were cautioned that things could go wrong, and some did, but they and Pearce persevered. The child still undergoes monthly evaluation at Amos Cottage, and his parents know that some problems could still occur. He has done remarkably well, however, and their vision for him goes in only

Pearce Dougan turned 10 on April 15, 2000. –CHRISTINE RUCKER

two directions: forward and upward.

For that, they feel, they have Brenner Children's Hospital to thank.

"At Brenner, they wouldn't let you have any negative thoughts. They always told you what could go wrong and what it would take to correct it, but they wouldn't let themselves become negative, because they didn't want you to fall into those thoughts. They were always optimistic....

"They treated him as if he was one of their own. There wasn't a single nurse or doctor or a single person in transport or respiratory therapy who did not treat him as if he was their own child. They just showed him that type of attention. He never lacked for attention the whole time he was there."

Today, Pearce seems healthy, weighing in at 20 pounds. And since he started crawling and standing several weeks ago, he is so active that his mother is sometimes worried.

"When he found out he could go forward, I had to block off parts of the house," she said. "His sole purpose in life seems to be to chase after my cats, Pebbles and Ciba. And he has a dog, a black Labrador named Tarheel. And Tarheel's sole purpose in life seems to be in taking care of that baby."

Mrs. Dougan had thought, as Pearce's birthday approached, of sending the people at the hospital a picture of him today as a kind of thank-you card, asking: "Do you recognize this child?"

Then she thought again.

"We owe a lot of his strength to the people at Brenner, because the Brenner strength rubbed off on him and gave him a determination to survive.

"How do you thank people who have given you your son and given you the opportunity to help him grow and learn and prosper?"

How, indeed?

Thanks, Brenner.

(4/7/91 WSJ)

EPILOGUE: *Tom Sieg had asked Mrs. Dougan to call the* Journal *when Pearce was about to turn 10. She did.*

"He is as healthy as a horse," she said. Pearce has a perfect-attendance record at school and at Sunday school. A straight-A student, he has taken part in an accelerated reading program. He has earned trophies playing basketball, his main sport, and also flag football and baseball. *(4/4/00 WSJ)*

Chance Photo Keeps Alive
Memory of One Veteran

Row upon row, the monuments stood like silent granite sentinels on military review, paying homage to Forsyth County's fallen 20th-century heroes.

The face of each stone bore the name of a veteran, and behind each name lay a poignant human story. I had come looking for the name and story of Billy Ray Anderson, who died in Vietnam in early January 1971.

Briefly, however, I found myself adrift in memories of Korea, and of my childhood during World War II, when so many men went off to war and never came home again.

This poster photo of Billy Ray Anderson, taken in the early 1950s, was long a trademark of the apple industry worldwide. –MAX THARPE

Beside me, Billy Ray's mother, Mildred L. Anderson, brushed away a tear and choked back another.

"I like this," she said. "This is nice. It's real nice.

"It's good that they think of the veterans this way. They *should* honor them. They should, because they fought for this country here—all of them."

In the array of markers, nothing distinguished her son's stone from neighboring ones honoring other veterans: Robah C. Shields Jr., World War II; Ronald Ray Hammett, Korea; Charles R. Pegg, World War I; and, in all, 481 others who fought and died.

Still, by odd coincidence, we had parked 20 feet from Anderson's monument and had walked directly to it.

Mrs. Anderson and I were together because of a telephone call from a reader, Dennis Bohannon, to SAM, the *Winston-Salem Journal's* answer man. Bohannon had visited the memorials outside the new Joel Coliseum and thought about Anderson, whose name he couldn't remember.

Every year at the Dixie Classic Fair, Bohannon said, he saw the same poster of the same smiling little boy, eating an apple. He knew that the boy was from Forsyth and had died in Vietnam.

"I would like his name," he said, "so I can see his marker."

The name was Billy Ray Anderson. And the poster photo, taken by Max Tharpe of Statesville in the early 1950s, was long a trademark of the apple industry worldwide.

It still graces the walls of expositions and fairs and is displayed at the International Apple Institute's offices in McLean, Va.

Mrs. Anderson, who is retired now and lives downtown in the Winston Apartments, winced at the memories evoked by the familiar picture.

"That's him," she said. "Yeah, that's him.

"Gosh. That picture is in the fair, and it's been in bank buildings....

"When I worked for the government, people would write letters and send him gifts.

"I don't mind seeing it. It's just that it brings back too many memories. I try to forget it...."

Her voice trailed off, then returned to tell the story.

She was reared in Moravian Falls in Wilkes County, married there and bore five sons, including Billy Ray, and a daughter.

While she and her husband were together, he worked in apple orchards and furniture factories. Sometimes they sold apples on the sides of the Brushy Mountains roads.

"We were over the line in Alexander County this one time, selling apples by the truckload," said Mrs. Anderson. "This guy in Statesville, Max Tharpe, he comes along, and he wants to take this picture of my son.

"He said, 'I want to adopt that boy there.' I said, 'No way!' He said to Billy Ray,

'How's that apple taste? Why don't you take a bite?' And he took his picture."

The chance encounter with a little charmer produced Tharpe's most famous photograph, the one he named "Juicy Fruit Smile" for Billy Ray's infectious grin. Soon, the picture began to appear everywhere.

It followed Mrs. Anderson 30 years ago when she left her husband—his drinking and abuse became intolerable, she said—and brought her brood to Winston-Salem, where she went to work.

"I worked in restaurants," she said. "I worked in a cold-storage plant; I crated apples. I taught school, believe it or not, as a substitute teacher."

She also finished raising her family, and when Billy Ray was 17, before Vietnam had become an American war, he charmed her into signing his papers for enlistment in the U.S. Army.

Almost nine years later, as a volunteer for a third Vietnam tour and winner of eight Bronze Stars and four Purple hearts, he was killed in a Viet Cong ambush.

Now, almost 19 years after her son's death, Mrs. Anderson stood at his monument, a granite shaft 3 feet high and 8 inches square. She was glad she had come, impressed by the tribute to all veterans, as equal at the memorial as they would be in a national cemetery.

"It's a great thing," she said, visibly moved by the experience. "It's really well done...."

Again, her voice trailed off. Clearly, she agreed with Dennis Bohannon, who had made the telephone call that brought us together.

After visiting the memorial, Bohannon had come away baffled by the bickering among local veterans over naming the coliseum for Lawrence Joel, who won the Medal of Honor for service as a medical corpsman in the Vietnam war.

"When I saw it," Bohannon said of the memorial, "I really got the sense that it is for all the veterans.

"When anybody walks in front of that coliseum, it projects that it is honoring all men who served—and especially Forsyth County men. It gives them respect. It gives them honor.

"I wish they'd quit fighting."

The wish is well and aptly made.

If you spend time at the memorial and come away without even a small surge of emotion, let me know. I'll be surprised.

So will Bohannon.

And so will Mildred Anderson.   *(9/10/89 WSJ)*

Breaking the Line Wasn't Easy

Alex Morisey is the Jackie Robinson of southern journalism.

Just as Robinson broke the color line in major-league baseball, Morisey broke the line in southern newspapers, becoming the first black reporter on a daily newspaper south of Washington.

He also was instrumental in getting news of the black community out of the specialized "colored section" and into the general news pages.

As Morisey lay in his bed at Baptist Hospital yesterday, it was still easy to see in him the qualities friends had described earlier: the erect, dignified bearing, the preciseness of mind, the tactfulness in describing his life and times.

Morisey's effect on journalism began being felt in the 1940s when he was North Carolina correspondent for the *Journal and Guide* of Norfolk, Va. "I wrote some columns, editorials, feature stories," he said. "But naturally all the stuff was black news…I made a strong effort to expand what might be called traditional black news, to show how the general news was impending upon their lives."

One aspect of that expansion was to have an impact on Morisey's career, on the *Winston-Salem Journal* and *The Sentinel*—and on journalism itself. "Since my interest to this point was watching the governor's office and state," he said, "it occurred to me, 'Why shouldn't I be going to the governor's press conferences?' So I decided to go. I just walked in like everybody else and stood around and started talking. I asked a question related to registration of black people in Eastern North Carolina."

In those days, that in itself was news, and the Associated Press reported Morisey's attendance and questioning.

"Then came the *Journal* and *Sentinel*," said Morisey. "They wanted a black reporter. I went over to see Wally Carroll [then executive editor]. They saw my clippings and they made me an offer."

Morisey didn't relish putting out a "black news" section every Sunday, but he thought he might have a chance to expand and extend that traditional coverage in a way similar to what he had done with the *Journal and Guide*.

"I didn't see this as just a black news assignment," he said. "I saw it as coverage of the community. Newspapers in that day just weren't doing the job in the black community. A hell of a lot of them still aren't.

"I felt that for human relations and race relations—for it to improve, there had to be more understanding. I thought the press could do some of that by writing about what the people on the other side of the tracks were doing in the arts, in education, in politics.

"I don't know how or when the line broke, but all of a sudden I began to get in the paper during the week. I covered spot news....I had front-page by-lines. I put in full-time on it and I was able to turn out stories they thought were important."

Morisey covered everything from sports to social programs, but his special interest was politics. He kept track of black candidates in the state and who won and who lost.

And he found that blacks who won sometimes didn't quite win in the same way that whites did. "In the Greensboro council election one year," he said, "they had a black candidate. After the election, they [council members] would elect their own mayor. The general rule was that the man who got the most votes would become mayor.

"And you know, this black man got the most number of votes. But they changed the rules. They elected somebody else."

Morisey eventually left, in the 1950s, to go to work for the American Friends Service Committee, and later he worked in public relations for *The New York Times* and two colleges. But by the time he left here, he had helped create a growing awareness that Winston-Salem was a community, not two communities that could coexist and generally ignore each other.

Morisey takes great satisfaction in what he was able to do here, and it especially pleases him that he was accepted in the newsroom from the start. But he doesn't pretend that there were no rough spots, and he obviously knows that his white friends—no matter how dear—did not fully comprehend the meaning of being black.

There was, for example, the matter of the restroom. In 1950, the law said there had to be separate facilities for whites and blacks, so a special restroom was built for Morisey. People talk about that situation today almost with amusement, indicating that Morisey didn't mind.

"I didn't like it," said Morisey. "That was one of the most exasperating and painful experiences I ever had. But at that point I was a mature man and I knew that life required compromises. And I knew that someday black people would be in the mainstream of journalism.

"I thought that somehow the damn thing had to be broken. And I thought that if I broke it, it probably would be a great advantage to me. And it was."

(7/14/79 The Sentinel)

EPILOGUE: *After leaving Baptist Hospital, Morisey returned home to Manhattan, where friends said that he fell at home. He was taken to St. Luke's Hospital, in New York City, where he died of cancer on July 23. He was 65 years old.*

(7/24/79 The Sentinel; 7/25/79 The New York Times)

One Good Turn Deserves Another

When Mary Margaret Losier faced the prospect of taking her dog Luke to the veterinarian for the "last time," it was the most difficult, most painful, decision of her life.

Luke, a cocker spaniel, had been treated for chronic ear infections for months without relief and was in terrible pain. With his inner ears swollen shut, his only hope was complicated surgery.

On their veterinarian's recommendation, Mrs. Losier and her husband, Earl, went to a veterinary surgeon. The bill for the surgery, they were told, would be $850. Both ear canals would have to be removed, and Luke would be left deaf.

The Losiers were trapped in a dilemma. They loved Luke, loved dogs in general.

They were volunteers at the Humane Society. Dog figurines were everywhere in their home. A life-size statue of a Doberman Pinscher stood in their kitchen, and even their shower curtain had a dog motif.

It would be terribly hard to let go. "Luke is just a special dog," Mrs. Losier said. "He's black and white with black freckles on his nose. We've watched him grow up. He was a fun puppy....You could sit and look at him for hours at a time because he was so entertaining."

On the other hand, the Losiers, married a year, were still getting started in life together, she as a loan officer in a mortgage-banking company and he in sales. They had no money to spare, and they worried about the implications of Luke's deafness if they did somehow scrape together the cash.

Mrs. Losier said: "We decided after a couple of days of deliberating that we would have to have him put to sleep. It was the hardest decision that we've ever had to make in our lives. It was awful."

And so, with her husband out of town, Mrs. Losier took Luke to the veterinarian's office.

There, oblivious to others, they played out a scene that must have been almost as painful to watch as to be part of.

"I remember in the car on the way over there, it was all very emotional. I felt like somebody was just jerking my heart out," Mrs. Losier said.

"It was awful. It was just like we were in our own little world in the corner of the office, saying our goodbyes to each other, me and Luke. They took his collar off with the tags on it, for me to keep....

"And they took Luke off around the corner. And they let me stay in the office until I could—until I was OK to drive home.

"I came home and wrote in my memory book about Luke and put a picture in there of him…and basically mourned all night."

The next morning, still crushed at what she believed to be the loss of Luke, she went to her office. Shortly after she arrived, she received a telephone call. The caller was her veterinarian.

What could the veterinarian want? To console her, to tell her that Luke passed peacefully?

That alone would have been an act of kindness, and Mrs. Losier would have been appreciative.

This call, however, was more than that. Much more.

"The veterinarian said, 'Mary Margaret, you're not going to believe this.' She said there was a lady in the office while I was saying goodbye to Luke, and she was so upset about me having to lose Luke and have him put to sleep that she was crying after I left.

"She was in the examining room, crying and saying it broke her heart. She said she would be honored to pay for any surgery that had to be done to Luke, so that we could stay together. And she wanted to remain anonymous.

"I could feel my heart racing in my chest. All I could do was run out of my office and tell everyone….and the people in my office were in tears."

In the end, Luke had his surgery—and an ecstatic reunion with the Losiers. Today, at home and healed, he is a happy, pain-free dog who responds to affection and vibrations set up by stamping on the floor. He doesn't seem to know, or care, that he is deaf.

The anonymous good Samaritan is probably pleased to know all that. She will probably be pleased, too, to know that her kindness has meant even more than that in the lives of the Losiers.

"The lady who paid for Luke's treatment, she told the vet to tell me if I could ever help anyone in my lifetime, for me to do it," Mrs. Losier said.

The Losiers do help. In the weeks since Luke's surgery, they have rescued an abused dog and placed it in a good home. But now they hope to do more.

"I *look* for people I can help now," Mrs. Losier said. "And one day I'll do for someone the same thing that this lady did for me, because of the way it made me feel.

"To know there are people out there that are that caring….I could never explain the thankfulness, the appreciation I have for what the lady has done."

(8/4/91 WSJ)   *Mary Margaret and Luke reunited.* –ALLEN AYCOCK

She's Alive!
Birth Certificate Perks Up Woman Listed as Stillborn

KING—Margie Calloway looked better now that she was alive.

Not that she looked bad seven weeks ago, for someone who had been born dead 50 years earlier. This time, however, there was more color in her cheeks, more sparkle in her eyes, her smile, her voice.

"For the first time ever, I am alive," an excited and enthusiastic Mrs. Calloway said when we talked last week. "I am alive—*officially*. I can't *tell* you how good it feels."

Her excitement was occasioned by the arrival of a simple letter-size piece of paper: a birth certificate. For her, however, it was far from simple. It proved that she existed and was who she said and knew she was.

Some of Mrs. Calloway's story was told in this space on March 17, her 50th birthday.

She was born in 1941 in Chipley, Fla., to Claude and Mellie Everett. For some reason, her mother—involved with another man and preparing to leave her husband and children—had listed her as stillborn and declared her officially dead.

She didn't know that, then. No need arose for a birth certificate until much later, when she applied for a job with Southern Bell in Atlanta. That was when she learned what her mother had done.

For the next 30 years, she was unable to convince the Florida bureaucracy of her existence despite the diligent efforts of two congressmen and an attorney retained by Mrs. Calloway, and despite repeated applications and submission of affidavits and school records.

One problem was that she and her father lived with friends in 1950 and were missed in the U.S. Census. Another was her mother.

"My mother wouldn't help me," she said during our earlier visit. "I got a letter from a half-sister of mine, asking me to leave her [the mother] alone, saying this had really upset her. There was just some reason she didn't want it uncovered. I will never understand it."

About two months ago, however, her luck began changing when Charles C. Bolton Sr., a retired letter carrier and postal-union official, dropped by my office. Bolton had heard Mrs. Calloway's story and suggested that I look her up and perhaps write a column about her predicament.

I did. Then I telephoned Ted Brown, who is Lt. Gov. James Gardner's special assistant for constituent affairs, and transmitted copies of some of Mrs. Calloway's documents to him by facsimile. He called Florida officials, and he called Mrs. Calloway.

"The state of Florida called me just a few hours later," she said. "The woman there told me they had found me on the 1945 state census in Washington County.

"Just like that. That easy. She said I would be getting my birth certificate. All I had to do was fill out this final paper....I was very skeptical."

So she waited. And she wondered why, if the state could find a census record on her so quickly now, it couldn't find one in all the years before. She wondered how hard other state employees had tried, and whether they had known or cared how desperately she wanted that proof of her live birth. She wondered, too, if even the census record would be enough, after all her disappointments.

Her skepticism gave way to enthusiastic optimism 10 days ago, however, when—30 years after she first tried to get a delayed birth certificate—the precious document arrived in the mail.

"I told my family to go out and buy me a gold frame," she said. "I had always said if I got it, I was going to frame it in gold. But they haven't found one big enough yet, so I've got it in brass for now."

By the time we talked, Mrs. Calloway had already telephoned Brown in Raleigh to thank him.

"You know," she said, "you've always heard that knowing the right person is all it takes to get anything done. I didn't believe it. I really didn't. But it just so happens that's exactly the way it was."

Brown was happy to be that right person.

"I got a kick out of her," he said. "She called me and she said, 'Guess what I'm holding.' She's really a nice lady. I'm just thankful this thing worked out."

Mrs. Calloway is thankful, too—and not just because the birth certificate can simplify such important tasks as dealing with Social Security when retirement time comes. Her reason, and her gratitude, run deeper than that.

"The main feeling that I have now is, I don't have that sense of rejection that I lived with all my life," she said.

"How much deeper can rejection be than to be rejected at birth? That's about as deep as it can be.

"The way my mother had it listed...it sort of makes you insecure. You have to work on it.

"I guess I'll never know the real reason....It's in the past. It's something I'm not going to think about anymore."   *(5/5/91 WSJ)*

Competition "Fulfills a Desire...Inside You"

Elmer Clayton spends his leisure hours in the summer playing golf and in the winter playing basketball.

"Everybody needs to compete in something," he said in an interview. "It just fulfills a desire that you have inside you."

In Clayton's case, the desire is strong. It has had to be; he lost both legs just below the knee in Vietnam in 1967.

Asked how a person adapts and learns to get around on two artificial legs, Clayton replied:

"The main thing is, you've got to *want* to. I went through some physical therapy courses. The most important thing is getting your leg strengthened, broken in—it's really tender.

"When I got out of the hospital, I was still walking on crutches. I walked on them about a week until I was able to balance myself without them."

Then came the return to the sports he had loved as a youth in his native Roxboro.

"The fact that I'd played golf and really liked it before I lost my legs helped my rehabilitation," Clayton said.

"When I got out, a lot of the friends I had played golf, and they wanted me to play with them again. I remember the first time I went out to play, I guess I'd been out of the hospital about two months, and I could only play six holes. After six holes, I was so tired I could hardly stand it.

"Then each time thereafter I played just a few more holes and made my legs stronger by doing that. So I think that's been a large part of my being able to hold a job like the one I've got here [at ITT Grinnell], because I am on my feet quite a bit of time during the day."

Now, Clayton plays at least 18 holes, and 36 if time allows. He shoots in the low 70s—far better than most golfers without physical handicaps—and tries to play twice a week during the summer.

Clayton's basketball is the wheelchair variety, and he enjoys it just about as much as golf.

"I play for the Winston-Salem Smokers basketball team," he said. "It's a member of the Carolinas Conference...."

The Smokers, with a 5-15 record, are not burning up the league, but that doesn't bother Clayton.

"When I was in high school, I played on the basketball team," he said. "This gives me a chance to play again, and I just love to compete.

"I think one of the best things about it is that it gives a lot of people a chance to compete who wouldn't normally have that chance. The paraplegics [who are paralyzed from the waist down] are the ones I'm thinking about."

Clayton was married in 1971, and he and his wife have two young children. From all appearances, his life is as normal as most and more so than many.

And if there is one way he still feels his handicap, at least it's only one.

"The only way I feel limited," he said, "is that sometimes I just want to get out and really run. Just run for the hell of it."   *(2/3/77 The Sentinel)*

Faded and Torn, But It Persevered

Bob Tannehill took his flag down and put it away yesterday.

The banner was badly faded, tattered and beginning to shred in places, and it should have been. It had hung there, outside his western Forsyth County home, since shortly after the American hostages had been taken captive in November 1979.

"It's funny," he said, holding the folded flag after he took it down, "but now that it's deteriorated to the point that it has, I want to preserve it. It just might mean something to somebody one day."

It already meant something to Tannehill, a former newsman, who is now director of community relations for Forsyth Memorial Hospital—just as it had all during the time it had been up.

Originally, the idea of hanging a flag hadn't even been his own.

"My late neighbor, Bowman Brookbank, called me one morning the week the hostages were taken," he said, "and asked me if I would put up an American flag on the front of his house as a tribute to the hostages.

"I told him I'd be glad to do it and I thought it was a good idea. When I finished putting his up, I went out and bought a new one and put it up myself the same day."

The next afternoon it began to rain, and Brookbank took his flag down as the U.S. Flag Code says you should during bad weather. But Tannehill didn't touch his.

"I just left mine up," he said. "I had heard that under certain circumstances it was all right at a private residence to leave a flag up at night and in inclement weather. And I thought that these circumstances warranted it.

"Actually, I didn't think it would be necessary to leave it up 440 some days. I thought I would be taking it down before it became faded and tattered....I thought it would be a couple of weeks."

Although Tannehill isn't what you would think of as a flag-waver, he deeply respects the symbol of America.

"I normally put my flag up on appropriate holidays," he said yesterday afternoon, "but I never leave it out. I'm not sure I would have put it up if I'd have known it was going to be this long. I think so much of our flag that I'd be the last to dishonor it intentionally."

Tannehill, a former paratrooper and Korean war veteran, is of a generation that grew up with the American flag.

"You remember when we were kids," he said, taking a deep puff from his pipe, "and the cowboys and Indians were fighting. All of a sudden—da-da-da-tah-dah—the cavalry would come charging over the hill. It just thrilled me to death.

"As a kid, on my first bicycle, remember how they had those flags and they put them on the handlebars? I had to have one of those.

"And, of course, in the military academy [that he attended as a youngster], a lot of emphasis was put on the flag.

"I love the American flag, and I think that's nothing uncommon."

As for the condition of his flag—well, Tannehill thought that, perhaps, in the eyes of Americans and others around the world, that might have become symbolic, too.

"The flag, like the Bible, is a piece of material," he said. "It's what it stands for that is sacred....

"It didn't bother me as I noticed the flag deteriorating over the weeks and months because to me it stands for something. It's a symbol. It stands for the hostages."

He sat and stared straight ahead, across his living room, for perhaps a full minute.

And then, speaking at least partly of the long hostage ordeal and the American flag generally, he added: "I think, to a certain extent, the flag has been faded and tattered as a symbol of our country."

(1/21/81 The Sentinel, newsfeature)

EPILOGUE: *In the aftermath of the tragedies of Sept. 11, 2001, in which terrorists hijacked four American commercial airplanes and caused a monumental loss of life and destruction, Tannehill said that he thought people respected the flag even more than they had before the attacks. People who didn't give it much thought or had never displayed it have put it up now, he said. In fact, Tannehill said, after the attacks, a family friend, Mary Bones, had phoned to thank him for giving her a flag (much earlier), which she had just put up. (Television news commentators reported that flag sales in the days after the tragedies increased dramatically.)*

For several years, Tannehill, now retired, has permanently displayed a protected flag outside his home. And what happened to his old, faded, tattered flag from the earlier hostage era? Tannehill said, "I still have that flag. It's in a box in the attic."

(9/13/01 Interview)

"Making the Best of a Bad Thing"

Edward Paul Hull's split-level home alongside a rushing creek in southern Forsyth County isn't your everyday suburbanite's dream.

It's drafty, for one thing, and hard to keep clean; and it has only a roof and two walls.

Hull, 53, is living under a bridge, with his bedroom a bunk tucked into a nook on the underside of the abutment, his closet a wooden pole sunk into the ground and his kitchen and living room the bank above the stream.

"Come in, gentlemen," Hull said this morning as a reporter and photographer approached. He was huddled beside a cooking pit he had built from scavenged rocks. Beans and coffee were cooking on the fire, and leftover potatoes were in a pan on the back of the "stove," keeping warm.

"Have some breakfast," he said. "Have some beans, if you can stand 'em. Want a cup of coffee? I ain't got nothin' but creek water, but it's going."

Edward Paul Hull huddles beside a cooking pit built from scavenged rocks. –ALLIE BROWN

It was cold—"cold as hell," as Hull put it—but he didn't seem to mind. He was wrapped in two blankets, but under those, only a T-shirt covered the upper part of his body.

Despite the crudeness, the place seemed well organized. A board across the top of a barrel served as a kitchen counter, with each bit of food and supplies seeming to have its own place; and the cans and bottles and other litter that had been strewn all around were stacked together in a neat pile.

"Oh, it's a mess up here," Hull said. "The damnedest mess I ever seen in my life. People don't care about nothin'....I cleaned up around here a little bit, planted some seeds."

He had also been clearing brushwood around the area, but that was partly a matter of survival. On mornings like today's, a fire is a must.

Hull moved to his present quarters recently from a spot under another bridge. He has been living this way for about two years, he said, since he sold his car and could no longer sleep in it.

"See," he said, "I had lived some up here with my [late] mother. I lived in the car some. It was parked down here at our homeplace. I felt I was more comfortable there at times.

"This is just a temporary assignment, temporary quarters, as far as I'm concerned, because of lack of funds or more suitable housing accommodations.

"The main reason why I came here was because of the comforts I knew that I'd receive because of the water—running water. The sea will do the same thing for me. I can find comfort. It seems like tensions will just leave."

Those tensions, said Hull, are the reason he is in his present condition.

He came up in Forsyth County during the Depression in a family of 15 people. He quit school in sixth grade and, for a time, worked wherever a youngster could find work in those hard times.

"My first job was in a sawmill," he said. "I was working some for farmers around the farm—neighbors—priming tobacco or whatever, for 25 or 50 cents a day. If you could find somebody who had the 25 cents to pay you."

With the war taking older teen-agers away, Hull found a couple of more regular and better-paying jobs and then, in 1945, went into the Navy himself. Afterward, he became an over-the-road truck driver, married and settled down. But the marriage, like Hull, was fated to break down eventually.

He worked hard, he said—perhaps, too hard.

"I stayed in that as a driver 28 full years," said Hull. "But just like most people, I guess, I just tried to do too much too long and broke my health down. The way it was termed by the doctors was nervous tensions....I was in and out of John Umstead Hospital at Butner on three different occasions. The last time I was down there I had to go for shock treatments and medications of different types.

"I tried to work, do what I could do, different things. But I couldn't work in my own profession….For the past four years, I haven't been on anybody's payroll. Doin' pretty much just what you see, just trying to make the best of a bad thing."

One reason Hull is such a loner, he said, is that when he is around others, they want him to take the medications that had been prescribed for him during his worst years of emotional strain. He'd rather live under a bridge.

"I've been through some hellish problems with that medication," he said. "I was under all that stuff and me trying to work, too, for 18 or 19 years. I just had to drag myself. It was sapping me. It was taking all my energy. It ruint my life."

So now Hull stays under the bridge, willing to contend with the cold and discomfort, eat what little he can afford with the help of food stamps and wash in the icy water in exchange for what peace the solitude and running water give him.

And he dreams. He dreams of someday amassing a fortune and buying a mountain and building an open-door church and offering food and a clean, warm place for others who may have lost their way as he lost his.

For now, however, his dream is smaller.

"What I want now," he said, "I'd like to find some suitable employment where I could establish some comfortable living quarters. Just one room and a bath, where I could keep myself clean and comfortable."

And until and unless that comes, he said, he isn't feeling sorry for himself.

"There's others that might be less fortunate than I am," said Hull. "I'm not froze yet."

(1/8/82 The Sentinel)

EPILOGUE: *Hull came in from the bitter cold to the Rescue Mission for just a short time, but he couldn't stand the confinement that came with the warmth and comfort, and he missed the outdoors. He eventually found an empty house where he could sleep and he ate meals with various friends. He did come part-way in from the cold.*

(1/8/83 The Sentinel)

Happily Ever After
Cinderella Meets Prince

When Carl Taylor moved from Lexington to Winston-Salem's West Hill apartments on Dec. l, romance never entered his thoughts.

He was 70 years old, after all; and his wife of 42 years, Addie, had died only recently.

"I just wanted to stay here and live here and make it my home," he said.

Likewise, Louise Redmond, 64, was an unlikely candidate for romantic involvement.

From her early youth, Miss Redmond had been tied to her mother's apron strings, unable even to date young men except during a few months that she spent at a beauty school, where she managed to go to the movies with a couple of young men.

"My mother wouldn't let me date," she said.

"I had epileptic seizures. She was afraid that I'd have one and a boy would pitch me out on the side of the road. That's what happened to a girl in Washington, D.C., and she was always afraid that a boy would do me that way...."

"I've been a housekeeper all my life. I was my mother's Cinderella. I washed the windows. I scrubbed the floors. I did everything."

Over the years, she continued to play Cinderella, first hopeful that her handsome prince would come, then resigned to missing the ball altogether. Meanwhile, her epilepsy made it impossible for her to get a driver's license or become independent in other ways.

When she was 37, her seizures simply left her, never to come back.

"I don't give nobody the credit for that but God," she said.

Shortly after that small miracle occurred, she took a course to become a professional sitter for sick people. Among the people she cared for was her mother.

A dozen years ago, they took adjoining apartments at West Hill. She cared for her mother until six years ago, when her mother died.

At that moment, her mother seemed to realize her mistake in controlling her daughter's life for so long.

"When her death came," said Miss Redmond, "she told me, 'Louise, I was too hard on you. You should have been married a long time ago and had your family. I didn't do right by you.' She hated it."

By then, it was too late—or seemed to be.

When she met Taylor, who had come to town to be closer to his daughter, she was no longer even thinking happily-ever-after romantic thoughts.

Neither was he, as a recent and still-grieving widower.

Now, less than four months later, they're as giddy as a couple of teenagers, planning a wedding for 2 p.m., Sept. 1, at West Hill, so that residents who lack transportation will be able to attend.

Yesterday, they reflected on what had happened to them—how their lives had taken such a sharp and exciting turn at such an unlikely time.

"I met her in the hall out there the first day I come here, when I was moving in," said Taylor, a retired textile craftsman. "I didn't fall in love with her right then. It just gradually came along."

It began, said Miss Redmond, when she and a couple of other residents became ill and Taylor stepped in to cook for them and doctor them with home remedies.

"He just spoiled us," she said.

Taylor grinned in agreement.

"I waited on her when she got sick," he said. "I made her soups."

He also invited her to his Baptist church, and she invited him to hers. Soon they began going out for a sandwich or ice cream.

"Oh, we'd have a good time," he said. "And we would always agree with each other. We don't one go this way and the other go that way. We always agree…so far."

What about Taylor appealed to Miss Redmond?

"He was nice, kind, and he was a Christian. I really admired him."

And what in her appealed to him?

"Her kindness, her looks. She's good to everybody. She's friendly. She always meets you with a smile. She ain't got a frown on her face."

By last weekend, Taylor's mind was made up.

"He said, 'I sure would love to marry you,'" said Miss Redmond.

"I told him, 'Now, Mr. Taylor, I don't believe in jumping into a marriage. That's too sudden.'"

She wanted to allow a decent interval between his wife's death and his remarriage, however. Finally, they settled on Sept. l.

"I'd rather it'd have been May 4, so we could have all summer together," he said.

She didn't seem to mind waiting, however—perhaps, because she was accustomed to it.

"I've dreamed of having a home and family," she said. "I laid awake when I was a child dreaming of having a home and a family and a husband.…I built my castles and watched them fall."

Now, at 64, she's built a castle with Taylor.

Clearly, neither intends to let this one fall.

(3/22/90 WSJ)

Transplant Became Only Hope for Heart Recipient

Within 24 hours of 30-year-old Robin Grimes' death Nov. 23 at Forsyth Memorial Hospital, her heart was pumping life into Charles Madison, a retired math teacher at Surry Community College. (In addition, her organs and corneas were helping at least eight others.)

Ms. Grimes, who died last month after falling from a moving car, had been a Stokes County housing specialist for the Northwest Piedmont Council of Governments for seven years. She lived in Winston-Salem.

The transplant of the heart, performed at the Bowman Gray/Baptist Hospital Medical Center in Winston-Salem, had been Madison's only hope.

"For 10 years, I had looked at death," he said Wednesday at the center, where he had come for a follow-up biopsy.

"I knew 10 years ago that the only salvation I had was a transplant. And really, for the past 10 years I had not been free of pain. I always had some angina, from mild to severe."

There was no pain during the interview, and Madison, 55, appeared vigorous, if not yet robust.

His own heart had been damaged 12 years ago, when a strep-throat infection resulted in cardiomyopathy, a degenerative disease that causes the heart muscle to stop working. Once the disease was diagnosed, he said, his physician tried to keep him alive while transplant techniques were improved.

"He bought me time," Madison said. "He said: 'Charles, it's not working. The rejection factor has got to be overcome.'"

While he and his doctor waited, he became progressively weaker. In late August, he retired on disability from the community college.

"We finally reached a point this fall where no further treatment would do any good," Madison said. "That's when the transplant became my only option. I'd gotten to the point where I could not even take a shower without having to lie down and take a rest."

"The cardiologist who was taking care of me said it was time to come over and see [Dr.] Barry Hackshaw. So that's what we did."

Hackshaw and surgeon Dr. A. Robert Cordell head the heart-transplant team for the medical center.

By the time Madison was referred to the team, his doctor's wish had come true: The drug cyclosporine, in use at the center since the inception of its heart-transplant program more than a year earlier, had significantly reduced the risk that a recipient's immune system would reject a donated organ.

At 6 p.m., Nov. 23, shortly after Ms. Grimes' death, Madison received word that a suitable heart had been found for him. Ten hours later, the surgery began.

Afterward, Emma D. Bowman, the center's cardiac-transplant coordinator, said that it was probably the smoothest piece of surgery she had seen.

The center does not reveal donors' names to recipients or vice versa, but Ms. Grimes' parents, Therrell and Peggy Grimes of Thomasville, quickly knew by piecing together media reports that their daughter's heart had gone to Madison. He agreed to be interviewed knowing that, in the process, he would learn their identities, too.

Even before he knew who they were, however, he had spoken with Ms. Bowman about them and been touched by their willingness to donate their daughter's organs to help others.

"I wrote them a letter anonymously [through Ms. Bowman]," he said. "I explained how I felt and thanked them."

As he discussed what their decision had meant to him—and to perhaps eight others who received organs or corneas from their daughter—tears welled in his eyes, and his voice choked at times.

"This gave me the only hope that I've had in 10 years," he said. "I felt nothing but compassion for someone who cared enough for someone they did not know to make such a gift—give them a life…

"They gave the greatest gift that they could give to someone who was dying. I realize now that I did have less than six months to live. I did not know it at the time. I just cannot think of a greater gift that anyone could give.

"This donor…is living through at least nine other people. It's difficult to describe. The main feeling you have is gratitude for people in this world that will help their fellow man."

Today, Madison—his full name is James Charles, but he uses only Charles—is taking a long-term forward look at his life for the first time in more than 10 years.

"I feel the best that I have felt in 10 years," he said. "I am feeling stronger…. I'm riding an exercise bike. Yesterday, I rode 25 minutes. I can get out and walk without tiring."

There are other activities that seem important now, too. Madison knows the grim statistics: Half of those who manage to get as far as the computerized list of heart-recipient candidates die while waiting; for other organs, the figures are even worse.

"There are so many accidents.…Organs could be used if people were just aware and knew of the need of other people," he said.

"I want to go out and talk to civic groups and church groups and explain, as a living example—as a recipient of a donor heart—and try to promote the donor program as much as I can." *(12/27/87 WSJ, newsfeature)*

EPILOGUE: *Ms. Grimes' other gifts included: kidneys to a man and a young woman in North Carolina; her liver, to a patient in Missouri, where cells extracted from her pancreas also were used to control at least three patients' diabetes; and her corneas to patients through the North Carolina Eye Bank.*

(12/27/87 WSJ)

"I cannot give the Lord enough credit for the happiness He has sent my way," Charles Madison said 13 years after the transplant. He just received an excellent report on the state of his heart after his recent annual biopsy at Carolinas Medical Center in Charlotte.

Today, Madison, who has remarried, talks to schools and civic, religious and medical groups about the need for transplants. After one of his talks, two of Robin's cousins and an aunt spoke to him. Madison said, "It was so thrilling to meet some of her people.

"I have had 13 years of life that I would not have had, had it not been for the love of Robin Grimes [for others]," Madison said. "Her whole family had love." To be thinking of others when their child was brain dead—"That impresses me to no end." *(2/5/01 Interview)*

Betty Lyons Celebrates Her 118th Birthday

Betty Lyons has aged a good deal since a year ago, when she observed her 107th birthday at her Lewisville home.

She's celebrating her 118th today.

Mrs. Lyons, the oldest person in North Carolina, and perhaps in the United States, might never have discovered the 10-year error that was made in her age somewhere along the way if she hadn't become ill last December.

Her need to enter a nursing home led the Department of Social Services to check old U.S. Census Bureau records. She was listed during the 19th century as having been born in 1866, a year after the end of the Civil War.

"I just go by what the Good Book said," Mrs. Lyons said this morning, trying to explain her unusual number of years on earth. "It said honor your mother and your father so that your days might be long on the land. I've tried to do that."

Mrs. Lyons is a bit—and only a bit—hard of hearing, and her mind is sharper than those of many whippersnappers of 80 or less.

Until her illness slowed her down, she was able to do most things for herself in Lewisville, where she shared her home with a grandson. She still washed clothes on a washboard, although she had slowed down on such other activities as splitting her own firewood.

"I was doing my housework and all that—washing and ironing and keeping clean—until I got to the point where I couldn't do for myself," she said.

"I haven't been doing much from that time to this. I haven't felt like much."

She wasn't even sure she was going to celebrate her birthday.

"This might be the only party I'll have, you-all coming out," she said.

State Sen. Marvin Ward was already in the wings, however, waiting for other dignitaries to join him in presenting her a certificate making her a much-belatedly official member of the state's Century Club. Ward had spoken with June Barbour, a spokesman for the N.C. Division of Aging, who had confirmed Mrs. Lyons' age.

"She is the oldest person in North Carolina," said Ward, "and they raised the question, Is she the oldest person in the United States?"

A birthday cake was ready for the occasion, and more celebrating was planned for the weekend by her friends and fellow members of New Hope AME Zion Church, where she still goes to worship the Lord and sing His praises.

"She loves to sing, she loves to go to church," said Paul Thombs, pastor of the church. "As a matter of fact, she came to church last Sunday. She has a lot of life. She's a fighter. She's very religious, believes in God. She believes in hope in the life to come."

Thomasina Hawkins, a long-time and dear friend, enjoys a special status with Mrs. Lyons.

"She's my daughter," said Mrs. Hawkins. "She says that [normally] a parent adopts a child, but when you get her age you adopt your own parents. So my husband [Howard] and I are her parents…

"She is just the most sweet and lovable old lady I've ever known. She is caring and sharing for others.…To be her age, she has the best mind."

Mrs. Hawkins said Mrs. Lyons has been happy during her four months at Rogers Family Care Home—so much so that she has decided to adopt Ann Rogers, the administrator, as still another mother.

Mrs. Lyons was born in Davie County and later lived in Yadkin and Forsyth. She and her late husband, Albert Lyons, bought an old schoolhouse in Lewisville many years ago—she doesn't remember exactly when—and worked as sharecroppers in tobacco, wheat and cotton.

"I worked on the farm," she said. "I went from one thing to another.

"After I got older, I went to work in the tobacco factory in Winston-Salem, where you make plug tobacco. I was a stemmer. You had to stem that tobacco.

"I worked in the cook kitchen, did washing and ironing and all that. I stayed on the job for a long time cooking. I had to give it up on account of my health. The last work I did was domestic work. It's been a long good little bit. I won't say when because I don't remember. I always try to tell the truth.

"I'd be doing something now if I was able. But I thank the Lord I've got a good home."

There was no chance for any real education in Mrs. Lyons' early years, and times were hard. But there were good times and good people then, she said.

"Everybody was loving and friendly to each other and would go to church and have good meetings," she said. "It wasn't like it is now. They loved each other better then."

Mrs. Lyons has lost track of the number of great- and great-great-grandchildren, just as she lost track of her own age. She doesn't know how much longer she'll be on this earth, although she suspects it won't be a lot longer, and she seems more concerned with where she's going when she leaves it.

"I try to be nice to everybody and share the Lord as best I know how," she said. "That's the main thing.

"I sing a whole lot. I try to live right every day. I know I don't have much longer to be here, and I want to go to a better place when I leave this world."

(6/1/84 The Sentinel)

EPILOGUE: *Mrs. Lyons died on April 21, 1986, in Forsyth County, shortly before she would have celebrated her 120th birthday on June 1.*

(4/23/86 WSJ)

Couple May Seem Odd, But They're Lucky

As older people around him talked of times and issues he knew nothing of, Albert Lee Stout leaned over and kissed his mother on the top of her gray head. Then, he clasped her face gently between his hands and, gazing directly into her eyes, asked: "Are you happy?"

"Yes," Pansy Stout replied. Fleetingly, they embraced.

Earlier, Albert had kissed a friend and neighbor, Jeff McMillan. Before the gathering ended, he would also kiss the reporter who had come to talk with him and his mother.

"Down's syndrome children are the most loving children you'll ever see," Mrs. Stout said of her retarded son. "I'd rather have a Down's syndrome child than a normal child. And they're made just like God wanted them to be. God put them here for a purpose, and it wasn't to be mistreated and made fun of."

To some, Pansy and Albert Stout may seem an odd couple. He is 15, a victim of a traumatic early life and Down's syndrome, formerly called Mongolism. She was 72 when she adopted him last year.

Friends say they're a perfect match. For years, Mrs. Stout outdid the nursery-rhyme woman who lived in a shoe, helping raise 125 foster children as well as three of her own.

Unlike the old woman of the rhyme, however, she knew exactly what to do. The grandmotherly patience and tolerance she developed then seem perfect, now, for Albert, who is happiest when he can give and receive love with no strings or conditions.

Mrs. Stout's life as proxy mother began in 1953, in Davidson County. While raising her own family with her late husband, James Albert, she was also caring for an elderly uncle. When he died, she had space and time on her hands.

"My children were grown, practically," she said. "I had to have something.... I asked for a baby and they brought me one the next week, 11 years old. She was mentally retarded. Then, I got a little boy, 6, and that's how it started.

"I've had so many children I wouldn't even have beds to put 'em in. I'd have 'em on pallets. I'd never know how many I had from one meal to the other. I've kept 'em while they were waiting to go to court. I had nine at one time. It was just one right after another."

Her willingness to share may spring, in part, from her own roots. Reared in Alexander County in lean times, she married her husband, who lived in Iredell, in 1933—the year that the Great Depression tightened its cruel grip on all of America.

Millions of people took to the roads in those days, forming an American hobo army. Mrs. Stout and her husband were among them. For them and others, first-class travel was finding a soft-riding railroad fruit car to hop. They harvested wheat in Kansas and apples in Washington until she got pregnant, and then, they came home to North Carolina. They farmed in Iredell, worked in a cotton mill in China Grove and then, in 1944, found jobs in Winston-Salem. They moved to Davidson County in 1951, and two years later she became a foster mother to her own little hobo army of troubled children.

Some of the youngsters were retarded, and Mrs. Stout had a special way with them. One of them, who stayed with her summers and part-time in other seasons, was Albert.

"He was three years old before he ever tried to walk," Mrs. Stout said. "The doctor told me I had a live doll to play with all his life, because he'd never walk and he'd never talk. I said, 'He *will* walk, and he *will* talk.'"

In time, Albert's situation at home became impossible. Abused and ill, he was taken away from his natural mother. He was in the hospital when he and Mrs. Stout were reunited. She took him in, then adopted him.

There have been problems. Albert is a timid boy who has still not shaken all the fears and traumas of his early life. Like all Down's syndrome children, he requires loving patience from those around him. When he doesn't get it— when other children tease him or adults ridicule him or shout at him, for example—he sometimes strikes back.

Once, his mother recalls, a neighbor in Davidson County saw him down on his knees praying and made fun of him.

"I told that woman, 'God hears his prayers. How far do you think yours go?'" Mrs. Stout said.

There are few such problems now. No longer in school, Albert is tutored by his neighbors, Jeff and Georgia McMillan, and by others who understand and care for him.

Life is pleasant and easy now. You can see that in Albert's face as he responds to each word or touch, willingly doing what is asked, especially when he thinks it will please someone who cares about him.

"He is one of the best-behaved children I have ever had anything to do with," said Mrs. Stout. "Discipline is no problem. Not for me."

Albert liked hearing that, and he had something he wanted to add.

"Write 'Good boy,'" he said.

It was an easy request to grant. He is a good boy. He is a lucky one, too, to have Pansy Stout to fill his Christmas stocking—and his life—with the good things many Down's syndrome children never find. *(12/15/85 WSJ)*

Simple Gifts Are Precious on the Road to Recovery

You won't find material possessions among the wishes hanging on a holiday tree at Whitaker Regional Rehabilitation Center here.

The wishes, written on paper-cutout ornaments in the shapes of candles, trees and stars, come from patients of the center—people with debilitating illnesses or injuries, some of which will be with them the rest of their days and nights.

Invariably, the patients ask for the important things of life.

"My wish," says one, "is to go home."

Another is even briefer: "Good health."

Others ask simply to be able to walk again, to have a better year in 1992, to be able to use a hand to write again, or to have "no more bad luck."

Charles Hooker, a retiree from Mount Airy, is among the patients who hung their wishes on the tree this season. His wish? "To get well soon."

Like others in the center, Hooker no longer ranks material things very high on his list of life's priorities. "I found out I didn't always really want what I thought I wanted," he said. "I'm like the guy that said, 'When you get what you want, do you have what you need?'

"I'd be happy just to get home and be with the family. That's enough happiness. What else could you ask for? There's nothing else that compares."

Hooker has come a long way back since his stroke a month ago, and he credits "these fine people here" for showing him how to overcome some of the loss of feeling and control of his limbs. He says he has also gained new respect for the fragility of life and the suddenness with which it can change.

"It didn't give me any warning," he said. "You can be feeling good one minute and on the floor the next. It's a funny feeling. You get scared."

He didn't seem scared when we talked on Tuesday. He had learned that his rapid progress had earned him a very special gift: release from the center on Christmas Eve.

"I'll be home for Christmas," he said, smiling broadly.

Nearby, in a large room for patients who are undergoing therapy and training, Mildred Thompson, a diabetic who had recently lost both legs to poor circulation and gangrene, sat in her wheelchair.

Mrs. Thompson, whose therapy had included strengthening her arms so that she could learn new ways of doing old chores without walking, also hung her wish on the holiday tree: "Wish I could help myself do most of the things I used to do myself."

"I want to do my housework, my cooking….I would love to do the things I used to do," she said. "Make my own bed, do my washing. And take my own bath.

"I'm going to miss my sewing, because I can't use the pedal on my sewing machine anymore….And I hope I can continue to go fishing. I love to go fishing…

"It's going to be difficult, but I'm going to do it. I've been looking at the different people in here and the conditions that they're in. It made me stop feeling sorry for myself. That's one of my biggest problems.

"It takes prayer. Constant prayer. That's what I've been doing. I feel like I'm going to be all right. I'm going to make it."

With luck, Mrs. Thompson was to go home sometime today.

Mildred Loos, a widow from Winston-Salem, will also be leaving soon to spend Christmas with a daughter in Virginia. She won't have her wish of "a good foot," however. Not yet.

Mrs. Loos, who broke her foot in three places simply by turning the wrong way in her kitchen, has just begun her road to total recovery. Her experience has been frustrating, but, as with other patients, it has left her focused on what is truly important in life, at Christmas or at any time.

"You find out what you can do without," she said.

Doris Siceloff, whose wish "to walk in the year 1992" also hangs on the tree, shares that perspective. Mrs. Siceloff, an 82-year-old resident of Davidson County, worked at the old Montaldo's in downtown Winston-Salem for 35 years. She is also a stroke victim.

"I was at home in the evening, and this hit me, and I just went over," she said. "I knew what was happening. I called to my sister. I told her I was having a stroke."

Mrs. Siceloff's progress has been slower than Hooker's during the month since she suffered her stroke, but she remains hopeful.

"Oh, yes, yes," she said. "At my age I wish to walk. You know, that just bothers me a lot. I've always been active and able to do things. It's such a change that I can hardly take it in.

"It's taken everything away from me. I just don't seem interested in getting things—material things—at Christmas. I just want to walk like I used to."

All the wishes seemed so simple, so basic. But they *would* seem that way, wouldn't they, to someone who can walk, who hasn't suffered a stroke and who has both legs?

So simple, so basic—and so precious, to those who lack them.

Happy holidays. May your gifts be as precious as theirs. *(12/20/91 WSJ)*

CHAPTER 3

Home Folks

"**H**ome Folks" are people like your neighbors who maybe pulled a prank or two or spent many years in a home, only to have to move away from familiar roots. An elderly lady struggled with Alzheimer's disease. Another woman, Mrs. Fannie Ogburn of Clemmons, spent most of her life in the house of her youth in a historical stagecoach inn on the old route from the mountains to the coastal plain. A Salem College student and an Old Salem tinsmith—both descended from early Moravians—are profiled. Another local man, Mr. Harry, brightened the lives of those around him, with his cheerfulness and appreciativeness. Then there was the young man who found a novel way to propose to his sweetheart. A merchant persevered to capture a shoplifter who almost eluded him in a situation taking on the aspects of an old Alec Guinness comedy. An old-timer reminisced fondly about his travails while working the elections in the "Good Old Days." Then there was the friendship between a local high-school teacher and a friend who drove her around late in her life and helped her take care of her apartment—a tale akin to "Driving Miss Daisy."

These are some of the many entertaining personalities in this chapter.

You Didn't Know that You Saved Sweet Little Shirley's...

We know you're out there in readerland, Scapegoat.

Do you remember, back in the 1940s when you were growing up in Ogburn Station and took a bum rap—and a hard whipping—for something you didn't do?

Well, I'm going to give you your chance for revenge. You remember Shirley, that "sweet" little 8-year-old who used to play with your sister? Well, Shirley did it.

As you know, back during World War II, kids didn't have much, and they had to create their own recreation. You may not have realized it at the time, but Shirley was—well, creative.

To hear her tell it, living out there in the country, with nothing but gardens and dirt roads, there just wasn't a whole lot to occupy the time.

Your sister, whom we'll call Betty Ann, was only 6, so it fell to Shirley to be the leader, to come up with things for them to do.

"We didn't have a lot to play with, so we'd find us something—mudpies and stuff," she said. "And we'd have biddy funerals—dead chickens, dead anything. We had funerals and got all dressed up and cried and preached and prayed. We really did."

Another favorite pastime was abusing a player piano owned by your family. (You may have been blamed for that too, for all I know.) It was the kind of piano that you pumped with your feet, and the harder you pumped, the faster it would go. Shirley and Betty Ann would wait until no one was around and try to pump the thing so fast and hard that it couldn't keep up.

All that, though, was good, clean fun.

Compared to the cigarettes, that is.

"Back then," said Shirley, "smoking was next to sin. For girls, anyhow."

The girls had to be careful and furtive about smoking, since they were left during the day in custody of the older children. You remember that, don't you, Scapegoat? Usually, they could do little better than sneak a cigarette or two, sometimes a pack.

But one day they got really lucky.

"Betty Ann's father drank a bit," said Shirley, "and he happened to go out and she went in and instead of a pack, got us a whole carton of cigarettes to smoke.

"In that time, everybody had an outhouse, except somebody who was very rich. We went in their outhouse—it was a two-holer—in order to be undetected.

"I'm the oldest, so I'm very careful. I'm the leader. We light us up a cigarette and we put it out. We light up another and put it out. All the time, we're wrapping 'em up in leaves and papers and whatnot after we smoke them, and we're throwing them down the holes. I was telling her, 'Now, we can't catch nothing on fire. If we get caught, they'll beat us to death.'

"So we sit there like Marlene Dietrich in all her glory, lighting her cigarettes and putting them out. It must have taken us two hours to light 'em all up and put 'em out. We smoked every one of them.

"We got dizzy, but I was still thinking…We ate onions to cover up the smoking. We went on with our playing; we had forgotten for the time being about the cigarettes. We were in the house getting on high heels and long dresses for a biddy funeral."

At that point everything—the outhouse and its contents—hit the fan, if I may coin a phrase.

"It was the loudest explosion I have ever heard in my life," said Shirley. "I can still see the burning toilet flying through the air, the pieces burning."

Fortunately, when the spark hit the trapped methane gas, the place was unoccupied. (It would have been a rude way to be dethroned.) But as the fire brigade formed, that was little comfort.

"You can see me and this little girl standing back in the weeds," said Shirley. "Long dresses, heels, hat, gloves—we had it all. We watched till it was all over with—grown people carrying water and wondering what happened to the toilet. We were scared to death, just waiting for the sheriff to come get us."

That's where you came in, Scapegoat. In those days, it would never have entered an adult mind that sweet little girls like Shirley and Betty Ann would do something as nasty as smoke—and it seemed obvious that somebody had been smoking.

You were older. You were a boy. You were, therefore, guilty.

You remember the razor strap, of course, and the protestations of innocence that got you nothing but bigger and redder welts. It may be of some comfort to you that Shirley and Betty Ann felt sorry for you.

"We felt bad about that," said Shirley. "Real bad. We really did."

But not bad enough to confess?

"Well, no, not so we'd get the whipping."

So there you have it, Scapegoat: the truth at last. Just don't let Shirley know I was the one who told you.

(8/18/83 The Sentinel)

A Home Can Become a Memory's Storehouse

If you live long enough in one place, it becomes an archive of your life, a repository of its joys and sorrows and its prayers and dreams, fulfilled and unfulfilled.

It may also become very hard to leave, even when there is no choice.

Dallas Lewis has faced that reality and prospect for many months as more and more of the homes of neighbors on Queen Street became the property of Baptist Hospital.

In fact, she and her late husband, Gaither C. Lewis, had originally bought the house largely because they thought that its location near a growing hospital would make it a good investment.

"We bought it in 1944," Mrs. Lewis said in a conversation yesterday. "It was wartime, and we had looked and looked for a house at our price. When we saw it, we said, 'This is it.' We bought it as an investment, thinking we would build later. I still have the house plans."

As life worked out, they never used those plans.

Today is Mrs. Lewis' last official day on Queen Street, the day the keys as well as the house itself belong to Baptist Hospital. She has actually been out of the house for over a week, except for short visits to pick up some things she left behind or to water shrubs that she hasn't moved yet.

She isn't upset with the hospital. Far from it.

"Baptist Hospital has been very nice to me," she said. "I enjoyed having them for a neighbor. And I enjoyed sitting on the front porch to watch the activities at the hospital—even down to the helicopter....

"Recently, it had become increasingly apparent that I would have to leave. They had all the property in front of me and beside me....I felt I needed to be somewhere where there were people around me."

As the time to sell and vacate neared, she tried to avoid dwelling on nostalgic memories.

She was not entirely successful.

She remembered what a good neighborhood Queen Street was part of, then, for young married people raising a family.

"There were no houses in back of us," Mrs. Lewis said. "Just vacant lots. Gaither Jr. used to play with the neighborhood children in the back yard. They would climb the apple tree....None of the women worked then. We would have coffee in the morning, and lunches....If we wanted to shop, we had to go downtown."

She was describing a different neighborhood, and a different world, from what exists today.

But that was where Gaither Jr. grew up and where the Lewises' daughter, Beverley, was born 11 years after her brother. Both started school at Ardmore and finished at Reynolds—and Beverley was Reynolds' senior-class mascot in Gaither's senior year.

They'd gone off to college and returned, gotten married and had children of their own—and come home to visit frequently, bringing the grandchildren.

Through most of those years, until his death in 1983, Gaither Lewis Sr. was a part of all the scenes and activities.

He had made a career in tire sales and was active in church and civic groups—as a Mason, he became master of Salem Lodge—and he was a devoted husband, father and grandfather.

All of the people and activity made for thousands of memories. And if there had been any danger of those memories being lost—well, Mrs. Lewis probably stored them somewhere, even after the place seemed about to burst at the joints—attic and all.

In talking about her discoveries and memories, Mrs. Lewis did her best not to be soggy or sentimental. She was successful—most of the time.

"I found a red fire engine that Gaither Jr. had when he was little," she said. "I found Beverley's dolls and doll-clothes trunks...."

"I found the corsage I wore when I got married, from Morganroth Florist....It brought back memories of being a bride....I found a box of canceled checks that Gaither and I kept the first year we got married. We were paying $3 and $4 a week for groceries."

With family members and friends from New Friendship Baptist Church, she had plenty of help packing for her move. It was a good thing.

"I'd want to stop to read the old letters and newspapers....," she said.

"It was hard. I'd pack a while and cry a while, and then when it got too much, I'd just shut down and leave for a while."

There was nostalgia even in the shrubbery, which Mrs. Lewis will move to her new home, just a bit deeper in the heart of Ardmore. "Some of the shrubs came from my grandmother's," she said. "They went from there to my mother's to Queen Street, and now they'll be coming here."

For Mrs. Lewis, the shrubs also represent a continuity of living things, an extension of the certainty of life's continuing in a world that often seems uncertain at best.

Today, she is settled in a larger house that doesn't seem strained by her worldly goods and memories. She reserves the rooms upstairs for her grandchildren and looks forward to their visits.

But she has limited her visits to the old place, because parts of her life are still there, even though the mementoes aren't. There, she can't overcome, or even effectively mask, the sentiment. Once all her business is done, she'll avoid it. She certainly doesn't want to see the bulldozers come.

"I won't be going to Queen Street for a while," she said. "I'm just not going to go that way. I don't want to see it for a while."

A good long while, I suspect.

(12/15/87 WSJ)

EPILOGUE: *Mrs. Lewis spent more than 13 years in her new home, happily making her house and garden a haven for her family and many friends, before she died on May 21, 2001.*

Blum Is Part of Salem

Peter Blum Jr. looks the way a tinsmith at Old Salem ought to look.

That's why he has a well-known face. It's been published in newspapers and magazines—including *National Geographic*. (It's been featured in a movie at the Carowinds amusement park near Charlotte.)

Blum also has one of the more familiar names in Winston-Salem, associated as it is with such institutions as Salem Tavern and Blum's Almanac. But, perhaps, because he is so modestly quiet, the man himself is not nearly as well known as the name and face.

"I've been here since 1964," he said in an interview yesterday at the Single Brothers house. "That makes it 11 years—going on 12—doesn't it?"

Why is he there?

"I just like it," he said. "I've been interested in the buildings for years. I was in on the original meeting to start the restoration."

And besides, could Old Salem really be Salem without a Blum?

"Franz Blum came over from Austria and on down to Germantown [Pa.] in the 1730s," Blum said.

"His son, Jacob, brought a group to Bethabara, where he ran a tavern. He came here [Salem] sometime after the tavern burned in 1784, and he ran the tavern here until 1802, when he died.

"His son, John Jacob Blum, ran the tavern for a while and then went into the mercantile business.

"John Jacob's son, Alexander Christian, went into business with his father.

"Alexander Christian's son was James Alfred, who was a dentist in Winston. His dental chair and his tools are over there in the museum.

"His son, Peter Blum, started the tinsmith shop (which is still in business as a sheet-metal shop)."

Which brings us to Peter Blum Jr., sixth-generation Moravian of Forsyth County, 50-year member of the Moravian Band, and, perhaps, best known as a tinsmith, although he didn't even start working with the metal until about eight years ago.

"I'd messed with woodwork, electricity and photography," Blum said. Then he saw the need for another tinsmith at Old Salem and did the natural thing: He filled the need.

"It's just another hobby," he said, explaining that it had come easily. Craft skills have been passed down through the generations, and Blum's wife—"Miss Lucy"—is known for her ceramics and pottery.

"The whole 'Blum-in' family can use their hands," he said, laughing softly at his pun.

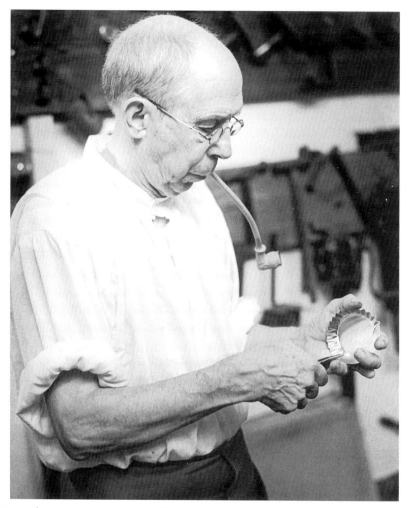
Peter Blum Jr. carries on his family tradition as a second generation tinsmith. —WSJ

But history and family ties and skills aren't the only reasons Peter Blum Jr. is at Old Salem.

"It gives me something to do," he said, "something to occupy my time. Most people retire and sit down. It gives me a chance to meet people from all over the world. It really broadens your outlook on life.

"The people coming in actually see hardware being made. For a lot of people, it brings back memories of their childhood. For the youngsters, I think it gives them a look back at how life was many years ago....

"It's a history lesson, but what we might call living history."

Appropriate, coming from a man who *is* living history, and who brings history alive.

(*9/25/75 The Sentinel*)

EPILOGUE: *Today, Peter Blum III, who lives near Elkin, is a tinsmith, carrying on the family tradition.*

"I learned from my daddy [Peter Blum Jr.] and my granddaddy. I'm the third generation at it," Blum said.

Blum made tinware for the movies, "The Patriot," and "The Last of the Mohicans." Among his creations are lanterns, wall sconces, kitchenware and candlesticks. He said, "It's been interesting; I get to do the research."

He also makes beeswax candles. He made eight street lamps for Old Salem for the landscaping of its new Moravian Archives and Moravian Music Foundation building. He has turned out angels and cookie cutters and done reproduction work for Old Salem, "just as my daddy did," he said.

He has been written up in the Winston-Salem Journal *and* Country Home *magazine, and he has appeared on PBS' "The Woodwright Shop."*

(10/5/00 Interview)

She's Keeping Up with a Tradition

Salem College likes to know if its freshmen had any relatives who attended the school.

But it doesn't often get lists that say "Mother…Grandmothers…Great-Grandmothers…Great-Great Grandmothers…Great-Great-Great Grandmothers…Great-Great-Great-Great Grandmothers…Great Aunts…Great-Great-Aunt…Great-Great-Great Aunt…Cousins…"

For Elizabeth Marie Weber, even that was leaving out a lot for the sake of conciseness.

Miss Weber, a spunky 18-year-old, began classes today at Salem. In an interview earlier this week, she said she had felt no family pressure to preserve the seven-generation tradition that goes back the better part of 200 years.

"I applied to two other colleges," she said.

"One reason I came here is the small size…and a lot of people I talked to really liked it.

"I really like it so far. From the time I came here, I've felt like an individual."

Miss Weber admits that "family dedication" played a part, though not as big a part as the fact that "In a way, it's like coming home…."

Indeed it is. Her father, the Rev. F. Herbert Weber, is a Winston-Salem native who served from August 1966, to December 1972, as minister at Fries Memorial Moravian Church before going to Charlotte's Little Church on the Lane. And her mother, the former Emma Elizabeth Kapp, was born in Bethania. She attended Salem, and *her* mother was one of several in the family who held positions at the school over the long years.

"I knew my mother had attended Salem," said Miss Weber, "and my grandmother had attended and taught there, but I didn't realize how vast it [her Salem background] was."

Vast? Yes. It goes back to residents of the original Bethabara, people born well before 1800, and includes so many dedicated Moravians it would be impossible to list them. One was Agnes Fogle Pfohl Eller, whose husband, Ernest, authored several Moravian books, including *House of Peace;* another was Emma Augusta Lehman, who taught at Salem from 1864 to 1916—almost 52 years.

"That's one reason I have always respected Moravians," said Miss Weber, "because they've always believed that education was important for the women as well as the men."

If she fit in and felt comfortable as she was about to begin a long step in her adult life, it was little wonder.

"I took music here at the Fine Arts Center for about seven years," she said.

"After we moved to Charlotte, I came back for about half a year or so."

That interest in music, plus her own strong religion, gives her a list of stage credits and church activities that, combined with an outstanding high school scholastic record, is about as long as her list of "relatives who attended Salem."

At this point, Miss Weber, who finds Charlotte a bit big for her, is just happy to be back and at the college; she isn't sure what she wants to do, but she said there has been no pressure on her to do or be anything in particular.

"Whatever it is" that she goes on to, she said, "I'd like to work with people....I'm not really interested in an office job or gaining a lot of money....

"I feel like whatever God wants me to do, if I pray about it, He'll reveal to me how He wants to use me."

As with attending Salem, that attitude appears to be a long-standing family tradition.

(9/4/75 The Sentinel)

EPILOGUE: *Today, Elizabeth Marie Weber Nodine lives in Charlotte with her husband Dennis and their two daughters, Jennifer (Jenna) Elizabeth, six years old, and Emma Kristen Abigail (Abbey), three years old. Mrs. Nodine teaches part-time at the Charlotte Children's Theatre.*

She graduated from Salem College in 1979, with a B.A. in Spanish, although her main interest was drama. After graduation, Mrs. Nodine said that she "mostly worked in education with children, whether in church or drama."

She also has appeared in commercials. Abbey is following in her mother's footsteps with one commercial to her credit. *(10/00 Interview)*

Reaching the Person Within the Patient

An old woman moved haltingly along the corridor, using her walker as much for orientation as for support, her eyes darting about in search of some reassuring landmark.

Susan Holmes, the health-care administrator at the Arbor Acres retirement community, called out a cheery hello and asked, "How are you?"

"I'm sick," said the woman, who suffers from Alzheimer's disease.

"What's wrong?" asked Ms. Holmes.

"I don't know. I'm just lost. Your hair is so pretty....What am I going to do?...I don't care what I do. I've just got to walk."

The conversation was typical: the feeling of being lost, the disconnected thought, the desperation and, in particular, the need to walk or wander.

"Well," said Ms. Holmes, grasping the old woman's shoulder, "we're out for a little walk. Why don't you just walk along with us?"

She did, and soon we were joined by another resident, a man, on our stroll through the new Alzheimer's unit at the Health Care Center of Triad United Methodist Home.

The unit, opened in June with 22 beds, was designed to meet the special needs of Alzheimer's victims, as well as human needs in general.

Its intersecting corridors and unlocked doors, opening onto outdoor court-yard walkways, allow residents to wander almost at will without becoming lost, as Alzheimer's patients so often do.

"We developed our program around the behaviors of this disease: the confusion, the wandering," said Ms. Holmes, who came to the Arbor Acres community four years ago from Blumenthal Jewish Home in Clemmons.

"The wandering is a need. The residents, because of the intense frustration, they need a release," she said.

"The wandering, in my opinion, is a response to the frustration caused by the loss of memory."

In the past, at the Methodist Home and elsewhere, staff members had to watch doors almost like military sentinels, barring patients from leaving—and piling new frustration on old.

"We needed a building that let us stop saying no to our residents," Ms. Holmes said.

"We don't believe in any across-the-board use of chemical or physical restraints. We don't use a lot of medications to control behavior."

Without such controls, and without the continual "No's," the unit is able to emphasize the human dignity that is often among the first casualties of Alzheimer's.

Surroundings are spacious, bright and attractive; residents live in private rooms with furnishings taken, at least in part, from their own homes.

They wear street clothes, even if someone has to dress them; eat at tables in a dining room with compatible companions, even if someone has to sit with them and feed them; walk on carpeted floors and sit on attractive—but waterproof—sofas and chairs, although devices such as catheters are not routinely used.

Rather than issue orders, staff members engage residents in conversation.

And, although few can match the unfettered exuberance of Ms. Holmes, all seem friendly.

"If we focused on the tragedy and the loss, we would be mired in it," said Ms. Holmes. "We have to leave to the researchers the task of finding out why.

"I have to ask, 'How can I make the residents' lives as meaningful as possible?'

"I can't judge what that is. I just have to put as many tools as I have at my disposal in front of them."

Among the tools are activities, including crafts classes and bird watching, made easy with the placement of feeders almost everywhere around the property.

Some residents pursue such personal interests as gardening or art, as evidenced by the flowers one man cultivates and by a colorful painting of a spring-flower arrangement, hanging on a wall in the administrator's office.

"One of my Alzheimer's residents did that painting," Ms. Holmes said. "She was one of the gentle souls. She relieved the anxiety by painting." Now, despite her earlier protests, Ms. Holmes was focused on tragedy and loss, and wondering aloud just how much Alzheimer's victims may understand about their own personal tragedies.

She recalled the time that her artist-resident, confused and disoriented, was prevented from leaving the old unit by a staff member who reached out to her and asked: "Why don't you come on back this way with me?"

The old woman refused, and the staff member asked her, "Are you looking for something?"

"Yes," she replied. "I'm looking for myself."

As Ms. Holmes told the story, she lost her battle to hold back the tears that welled in her eyes—but only momentarily.

"It *is* tragic," she said. "I have to feel it, but I can't dwell on it....

"There comes a point where I have to just wipe the tears away and act," she said.

(10/1/89 WSJ)

When Hearts Were Pure and Dead Men Voted

Oh, for the Good Old Days.

I mean the really old days—the times when hearts and motives were pure, when even politics was simply a matter of doing one's best to see that the best man, the one who would serve his constituency the most honorably, was elected.

A recent conversation with a very old man, who hailed originally from a southern county that was not named Forsyth, gave me some inkling of what I have missed.

The man asked for anonymity, so I shall call him Seth.

"In 1928," said Seth, "when [name omitted] first ran, we got absentee ballots from a lot of people. When they're sick in bed, you have to get a ballot and take it to them.

"Now, it's necessary that you have a notary public to put the seal on the ballot. She [the notary] would go around with me...I would go in and get the votes marked and get them to sign the bottom of the ballot. All she has to testify is that she saw the person sign the ballot.

"We got quite a number of them [absentees]—20 to 25, which was good back then. It was all Democrat. If it was Republican, it'd be burned before it ever got to the ballot box."

You know, you hardly see dedication like that anymore. But there was more.

"We was up in [another county] one time, about 1940," said Seth. "It was two nights before election. Young high-school girls were in the back room marking ballots, putting them in ballot boxes by the hundreds.

"There were about five or six of them, and they had one supervisor telling them how this operation should be handled. Myself and a friend recognized what was going on.

"The election was held two days later. This county went over 96 percent the way those ballots were marked. What happened to the legal ballots, I do not know.

"After the election, there was to be an investigation. A number of [investigators] went to the town....Farmers in bib overalls were aggravated to the extent of violence. They were mean mad. They showed their anger to the extent that the investigators were glad to get out of the county."

Gosh. Where can you find that kind of dedication today?

These weren't the only methods used, back then, to see that justice triumphed.

"They'd vote tombstones, telephone poles, anything," said Seth. "They'd get names of people who'd been dead four or five years, and people who'd moved, but their names were still on the books. They didn't go around and check on who's dead."

But how did the politicians know the names were still there?

"They had copies of the registrar's book. They couldn't vote for anyone whose name wasn't on the book. They didn't vote telephone poles. That was an exaggeration."

It was a relief to hear that. Telephone poles seemed, to me, to be stretching ethics a bit.

Seth had duties other than collecting absentee ballots. For example, he would assist illiterate people in the voting booth—a practice that illustrated this fine man's altruism.

"You'd have to ask the registrar can you go into the booth with another voter," he said. "They'd ask him if it's all right. One time I carried a family of five and had to go through this rigmarole. I voted them just like I wanted to.

"Some people were stubborn. They knew what they wanted to vote for, but they couldn't read the names. I would read the names out to them and they would say who they wanted to vote for. I would tell them, 'Let's mark this man out. You don't want him—isn't that correct?'

"I'd put an 'X' right by the candidate's name. That's what we called marking them out."

One time, Seth almost got into a bit of trouble. He had been in charge of the absentee ballots, and after the election, an investigation was called for.

"I had to go around," he said, "and tell the people how they voted."

As admirable as such dedication might seem to most of us, I felt compelled to ask Seth if he felt at least a twinge of conscience, since such activity was at least technically illegal.

"Hell," he said. "It was fair and square. I got it just like they were trying to get it from us."
(*11/21/78 The Sentinel*)

Romance Is Star of Balcony Scene

But for the brevity of its oratory, the balcony scene that played at the Stevens Center this month might have been worthy of one of the old master playwrights.

As it was, it was received with rare enthusiasm and animation.

The stars on the evening of Jan. 11, before the curtain went up on Neil Simon's *Lost in Yonkers,* were Mardee Hedrick, a graduate student in speech and language pathology at the University of North Carolina at Greensboro, and Alan Houston Johnson, a Wachovia banking-operations manager.

Ms. Hedrick had no idea, when they arrived at the theater, that she was about to be thrust into the limelight.

"We went to the balcony. Then he piped up and said, 'I got my camera fixed.' And he patted his pocket. 'I'm going to go downstairs and take a picture of you looking over the balcony before the play starts.'"

Ms. Hedrick fell for it.

She couldn't help it. In some ways and manners, she is a 1950s woman in a 1990s setting, conservative in values and trusting, sometimes, to the point of—well, innocence is perhaps a better word than naivete.

For her, there was no reason to think that Johnson, who is normally a fairly conservative person himself, might be so wild and foolish as to stand beneath the balcony and propose. Oh, they had dated since March, first casually and then seriously; and she *had* gone home to Virginia with him to meet his parents at Christmastime—a visit that she felt put them on the road to marriage talk. But they hadn't been dating for a full year yet, for goodness' sake, and she had made it clear that there should be no such talk until they had.

"I was sort of on a wing and a prayer," Johnson said. "I came up with the camera idea when I realized that she was seven rows back from the edge of the balcony. I had to get her to the very front. It sort of lent credence when I patted something in my pocket, suggesting it was a camera."

It wasn't, of course. It was a ring case.

Johnson made his way down several flights of stairs to the theater floor. Possessed of a commanding voice, he planned to get the crowd's attention first, and then Ms. Hedrick's. It was minutes before curtain time as he looked for a strategic spot in the left aisle near the stage.

"I was about five or 10 yards from the stage," he said. "It was hard to see her, because there are no lights up in the balcony, plus it's five flights above the floor. As soon as I got to where I could see her well and she could see me, I turned to the crowd."

And Ms. Hedrick?

Mardee Hedrick and Alan Johnson put the Stevens Center to dramatic use. –COOKIE SNYDER

"I was waving and smiling and getting ready for my picture to be taken," she said.

Now Johnson made his move.

"I turned to the crowd and said, 'Could I have your attention, please?' The crowd reacted immediately. Everybody got quiet."

At this point, Ms. Hedrick was wondering why he needed the crowd to be quiet in order to take her picture.

After calling the crowd to attention, Johnson moved into Phase Two of his plan.

"I said, 'I have something that I would like to ask my girlfriend, and I would like as many witnesses as possible,'" he said. "As soon as I said that, the crowd picked up on what I was getting ready to do. Plus, I was reaching for the ring case in my pocket."

At that point, people in the crowd began to clap and shout.

Upstairs, meanwhile, Ms. Hedrick blushed silently.

"The crowd is making a lot of noise as I'm talking," Johnson said. "So basically I had to scream her a couple of mushy things."

And what were those things, which even Ms. Hedrick didn't fully catch over the rising noise of the crowd?

"I haven't told *her* since then," Johnson said. "I don't want to tell everybody what I said to her."

What? He gets up in a crowded theater and screams these things at her and the mob, and he doesn't want them quoted in a newspaper?

Aw, come on, Al. We've come this far, after all…."I said, 'I'm hopelessly and irreversibly in love with you. Will you marry me?'"

And Ms. Hedrick, who, of course, caught the "marry me" part?

"I was going, 'Oh, my Lord, what is he doing?'" she said. "I remember going like this [covering her face] and hoping that this wasn't really happening or something."

Nevertheless, she managed to squeak a "yes."

By the time she added, "I'm going to kill him," the crowd was paying no attention. On hearing that she had said "yes," people leapt up and stomped, clapped and yelled like a bunch of good ol' boys at a George Jones concert.

As Johnson tried to make his way back upstairs, he was stopped again by well-wishers wanting to pat him on the back, shake his hand or offer encouraging words.

In the balcony, meanwhile…

"I was frozen at the rail," Ms. Hedrick said. "My knees were shaking so badly that the two girls behind me were saying, 'She's going to fall. She's going to fall.'"

Finally, Johnson appeared at the balcony rail. Now the crowd really went wild. "Give her the ring! Give her the ring! Kiss her! Go ahead!"

Ms. Hedrick was shaking so badly that Johnson had difficulty finding her lips with his when they embraced, but he managed. As he did, a man who had followed him from the floor of the theater said, "Bring her back downstairs! We want to see who you're going to marry!"

It was bedlam again.

They went to the floor of the theater, where, at this point, even Johnson was getting a bit embarrassed as the crowd's cheering and clapping continued. "The only thing I could do was hold up her ring finger," he said. "I picked her up. She's small…So I wrapped my arms around her and gave her a big bear hug" and lifted her.

As she rose in the air, Ms. Hedrick was still repeating, more to herself than to anyone else, "I can't believe he's doing this."

Finally, they were able to take their seats, where they stayed until the end of the first act.

Then they retreated to the pay telephone in the lobby—Johnson had come prepared with quarters—to call family and friends and announce their engagement.

They have since announced the date and place: Sept. 28 at Wake Forest University's Davis Chapel, where Ms. Hedrick's parents were married.

Now, Ms. Hedrick is looking forward to becoming Mrs. Johnson. "If the rest of my life is as exciting as the proposal," she said, "I think I've got the right man for the job."

Perhaps. On the other hand, if the rest of her life is as exciting as the proposal, she might have a heart attack before she's 35. *(1/27/91 WSJ)*

EPILOGUE: *Has the Johnsons' marriage been as exciting as the night of the proposal?*

"Yes," said Mardee Johnson, a speech/language pathologist at Whitaker Elementary School. "A lot of people don't go out...but we do. If there is an activity out there...we want to do it. We've been happy."

Al Johnson, who works at Wachovia in capital markets risk management, credits his wife. "My wife has boundless energy and organizational skills," he said. "She makes sure we stay involved with all the civic and artistic activities.

"She is just an incredible mother to our children," he adds. "This has been the greatest surprise and the biggest joy [to me]."

The Johnsons have a boy and a girl: Baily, four and one-half years old, and Taylor Jane, two years old. *(9/16/00 Interview)*

Many Years, Good Memories in the Inn

CLEMMONS—Fannie Sprinkle Ogburn has spent 74 of her 88 years living in a 14-room frame house built by Peter Clemmons, who came here in the late 1700s and left his name on the community.

"There's a lot of history here," Mrs. Ogburn said during a recent visit.

Indeed there is—from the rooms that once echoed with the sounds of guests taking advantage of an overnight respite from the rigors of a long stagecoach ride, to a nearby cemetery dating back at least to the early 1800s.

"This used to be a stagecoach inn," said Mrs. Ogburn. "The stagecoach came through here from—I don't know." (It was from Asheville to Edenton.)

"This was a stopping place, and that room in there was the waiting room or lobby. It was where they all met, and they told us they had dances in there."

The stagecoach line was operated by Clemmons' grandson, Edwin Clemmons, from 1840 to 1875 over several routes. When Edwin Clemmons bought his last coach, in 1857, he named it the Hattie Butner, after his wife. That stagecoach is now in the Wachovia Museum in Old Salem.

It's said that Peter Clemmons is buried in the cemetery out back, but there's no way to be sure. The names have worn off some of the stones, and other old stones probably are missing.

As for Mrs. Ogburn's personal memories of life in the house, they go back "only" to 1903.

"My father bought this place here in 1903," she said, "but we didn't get possession of it till 1904, for the reason that the man that was living in it was a renter and he had it for that year.

"It was a big farm; there was over 400 acres of it.

"Before Papa bought it, the dining room and kitchen was out yonder; I think in an old log house. I came here with my daddy one time and we ate dinner.

"My father was a sawmill man, and there was a lot of timber. When he had a sawmill, he boarded and roomed the men who worked there."

Her father also raised cows and horses and hogs and grew his own feed, so there was no lack of chores to be done. But Mrs. Ogburn managed to keep up with her schooling, and in 1908, at age 18, she became a teacher in Donnaha on the Yadkin River in Forsyth County.

"I started teaching school for $25 a month," she said. "We had school six months, and I paid my board and bought my clothes and transportation—there was no way to go but the train—and I saved $75 [in the first six months of teaching].

"But board didn't cost but $7 to $9 a month—board and room and all. I think when I quit teaching I was getting $55 a month."

She quit in 1918, a year after marrying Henly Ogburn. They were both 28 years old when they married. They celebrated their golden anniversary in 1967.

Over the years, Ogburn worked at Hanes Knitting and Mrs. Ogburn spent more and more of her time caring for her aging parents. The arrangement was a good one, according to Mrs. Ogburn.

"We just enjoyed it," she said, "because we were compatible…all good church people. They had a happy life, and we did, too."

And what were her fondest memories of the family's long years in the house? She paused for a time, thinking.

"Being together," she said. "Just being together."

(6/19/78 The Sentinel, newsfeature)

EPILOGUE: *Mrs. Ogburn died July 9, 1985.*

"A lot of history left with her," said Cookie Snyder, a niece who was really like a daughter to Mrs. Ogburn and her husband. "I think of all the things she knew, and we can't remember it all—all the family and who was kin to whom, and who did what in Clemmons." (7/12/85 WSJ)

Jim Ogburn, Mrs. Ogburn's son, and his wife, Frances, are now fixing up the house and living in it part-time. (9/13/00 Interview)

She Threw It Back and Then Ran Away

It is not normal for Hill Stockton to lie on the floor and look up a customer's skirt.

He doesn't often jog up and down Stratford Road in his expensive business clothes, either.

And you will seldom see him in a police car, directing a chase.

But Oct. 15 was kind of a funny day.

The funny business started at the Norman Stockton clothing store on Stratford Road.

"The Astros and the Mets were playing that long 16-inning [baseball] game," Stockton said. "We didn't have any customers. It was around 5:30, and all the men were watching the game."

During that time a couple of women entered the store to "look around," but the men paid little attention.

"In the middle of the seventh inning, there was a commercial," Stockton said, "so I went to talk to the head of the ladies' department, and she informed me that one of these ladies had just stuck a sweater, complete with hanger, up underneath her skirt.

"I said, 'Are you sure about that?' You know, that's not something that happens all the time. She said she was positive."

Shoplifting laws being as tricky as they are, nobody wanted to bring in the police just yet even though everyone was certain that one of the women, at least, had come to the store to steal.

The men began wandering away from the television set, and a different kind of game began.

Hill Stockton's father, Richard, was among them, moving over in front of the women and doing little to hide the fact that he was watching them.

Unbeknownst to Richard Stockton, at least until he finally gazed behind the women, son James Hill Stockton and a salesman had crawled under a fixture on the floor. They were, "lying on the floor trying to look up underneath her dress."

It was unorthodox, but effective.

"There was obviously something not normal under her skirt," Hill Stockton said. "She had some kind of pouch under there....I mean, we weren't looking straight up, but...Dad almost fell out when he saw us lying there.

"That's when I said, 'I believe you've got a sweater underneath your skirt.'"

The woman probably was not accustomed to replying to voices from under store fixtures, but she managed to retain her composure. She denied the charge.

Hill Stockton called the police.

"She was uncomfortable," Stockton said of the woman with the pouch, sweater, hanger and nobody-was-sure-what-else. "She was saying, 'This is ridiculous. We don't have to take this. We'll just leave. I don't have anything under my skirt.'"

The manager of the women's department reaffirmed that she had seen a theft, and Richard Stockton told the woman to wait for the police.

The woman's companion didn't get involved in what was to come next, and she was never suspected of any criminal activity.

"The woman realized that we weren't going to bargain with her," Hill Stockton said, "so she picked up her skirt and took the sweater out of her pouch and threw it at Dad, turned and ran out of the store. In the process, she knocked over one salesman and the two ladies in the ladies' department."

As the woman ran down Stratford Road, young Stockton began jogging after her.

She ran into the access road leading to the Bocock-Stroud Team Division, tried unsuccessfully to get a woman to give her a ride, and became trapped in the area by a chain-link fence.

Unfortunately, she wasn't trapped long.

Despite the admonitions of Stockton and two salesmen who had joined the race and caught up, she did not heed their advice to wait for the police. Instead, she began climbing the fence, displaying great agility—until she fell over to the Interstate 40 side.

Now Stockton ran back to the store, leaving the salesman to try to keep track of the suspect, to let the police know that their quarry was loose along I-40.

Meanwhile, the woman had managed to flag down a tractor-trailer. With the salesman in hot pursuit—he had climbed the fence too—she fell a couple of times trying to get into the cab of the truck, but she finally made it.

As the truck pulled off, the salesman was banging on it and shouting, but the driver, possibly thinking that he was being Sir Galahad, paid no attention.

The situation now was taking on some of the finest characteristics of an old Alec Guinness movie. And it didn't stop there; just after the tractor-trailer pulled out, the driver of a pickup truck stopped and offered the salesman a lift and the use of his Citizens Band radio.

Also, two police cars, one of them carrying Hill Stockton, were now in hot pursuit.

"There was a wreck down on the Hawthorne Curve that day," said Stockton. "So that slowed everybody down."

Meanwhile, people were trying to use CB radios to explain to the truck driver that he was helping a fugitive.

"We got to Highway 52," Stockton said, "at which point the truck driver heard over his CB that he was carrying a shoplifter.

"He pulled over along with the pickup truck and two police cars.

"When we stopped that lady, we were howling. The police were laughing.

"The truck driver was afraid he was going to be arrested for aiding and abetting."

The woman was taken downtown. Charges were filed and bond was set.

It was a lot of trouble to go to, Stockton said, but it is important at this time of year to stop shoplifting before it becomes an epidemic during the Christmas season.

"If one thing is shoplifted," he said, "you have to sell a ton to make up for that one item…and the sweater was worth $300."

As luck would have it, however, the "happy ending" wasn't the end of the story of the funny day at Norman Stockton.

Last Monday, the woman's case came up in court.

"She was nowhere to be seen," Stockton said. "She jumped bond."

The way she ran the first time, it shouldn't have been unexpected.

(11/2/86 WSJ)

Mr. Murray Has Made a Name for Himself

The sign on the apartment door says "William P. Murray," but the mail on the kitchen table says otherwise.

Medicare knows him as George. To his brother Jim and a few others who have known him a very long time, he is Paul. And friends that he has made during his 65 years in Winston-Salem call him Oscar, the nickname he acquired in the 35 years he worked at the old O'Hanlon's drug store and his 15 at Bobbitt's.

William P. Murray "trying to explore the extinct, the extant and the extent." –WSJ

Over the years, George William Paul "Oscar" Murray has used all the versions of his name, or at least allowed others to use them. To simplify matters, I have always called him by the affectionate term I prefer anyway: Mr. Murray.

Mr. Murray is the longtime resident raconteur-poet of downtown Winston-Salem, as recognizable as any politician or businessman. If he has been less visible in recent months, that is partly because such old haunts as Little Pep Restaurant have vanished—and partly because he was slowed a step by the heart attack he suffered July 1.

In Little Pep's heyday, which ended 13 months ago, the restaurant was a center of friendly political and philosophical debate that was often warm enough to make strangers worry that hostilities might erupt at any moment.

"I miss that," Mr. Murray said yesterday during a chat in his North Cherry Street apartment. "I miss Dennis [Canavos, the owner]. He was a good guy. I just enjoyed the sociability....I had a lot of fun out of the jovial disagreements."

Mr. Murray has been slowed down before and come back. Just over three years ago, at age 81, he broke a hip, giving rise to worry that he might never make his rounds again. But he came back, resuming his long walks, his luncheons and the hours spent presiding over a corner of the Hyatt lobby, where he sometimes worked on his poetry.

Then, on the first day of July, came the heart attack, which was to do what the broken hip and nearly 85 years of life couldn't: both slow him down and narrow his range.

At first, when visitors were unable to locate him in the hospital, they would gladly have settled for a slower, less mobile version of their friend. Briefly, they feared that he had died.

"That was amusing—and distressing, too," he said. "Friends would come—some would succeed in finding me and some wouldn't. They would come in and ask for 'Oscar' or 'William P.' Murray. It was under Medicare, so it was listed as 'George W.'"

Eventually, most of his friends found him. But by the time some did, he was back home—after only two weeks in the hospital.

And, slower or not, he still had the old resiliency. He didn't immediately tackle the 13 steps up to the front of his apartment building, but he was back on the downtown streets very soon.

"I went in and out the back—which is just one step up—for about two weeks," he said. "Then I started gradually coming up the front steps.

"I take a little walk in the morning and one in the afternoon, weather permitting. But I'm not in the mainstream, exactly. I wish I were."

Mainstream or not, his friends have been glad to see him back. He is a rarity: a human constant in the city's downtown, where he has lived and worked, for the 65 years since he came here from Rockingham County.

In that time, generations have come to know him for his dogged optimism and philosophy of human triumph. For years, he served up that philosophy, mostly orally, to acquaintances and customers.

It wasn't until he was 52, when he married a poet, Anne Spainhour, that he took up the hobby that so many now know him for.

His wife died 21 years later, but by then his own work had won literary contests and been published in national journals. He continued to write.

"It was a hobby, an avocation," he said, "but it became an obsession— almost a vocation."

Even today, Mr. Murray sometimes writes a poem a day. Often his recent work grapples with life's ironies, as in these lines penned just a week ago:

"Good and evil are implacable foes that have no common ground;

"In each, both friends and foes are invariably found."

He is perhaps better known, however, for his lighter poetry in a kind of 1950s magazine style, like this excerpt:

"When you're feeling blue, and melancholy too,

"Never say you're through; here's the thing to do:

"Buckle up and smile, and chuckle for a while

"And then good luck will come to you."

When Mr. Murray writes such lines, he means them. And whatever the tone or topic, the ending leaves room for hope for mankind, now and in the hereafter.

That's part of the charm that has cast its spell on so many people, over so many years, in the small place we call downtown.

"I love philosophy," he said, "and, of course, I've written quite a bit of religious material. I'm trying to run the gamut of life....You could say I'm trying to explore the extinct, the extant and the extent."

No wonder he's written enough poetry to fill books under every one of his names.

And no wonder his friends hope that he will continue to do so.

(11/3/87 WSJ)

Timing Can Create Strange Bedfellows

It was just another summer Saturday at the magistrate's office in a near-by city. There were warrants to be issued, prisoners to be released, a young couple to be married in a civil ceremony.

Across the street, the county jail teemed with new occupants, many of them victims of a youthful exuberance that, only the night before, had instilled in them an unshakable conviction that they could consume vast measures of alcohol with impunity.

In the magistrate's office that morning, a young man we will call Mack was earning his daily keep as an employee of the state of North Carolina.

"About 8:15," Mack told me the other day, "a gentleman arrived at the office in hopes of posting bond for a man who was being held in custody.

"I pulled the files, and it seemed that, during the early morning hours, he had been brought in and held on a charge of being intoxicated and disruptive. A white male, early 20s, kind of Irish-looking.... I was told he had gotten into a scuffle at a local bar, and when the police arrived, he was very boisterous, and his manner resulted in his being arrested and charged with being intoxicated and disruptive."

The magistrate on duty that Friday night had ordered the young man held without bond until 8 a.m. and then released if someone would post a $200 appearance bond.

"I asked the young man who came to my office if he had the $200," Mack said. "He did. He said: 'I was here at 2 this morning. Why would they not release him then?' I told him I imagined he had been rather disruptive, and the gentleman said, 'Yes, he *was* rather disruptive.'"

Mack called and arranged for the prisoner to be sent down to his office so he could sign the appearance bond and be released.

Meanwhile, to lend the scene a politically correct balance that would be the envy of Hollywood or the Equal Employment Opportunity Commission, a black man in his early 20s arrived with his prospective bride, a young woman of Oriental extraction.

"He was all dressed up, a clean-cut-looking fellow, and he had a marriage certificate from the register of deeds' office. She was quite attractive...

"He had all the information he needed and the certificate, and I asked him for the $10, and he had that. He had everything he needed except for the two witnesses."

Pay attention, dear reader. We're nearing the point where the plot thickens.

"The intake area outside our office was deserted except for the fellow who had come in to post bond. The gentleman who hoped to be married asked him if he would consider being a witness, and he said yes, he would be pleased to do that.

"So I assumed that the fellow being released from jail would also serve as a witness to this wedding."

Mack went to work, completing all the appearance-bond information, getting the $200, writing the receipt, getting the signature of the man supplying the bond.

"The only thing needed for that to be a done deal was to get the [prisoner's] signature on the appearance bond."

Meanwhile, Mack had also taken the $10 for the marriage, written a receipt and made sure he had all the paperwork for *that* matter in order.

Now, his paperwork in order, his bureaucratic fanny covered, he was ready to get on with both items of business at once.

"The jailer brought the young man down. He was a big fellow....His T-shirt was ripped off of one shoulder; there was blood all over his shirt. He looked like he'd been through a blender."

That was just the body. Apparently the man's mind was still well mixed, too.

"I gave him the appearance-bond form. I like to explain it to people, particularly if there has been alcohol involved. So I said: 'I need your signature here. Two hundred dollars has been posted for you by your friend, and he has the receipt. He'll get the money back when you come to court....All I need is your signature.'"

The prisoner, apparently grateful at the thought of getting out, signed the form with no questions. Next, the boldly lettered "Marriage Certificate" form had to be dealt with.

"I said, 'I also need your signature here to be part of this marriage ceremony.' He took the pen, and then he set the pen down. He said, '*Marriage?*'

"Now, I think he was still affected by the alcohol in his system. I don't know if he had a girlfriend or what, but he was single.

"Anyway, he just stood up and said: 'No, no, no. I'm not marrying *anybody*. Take me back to jail!'"

It took some doing, but later, reassured by Mack and the others, the man relented.

Mack described the scene:

"So we had this young couple being married with two witnesses they had just met and the one witness standing there with a shirt halfway torn off him, with bloodstains all across the front....

"But when I left them, they all seemed very happy." *(7/19/91 WSJ)*

Grandma Checkmates Check

A local woman, elderly but not confined in her movements, and by no means in her dotage, takes great pride in her grandchildren, as do most grandparents.

Recently, she sent a grandson, whom we shall call Johnny, a birthday card, along with a substantial enough check to provide him with spending money for a while.

Now, the lady's grandchildren are well-mannered and schooled in etiquette, and when she did not receive a thank-you note, she began to worry that perhaps the money had not arrived.

Johnny happened to call her on another matter and she asked him: "Did you get my card and check?"

"Yes, I did," said Johnny.

"Well," said the woman, "I was just wondering, because I hadn't heard from you."

"I didn't know what to do," replied Johnny, "because I couldn't cash it."

"What do you mean," asked the woman, "you couldn't cash it?"

"Well," said Johnny, "you signed it 'Grandma.'" *(7/11/81 The Sentinel)*

Friendship Captures Best of Human Spirit

If a movie were made about the last decade and a half of Annie Preston Fearrington's life, Willie Nash would be a major character.

The title might be "Driving Miss Annie."

The story would begin a dozen years after the retirement of Annie Preston, as she was known, as a teacher of French and other languages and the head of the foreign-language department at R.J. Reynolds High School. It would be just before the time she came to accept the fact that, at the age of 76, she shouldn't drive anymore—a decision that may have been made easier by Nash's presence.

She had begun driving only about 11 years earlier, in 1965, after the death of her husband, Amos Gregson Fearrington. Her decision to stop was occasioned, at least in part, by an accident.

"I got to know her through a friend of hers," said Nash, the long-time custodian at Centenary United Methodist Church, now retired.

"She asked me to come up and help her one day, help her clean up the house. And from then on, I started going around to help."

Nash had known for some time who Mrs. Fearrington was.

She was a fixture at the church, after all, as well as at Reynolds High, where she was a faculty member from the day the doors opened in 1923 until her retirement in 1964.

As they got to know each other better, mostly through the one day a week he spent chauffeuring her or seeing to her or her apartment's needs, they became close.

"She didn't feel too good about not driving," Nash said. "But after she had the wreck, she didn't do it anymore....

"I'd drive her to the store or to have her hair done, carry her to the doctor, to the bank. She'd go some down to the drug store, or to the place to have documents made.

"She was just real nice, is all I know. Wherever we went, she would always look out for me. We'd go to the doctor's office and she'd say: 'Don't you stay out there in the cold. You come in.'...

"In the car, we'd talk a little about politics or something. Sometimes things would come up in the paper or something. She'd say there were too many taxes and Social Security wasn't running right. And I'd tell her I thought so, too.

"We'd talk about everything. She was just glad to get out. She'd say: 'I'm going to have you carry me out around Reynolda Road, so I can see the dogwoods. It's so pretty.'"

Often, they would return to the house at lunchtime, carrying food that she had picked up for both of them at the K&W on Coliseum.

It was a good friendship, he said, and although Mrs. Fearrington was reared in a time when segregation was as much a part of life as education, race never entered into it.

"She thought a lot of me," he said. "And I did her."

When family and friends gathered here last week to say goodbye to Annie Preston Fearrington, who had died at the age of 91, several people recalled her friendship with Willie Nash as a positive force in her latter years.

By the summer of 1987, it was apparent to those who knew Mrs. Fearrington that she needed to live somewhere where she could be looked after more intently. She had begun showing such worrisome signs of forgetfulness as leaving gas burners partly turned on.

But she didn't want to become "dependent." That may have been one reason that she became so fond of Nash so quickly. His helping her once a week staved off that inevitable move to a center for the aging.

In the end, it was Nash who persuaded her to move to Arbor Acres, where she was to live until moving to Georgia a year and a half ago.

"Every time we'd go to the doctor," Nash said, "she'd say, 'We got a good report today.' I'd say: 'That's fine. I'm glad.'"

He didn't believe her, of course—not near the end, at least.

"She kept telling me she was thinking about moving. I said: 'Well, that would be a nice place for you to go. You'd have somebody to look after you.' Then she'd say, 'Oh, I don't know.'…I didn't want to push too much.

"She really didn't want to move, but she'd gotten to where she couldn't remember too good.…I finally said: 'I think it's better for you to go on. I think it's the best thing for you to do, Mrs. Fearrington, because at least you'll have somebody to look after you. You'd have help if you'd fall or something like that.'"

And in another scene that seemed to be made for a "Driving Miss Annie"— a la the movie "Driving Miss Daisy," which came later—Nash struck a bargain with his friend.

"I bought her old car from her, when she got ready to sell it. It was a 50-something Plymouth. I bought it when she moved out of her apartment."

(4/28/91 WSJ)

Life's Parade Marches Through the Checkout

The woman, expensively clad, shod and coiffed, stood at the meat counter, nervously glancing first over her left shoulder and then over her right.

Was the coast clear? Could she pick up that piece of marked-down beef without being seen by anyone who mattered?

Satisfied that she could, she whisked the roast from the counter and, in a single practiced movement, tucked it under a cereal box, where no one could see the "reduced" tag.

Now she had to get through checkout without being seen (by anyone she knew)—a chancier proposition. She checked again for familiar faces, then made a hurried getaway through the express line.

We don't want to seem less than affluent. We don't want our friends to think we are traveling through life any way but First Class.

I've witnessed the meat-counter scene before. So have you—that one, or another like it.

It's human nature. And it makes the grocery store a fascinating place.

From the tabloid reader who pretends to be disgusted at what he is reading…to the young man and woman pretending to pass the time of day while testing one another's potential availability…to the gentlemen who, on being told of an acquaintance's illness, replies, "That's too bad; would you *look* at the price of these corn flakes!"

Perhaps nowhere else is so much of humanity's passing parade visible in so few square feet as in the supermarket. There, little that we do or say goes unnoticed by strangers, and we often do and say much more than we intend to, or even realize.

I have often wondered what thoughts must course through the minds of the stores' cashiers as life's little dramas play out before their eyes every day.

And I wonder, from what they say or don't say on occasion, just how much they do see and hear on a typical workday.

Case in point: a small scenario in express checkout recently.

The silver-haired senior citizen, a tall woman with a face and frame that almost defined the word *angular*, pulled her cart behind her through the line. She emptied her cart and stood in front of it writing her check, making it difficult for the man behind her to load his items on the conveyor so that the line would keep moving in an express fashion.

The man leaned forward gingerly, managing to get a couple of jars to the conveyor and, in the process, brushing gently against the handle of the woman's cart.

"Stop!" the woman almost shouted. "Stop pushing my cart!"

From the defensive stance she assumed, hand held out to fend off attack, she obviously feared being rammed by that fearsome vehicle.

The man, who had not pushed the cart and caused no more movement of it than a slight trembling, replied:

"Ma'am, I'm sorry. But I didn't push your cart. I barely touched it."

Meanwhile, the cashier went about her business virtually expressionless, appearing unaffected by the small dispute that was breaking out at her duty station.

"You were pushing!" said the woman.

The man was becoming a bit impatient now himself.

"I didn't push it, lady," he said.

"Hmphh!" she snorted, grabbing the cart herself and jerking it away to a "safe" distance. "This has happened to me too many times!"

She went on, sniffing and snorting and glowering, and finally the cashier did look up just as the man, having decided to end the confrontation once and for all, said:

"Oh, [bleep-bleep] you old hag!"

That seemed to help the cashier size up the situation.

She moved the man's groceries toward the woman's and, glancing first at her and then at him, asked:

"Will this be together—or separate?"

The passing parade.

You can view it every day at your favorite grocery store.   *(9/8/88 WSJ)*

No Bed of Roses
Snake Discovered Inside Water Bed

If Taylor Vanhoy's friends ever want to hang a nickname on him, they should consider Mongoose.

What could be more fitting for a young man who, on Wednesday last, went eyeball-to-eyeball with a snake—and won? Of course, the snake was at a distinct disadvantage. It was swimming around inside a water-bed mattress at the time and had no way of fighting back.

But we're plunging ahead of the tale....

It began late Wednesday morning when young Vanhoy discovered a leak in his water-bed mattress and began casting about for a replacement.

"We called over at my uncle's house and asked if they had one," he said. "They had one. They told us to come and get it."

At the house, which has a stream and a lake nearby, his uncle, Bobby Durham, took his old water-bed mattress out of his storage building and put it in the car, driven by Taylor's grandmother, Vera Vanhoy. They took it to the Vanhoy home, near Walkertown, and Taylor hooked up a hose to it and went to the living room to watch television while it filled up.

In due time, accompanied by Grandma, he went back up to the bedroom to see if the mattress was full of water. Indeed, it was nearly full. However, looking through the top of the mattress, he noticed immediately that there was something in it besides water.

"I saw the snake. It was swimming around," he said. And what was his reaction to seeing a snake swimming around inside the mattress on his bed in his room?

"I didn't say anything. *She* did. She said, 'Lord, help us,' or something."

"It scared me, I'll tell you," said "Grandma" Durham. "It was just *wigglin'* in there. And about that time, Taylor picked up a bed rail and he hit at it."

"No," Taylor said. "I didn't have a bed rail."

The contradiction was understandable. Confusion reigned in the Vanhoy home for some time, what with Grandma running around yelling "Lord help us" and Taylor scrambling first to dispatch the 24-inch water snake to Reptile Heaven and then to get its body out of his water bed.

What choice of weapons did the young man actually make? "I hit it with my hand. It finally stopped, and blood started coming out of its mouth. It stopped and it just sat there. It was dead."

The beginning of the escapade had come to an end.

Now it was time to think snake-removal. How was Taylor going to get that snake out through the water valve in the mattress? To help meet that challenge, he called his 13-year-old cousin, Jerry Reddin.

"He said, 'Come over here and get this snake,'" Jerry said. "He said, 'It's wigglin' around.'…He told me he was scared."

At that, Taylor Vanhoy bristled. "I didn't say that," he said. "He told me just to lay on top of it, to sleep on it. I wasn't going to do that."

"He was scared," Grandma said.

"*She* was scared," Taylor responded. "I told him [Jerry] that Grandma was scared."

Finally, the finger of fear had pointed to someone who offered no protest. Grandma *was* scared. She was so scared she had to cancel an important errand at 4 p.m., after it was all over, because she was too shaky to drive.

"I was laughing at her," Taylor said. "Just her face. And she started screaming and yelling, 'Lord, help us.' She just kept coming back [to the bedroom] and saying: 'Get that thing out! Get that thing out!'"

Grandma rose to her own defense: "I didn't know it was dead. When I seen it, it was just swimmin' across there."

The reason she hadn't seen it since then is that she'd been downstairs hiding.

At any rate, by this time Taylor and Jerry were busily trying to remove the *corpus delicti,* first with a coat-hanger and then with a fishhook attached to the coat-hanger, but finding the snake too tubular to grasp—and too slithery as well, even in death.

At one stage in the pell-mell proceedings, Taylor talked on the telephone to his mother, Kathy Vanhoy, who in turn called the water-bed store and asked the people there if they knew how to get a snake out of a mattress. "They said they never had run across the situation before," she said.

Finally, the fishhook did snag something.

"It put a hole in the mattress," Jerry said.

It didn't really matter. By then, the young men had already spotted a leak from another hole, and they knew that the mattress was unusable.

"We drained the water bed with the hose," said Taylor. "We put the water hose outside, so it could drain." Then—*voila!*—they were able to bend the end of a clothes hanger into a hook and extract the scaly beast. They put it in a jar, and the mattress, which simply couldn't be used, in a Dumpster.

It was left to Kathy Vanhoy, Taylor's mother, to write the happy ending of the escapade by buying a new water-bed mattress.

Mrs. Vanhoy, who'd been kept abreast of the situation by telephone while at work—"I was in a meeting, and I had two messages in 10 minutes to call home"—was as relieved as anyone, with the possible exception of Grandma, when it was over.

"It wasn't a life-threatening situation," she said. "But it was the sort of thing that 14-year-olds and their 80-year-old grandmas don't deal with every day."

Indeed, it was an unusual day for Taylor and Grandma Vera.

But then, it wasn't exactly routine for the snake, either.   *(8/5/90 WSJ)*

Gonna Miss Ya, Mr. Harry

Mr. Harry's jowls could be described as Churchillian, but there was no bulldog in this gentle old man.

He was everybody's teddy bear.

In the morning, Mr. Harry would arrive at Hazel's Restaurant, short of breath from a too-brisk walk. He would remove the old coat that offered too little protection from the cold, but he would always leave on his well-worn little derby hat.

Before he could begin his breakfast routine, he might get a special greeting from Hazel John or one of her daughters, Mary Jo or Pat.

"I'd go over and hug his neck and rub his bald head," Mary Jo Tilley recalled last night as we paid our respects to Mr. Harry at Hayworth-Miller Funeral Home.

"I used to take his hat off and kiss his head," said Pat Lawing, "and he'd say, 'You're teasing me, you're teasing me.'"

Then it was time for Mr. Harry's aperitif: a single bottle of Budweiser and conversation in the bar.

After that, it was always the same: two scrambled eggs, bacon, tomato, coffee and the delicious, flaky biscuits made by his friend, Lucille Warren.

It was well known that Mr. Harry didn't have enough of a pension to live decently. Oh, he had a devoted sister in Baltimore (Sarah Costello), but everyone doubted that he would tell her when he needed something.

And when he came back in the afternoon, Hazel would see that he had a nutritious lunch of at least two vegetables and meat, and never mind if he had any money.

"Mama always thought of Harry as kind of like a father," said Pat. "He was at our house Thanksgiving and Christmases. He came to our house one Father's Day cookout we had. We bought him a Father's Day present—a blue shirt. He thought it was so much. It wasn't nothin' but an old blue shirt."

That brought to mind one of the adjectives that describe the special appeal the old man possessed: appreciative. Always.

It made you want to do something for Mr. Harry.

Except perhaps for Hazel, George Nichols did the most.

Mr. Harry had run off from home at 16 to join the Navy, and George tried long and hard to get him his veterans' benefits. The efforts were futile, because the Navy could not find the records, possibly because Mr. Harry's mother had gotten a lawyer to get him out of the Navy—a sort of annulment, if you will.

George also bought Mr. Harry a winter topcoat. (Someone—no one seems to remember who—provided warm gloves and a winter hat.) And he got the old man a place to live in Crystal Towers, where his rent would be based on ability to pay; and for a man with less than $200 a month total income, that was important.

Now, Mr. Harry did not drink all that much beer, but that beer in the morning and the one or two in the afternoon were part of his ritual.

And that ritual was important to a lot of us, because a chat with Harry, whether about his Navy days at Norfolk or about his friends on the street and their fortunes and misfortunes, was a reminder that there was, indeed, still such a thing as the milk of human kindness.

It can truly be said of Mr. Harry that he would not say an unkind word about anyone. He kept up with most of what was going on in the world, although—as I discovered much later—he could read little if at all, and when he didn't have something to say, he was the best darned listener on the street.

To be sure that Mr. Harry wouldn't be embarrassed to drop by when he was broke, and just because they wanted to do it, his friends took turns buying him his Bud-in-the-bottle.

There were Jimmy Stewart, Charlie Neyle, Bob Eaton, J.T. Joyner, Phil Separk and others too numerous to mention.

And when Hazel, the victim of seven break-ins and robberies, finally faced the fact that she was broke and had to close up shop, she could fight off the tears, except when she asked: "What is going to happen to Mr. Harry?"

The old man wasn't a charity case, of course. After all, he had that sister who would do anything she could for him when she knew what he needed.

But what happened to Mr. Harry, of course, was friends—new friends, plus the old.

He loved it at Crystal Towers and the people there—witness last night's funeral-home turnout in the cold rain—loved him.

He came to taking his daily beers at John Art Dombalis' place, and there he made friends of John, Charlie Evans, whom he had known before but who had been out of touch, and a gentleman known to me only as Sweet Willie, among others.

Now he would talk about that free midday meal that came with residence at Crystal Towers, about all he ate each day, and when asked how he could possibly eat so much, he replied with a sneaky little smile, "It's about the only meal I eat."

John Dombalis handled much of Mr. Harry's money for him, helping see that he made it from month to month. When the old man ran short, he got an advance, which he would conscientiously pay back as soon as the next check came.

And lest anyone think Mr. Harry was forgotten at other times, he wasn't. John and his friend, Bobbie Peeples, took him Thanksgiving dinner, among other things, and Charlie and Ruth Evans stopped by about once a week with food and treated him to Christmas dinner.

Almost everybody bought him Christmas gifts, even the women behind the counter at *The Sentinel*, where he bought his newspapers every day.

He appreciated it all, even as he appreciated an occasional ride home or to John's place when it was raining.

And he appreciated it ever so much when John would find that he had to leave for a few minutes and would ask Mr. Harry if he would do him the favor of taking care of the bar.

"He loved it," John said last night. "You know why? He loved it, being behind the bar and seeing people."

And he loved having the feeling that he, in his 80s, was contributing, doing something for a friend.

Finally, this week, for many of his friends, Mr. Harry got a last name. The obituary said he was Harry Nowlin, 83, a former roof repairman, and last night there were tears in the eyes of Pat and John and Mary Jo, who was happy that she had gotten a picture of Mr. Harry at her wedding.

Mr. Harry's friends had lost their lovable teddy bear, and Lord knows how the tears would have flowed if Hazel, who is now a traveling saleswoman and had been out of touch, had been there.

"Oh, I wish Mama was here," said Pat. "I hate to tell her. How do you tell Mama?

"You can't just say, 'Mr. Harry died.'"   *(1/23/80 The Sentinel)*

Nicole Broom's Journey Was Short

During a visit to Chapel Hill in January 1988, I felt a tug on my sleeve and turned to encounter a young lady gazing into my eyes, her face lit by a familiar impish grin.

As I groped momentarily for her name, she appeared mightily amused. "Do you know who I am?" she demanded.

After a brief-but-embarrassing hesitation, I replied: "Nicole."

Then, to rationalize my befuddlement:

"You look just great. Even prettier than the last time I saw you."

It was true, and she seemed to know why.

"I got married last month," she said.

So this was Nicole Broom—full name, Nicole Broom-Jones Anderson—all grown up, with a bachelor-of-arts degree in journalism from Chapel Hill, writing and editing for a living, and ready to conquer the world.

I had hoped that she would. From almost the moment she walked in the door as a correspondent for the old *Sentinel* newspaper's Teen Page in 1980, in her senior year at East Forsyth High School, she had warmed and won the hearts of skeptical old newsmen there.

Larry Queen, then the Teen Page editor and now a journalism instructor at UNC-Greensboro, became both her mentor and her friend. Once, I told Larry that she brought to mind the words of crusty old Alex Wilder, the late songwriter/composer, in expressing the simple qualities that impressed him:

"Magic and joy, beauty and love."

In both presence and promise, Nicole possessed those qualities—and an appreciation of them in others.

I could not have forgotten her or the infectious laugh that seemed to fade only when somebody pointed a camera toward her. As for her wedding—well, Larry had been there and filled me in.

I had thought about Nicole often since our brief meeting in Chapel Hill, but, of course, nothing in my wildest dreams or fears had prepared me for the telephone conversation with Larry five days ago.

"My God," he said. "I can't believe it. Nicole is dead. That vivacious young woman, so full of life. Twenty-six years old—and dead."

There was no groping for reasons. We were too old for that, too inured to loss. There was anger, however. Such a healthy young woman, dead of natural causes?

Her husband, Mark Anderson, explained on Friday as we sat in the living room of the home of Nicole's parents, Everette and Barbie Jones—six of us, including Nicole's brother, James Broome, Larry and me.

Nicole had suffered an asthma attack on May 9, Anderson said, but seemed much better after seeing her doctor.

"We had gone out on Thursday night," he said. "I had just gotten a raise… We had a really nice meal, and the atmosphere of the restaurant was just so beautiful…

"The next morning, before I went to work, I woke her up. Whenever I had to leave first, I would tell her, 'I love you. Be careful.' I was just so happy that I had the chance to say, 'I love you.'"

When he returned later that day, "She was gone," dead of a blood clot that moved from her lung to her heart—one of those awful things, the doctor said, that could happen to any of us.

Still, it was terribly painful, hard to accept. That was apparent in the tears that rimmed the eyes of the crowd—young, old, black, white, poor and affluent, from near and far—that lined the pews of Carver Road Church of Christ during Wednesday afternoon's funeral.

A day later, family members were able to fend off emotions with only occasional difficulty, and to express some of their feelings.

Very early, Jones said, he and his wife had decided to raise their children—James, Nicole and Dawn Jones, who suffers from Down's syndrome—in something other than the ghettolike conditions of the inner city. He had a good job at Reynolds Tobacco, and she went to business college and became able to hold responsible office positions.

"We took them away from the streets," Jones said. "Her mom wanted to give them the things she never had."

Nicole was given those things, including lessons to develop her dancing talent and assistance in developing her writing, which she wanted to make her life's work.

"From the time she was a little girl," Mrs. Jones said, "she always knew she wanted to work for a newspaper. I remember when she was in fourth grade at Prince Ibraham [school], her class decided to do a newspaper. She came home and said, 'I need you to help me.'

"She said, 'If you just help me, I think we can do it.' Between us, we did it.…

"I typed it, but even then, she would edit it. She'd look at it and say, 'Well, let's do this.' I said, 'Can you imagine—a fourth-grader telling me what to take out and what to put in!'"

Queen had no trouble imagining that. "She sometimes did me the same way," he said. "She had such a personality that she could be very determined without offending you with her determination."

Anderson smiled and said: "And she didn't have to say anything, either. People could just look at her and—she had a way of carrying herself that just brought so much pride and so much confidence.

"She was never egotistic, never conceited. She was just always very confident.

She wanted things to be done right…She got me to the point where I was the same way."

By all accounts, Nicole was a very sensitive, very concerned sister, daughter and wife—and also a friend and confidante, able to infect them all with her zest, optimism and pride.

"Nicole was my friend," Mrs. Jones said. "She was my daughter, but she was my friend. There were times when I went through things that I didn't think I could make it through, but my daughter sustained me.

"She would always tell me that she wanted me to be proud of her because she was so proud of me…

"You know, some people say, 'I don't know what's on my daughter's mind,' or 'son's mind.' I knew. There were nights that Nicole and I would sit up until 2 and 3 o'clock in the morning talking about what she wanted to do. I didn't worry about her when she went off to college."

The level-headedness she saw in her daughter was apparent to Anderson when they met in their freshman year at Chapel Hill.

"I'm not a very outgoing person," he said. "When I met her, I left a note on her door…and she sent one of her friends around to see what I looked like.

"So I went to see her. I knew I had someone special."

They didn't marry until several years later, on Dec. 12, 1987, after he had finished graduate school and gotten a good job as a counselor to head-injury victims.

"I'm so proud of what we had," Anderson said. "Other people talked about how they had problems with their marriages. Even our worst day was great. As long as we were together, everything was fine. She never asked for anything, never wanted anything.

"The only thing we wanted was to just be together. And she loved her family so much."

That love was—is—returned, full measure. "As many times as I told her I loved her," Mrs. Jones said, "it seems like I still want to say to her, 'I love you.' It still seems like you need to say it one more time.…

"We are born to die. Some journeys are longer than others, and Nicole's was a short one. That was the hardest thing for me.

"I won't see her physically anymore, but I have pictures of her, and she'll live forever in my heart. And I know she would say, 'Mom, you can do it.' She would say, 'I'm proud of you.' And I'm just so proud of her. I visualized her doing great things, and she's still doing great things." *(5/21/89 WSJ)*

Reflecting on Youth

Two Are Pleased to Find Somebody Who Knew How It Was in Those Dark Days

For most of us, there is something special in sharing memories of youth with others who can relate to them.

Unfortunately, those with the most memories—people who have lived well beyond the average span of years—often have the least opportunity to share them. Many of their friends have died and others find it hard to communicate, so reflecting on youth can become a solitary and frustrating pastime.

That irony helped make for a few rare moments recently for two rare old birds, Jesse G. Taylor and Richard Munsie Danner.

It began as Taylor, who will be 92 in July, trudged along Waughtown Street on one of the long walks he still takes—to the chagrin of some close to him—to town and back. Madge Boyles, Danner's daughter, stopped to give him a lift.

Danner, in his 91st year, was in town from Harmony visiting his daughter. Knowing that they were both veterans of World War I, she made a quick decision to get the two of them together.

It was like putting sparks to dry tinder.

The fire burned, in their eyes and in their words, through the morning and lunch at Mrs. Boyles' house, and into the afternoon. The oldsters talked of their growing-up years, Taylor's in Stokes County and Danner's in Iredell, in the dawn of the 20th century.

And they made an interesting discovery.

"I was in the 30th Division, Company D, 120th Infantry," Danner said of his wartime service in Europe.

Taylor said, "I was in the 39th Replacement Unit, Medical Corps, attached to the 30th Division."

They never served together or knew each other, although they were both stationed in St.-Nazaire, France, briefly after the Armistice on Nov. 11, 1918. But they had formed an immediate bond.

Although Danner normally shuns talk of the war, he found pleasure in being able to talk to somebody who knew how it was in those dark long-ago days.

"There's not a soul in Harmony that was there back when I went there," he said, trying to explain why it was so good to be able to talk to Taylor. "It's the old remembrances, I think, more than anything else."

Like others who served, Danner had seen man's inhumanity to man. He was mustard-gassed and seriously wounded by shrapnel. He saw Americans kill Germans unnecessarily, saw evidence of Americans being literally crucified by the enemy; and saw vats where soldiers boiled the heads of the dead—to get glycerin, he was told.

"War is something else, if you've never been in one," Danner said. "It's hell on earth. If it ain't, there's not any...."

Taylor, who arrived in France in August 1918—11 months after Danner and only three months before the Armistice—never got into the front lines. But he saw the kind of action Danner was wounded in: men emerging from trenches in waves to run hundreds of yards through gunfire and barbed wire to try to reach the entrenched enemy.

"When you jump into those trenches," said Taylor, "it's kill or be killed. The medical men [who were unarmed] would follow across to pick up the dead and the wounded and get them back any way they could."

That was the way war was before nations became mechanized enough to make machines do much of the fighting. The men attacked in waves, cruelly exposed, and often died that way.

When they died, gold stars went up at courthouses or other public buildings, as the cruelty of war came home to the United States. That happened, in fact, in Danner's case. When he was badly wounded and taken off to a hospital, somebody mistakenly believed he had died.

"They sent a telegram back [to Harmony] that I was killed in action," he said. "They put up a gold star at the schoolhouse....As I remember, it was two months afterward that they got a letter from me and knew that I was alive."

Danner escaped another enemy, one that killed some who had survived the front-line battle: the deadly influenza that gripped Europe and much of the rest of the world in 1918. Taylor was among the victims, and after he recovered he helped care for other victims in the hospital he was assigned to.

"The flu was raging all that winter," Taylor said. "I've seen the hospital yard covered with men on stretchers, waiting to get a bed....There was 50 to 60 men to a ward."

One truly pleasant memory, for both men, was born on Nov. 11, 1918, when the war was finally over.

Danner's eyes brightened as he recalled "those little French boys and girls walking around yelling, 'Finis la guerre! Finis la guerre!'...'The war is over.'"

So it went, two old men enjoying a conversation that evoked mostly unpleasant memories.

But the men were also discussing youth—a time when we all learn truths that will guide us the rest of our lives.

Danner spoke about one of those truths when he said: "You do your best.... It's the way you get home."

It's a simple lesson, one most of us learn somewhere, sometime. But the somewhere and sometime can be crucial, if the full meaning is to be shared.

That's what made the meeting of Jesse G. Taylor and Richard Munsie Danner so special.

(4/22/86 WSJ)

Each December Brings
Pearl Harbor Memories

Every early December, Helen Hays' thoughts turn to the distant past and the lessons that it taught her and others about the uncertainties that upset life's schemes and timetables.

It is a past that helped make Mrs. Hays what she remains today: a patriotic American who takes nothing for granted and who, when she sees others' suffering, feels some of their pain.

She was a young woman, a survivor of the Great Depression, in February 1941, when she got a rare opportunity: a chance to travel to Hawaii and live there with her husband, Harry, who was a petty officer in the U.S. Navy.

She was there as that long-ago December dawned, with its rumors of war and promises of peace. When a Japanese envoy stopped in Honolulu on his way to the United States mainland, supposedly to preserve the peace, she was on hand to welcome him.

And then, just a few days later, on the morning of Dec. 7, as Harry returned early from duty on Ford Island in Pearl Harbor, the brutal lessons began.

"I guess I kind of live through it again every year," Mrs. Hays said. "I think of the morning of the attack, of course. We lived in Pearl City....We were just saying good morning. Hardly more than that.

"I heard the noise, a roar, of airplanes. I got up and ran to the porch to see what it was, and I looked up and saw planes with the rising sun [insignia] on them. I said, 'Honey, it's Japanese planes.'

"He laughed. He said, 'This place is too fortified. It couldn't be Japanese planes. I think it's maneuvers.'

"We looked up about that time and saw this Japanese plane—poof!—explode in a million pieces, it seemed like....Then we saw another plane hit, and one wing was off, and it just went down.

"Then we knew, of course. It was war.

"My knees gave way. I couldn't walk. I was too weak. I crawled from the porch into the middle of the house. I just can't hardly describe the feeling, it was so deep: to realize that we were at war and all the suffering that would come out of that."

When she and her husband finally ventured outside, they encountered neighbors who were about to drive off in their cars. As they yelled to the neighbors, Japanese airplanes swooped in and began strafing the automobiles.

They ducked inside again—this time into a neighbor's house.

"I was at the stove getting a cup of coffee," Mrs. Hays said, "and a bullet came and lodged right between my feet. I just about passed out. I went into the dining room and got on my knees and started praying—praying and crying."

Finally, the action died down and she made her way to a friend's house in Honolulu and then to a giant cavelike bomb shelter. Her husband was able to catch a boat back to his duty station. There, he discovered that his bunk area was gone, blown away by a Japanese bomb a few minutes after he had left it early and gone home.

The harbor, America's naval stronghold, was a disaster: More than 2,000 Americans were dead and more were dying; the battleships *Arizona, West Virginia* and *Utah* were on their way to the harbor bottom, and other ships were sunk or badly damaged; and land installations and American aircraft had been devastated in the attack.

The loss of the ships hurt most, because we could not strike back without a powerful Navy.

"I don't think we really knew at the time how much of our fleet had been destroyed," Mrs. Hays said, "or we probably would have been a lot more frightened than we were."

As it was, she was frightened enough.

The first night in the rocky shelter, she and her friend heard airplane engines followed by anti-aircraft fire and explosions, and they assumed that the Japanese were back. They weren't; tragically, U.S. forces had shot down two of our own airplanes.

Later, they were able to go back and stay at the friend's house. Before she could leave for the mainland in May, she and her husband had begun learning of friends' being killed or taken prisoner in fighting that now raged through the Pacific.

"I didn't know whether we had a future together or not, really. I hated to leave. It broke my heart."

Fortunately for the United States, and perhaps for their future, the Japanese had made a monumental tactical error.

Intent on dramatic and symbolic victory, they had focused on ships and men and ignored the huge Hawaiian stocks of oil whose loss would have immobilized America.

Days after Mrs. Hays left, and only six months after the attack on Pearl Harbor, the U.S. turned the tide of battle in the Pacific with a dramatic victory in the Battle of Midway.

For most of the rest of the war, she stayed home and worked at the old Ideal store in downtown Winston-Salem.

Harry Hays survived the war, and so did most of their friends, some as prisoners until the Japanese surrender in 1945.

Afterward, she and her husband had that future together, but it would be disappointingly brief, lasting only until his death of a heart attack in 1965, at age 58.

But as she looks back each year, she looks back on times that left their imprint on most Americans who lived through them.

"It makes you know what war is like, if you've never been in a war," she said.

"I'm a patriotic person. I love my country. I love my flag."

Aside from patriotism, Mrs. Hays seems to share other qualities found so often in survivors of hard and perilous times: a sense of compassion, and a gratitude for what she has been given in life.

"As terrible as it was," she said of the war, "it's something that I wouldn't have missed. It made me more aware of the suffering of people, of the tragedy of war."

(12/4/88 WSJ)

Couple Finds Love in Classified Ads

What does a fellow do for female companionship if he's shy and doesn't hang out in bars or other places where modern dating games and mating dances play out?

Tim Gentry figured that one out a long time ago.

Oh, he hemmed, hawed and held back for a year and a half, but he finally did what he had to do.

He placed a classified ad in the *Journal*.

Male, 24, 5 ft. 6, 145 pounds, blue eyes, blond hair, seeking very affectionate... *Christian female, age 21–28, who is looking for possible long-term relationship, enjoys quiet activities.*

That was on Jan. 11, 1985. Gentry, a 1980 graduate of R.J. Reynolds High School in Winston-Salem, was managing and cooking in a pizza restaurant at the time.

Meanwhile, Bonnie Joyce, a 1982 graduate of South Stokes High, 25, also a bit shy, was working as a consumer correspondent at Sara Lee hosiery.

"The ladies that I work with, we all joke around and pick all the time," she said. "Every day at lunch, we would read the paper, and it's always been my job to read the personal ads. I read them out loud.

"So I was reading the ads one day and I casually said: 'This is the one. This is the one for me right here.' And they said, 'We dare you. We double-dare you.' I mean, double-D dare you!"

Ms. Joyce had never done that kind of thing before, she said, but...

"I went home and I wrote a letter. I thought, 'Well, I'm not going to send it.' But I said, 'Well, why not?'"

She sent it, and he telephoned her from the restaurant, where he worked at least 10 hours a night and at least six days a week.

"I went in to work the next day," she said, "and I said, 'Y'all are not going to believe this, but he called me.' They said, 'Well, what's his name?' I said, 'To tell you the truth, I don't know.' I had forgotten. He had said his name the very first sentence on the phone and we talked for two hours."

It didn't matter. He called again—and again. "The girls at work got concerned," she said. "They said, 'Well, wait a minute! This may be a lunatic. We're sending you out here to meet some crazy person who's going to kill you on the first date.'

"So they went to where he worked. They went incognito."

Some kind of lunatic.

For that matter, some kind of incognito.

One of the girls, Sarah—he couldn't give her full name because she had threatened to kill him if he did—walked boldly up to him as he worked pizza dough with both hands while talking into a telephone scrunched down on his shoulder and said, "Are you talking to Bonnie?"

Gentry's reaction?

"I said, 'Bonnie, it's for you.' And I handed the phone to Sarah."

Fortunately, even pizza-restaurant managers get a night off now and again. So a week after the first telephone call, the bride-and-groom-to-be—admit it; you'd already guessed—went on their first date.

Things moved quickly.

"He told me on that first date, when he brought me home, that he was going to marry me," said Ms. Gentry.

Why did he say that?

"I thought it was right. I just decided she was the one I was supposed to marry."

"It was funny," she said. "It was like we had known each other all our lives. Now it's five years, and it seems like we've been together forever. I can't remember ever being without him."

The Gentrys were married Aug. 31, 1985—Friday will be their fifth anniversary—at Olive Grove Baptist Church in Pinnacle, where they now live next to her parents.

On their first anniversary nearly four years ago, Ms. Gentry, a poet and songwriter, took out a *Journal* personal ad of her own:

TIM: Roses are red/violets are blue/it was through this ad/that I met and married you. Happy first anniversary! Love, Bonnie.

From the beginning, Gentry was a romantic, leaving poetry or candy or perfume around where his wife would find it, even hiding a real diamond ring in a CrackerJacks box to surprise her.

As recently as Thursday, he surprised her with another gift: a five-year anniversary ring.

Lately, however, both he and his gifts seem to have taken a more practical turn.

"I tell everybody at work that he went from diamonds and rubies to concrete deers!" said Ms. Gentry.

"That's what he got me for Valentine's Day. Two o'clock in the morning, he brings it and plops it down beside the bed. 'Look what I got you, honey!'"

Gentry, who left the 70-hour weeks behind some time ago, works for Food Fair today. Ms. Gentry remains at Sara Lee, but has become a dye-lab technician.

They still shun the high life. They stargaze with their telescopes, play computer games, watch television movies; she writes, plays guitar and paints—he wanted to learn, so she got him a paint-by-numbers set; they play golf together on Saturdays; and he does some cooking.

Their 2-year-old Chihuahua, Cricket, seems a constant companion—"If he learns to speak English, we'll have to shoot him," she said—and they all seem very happy.

For the Gentrys, the personal-ad route worked—the first time they tried it.

While they advise caution and honesty, they think it might work for some others.

So, as that fifth anniversary approaches, do they have any advice for others contemplating marriage?

"The best advice I can give," she said, "is a prayer said at our wedding: 'Let God be the head of the household, and the unseen guest at every meal.'

"It doesn't help much on your taxes, but it does a lot for our marriage!"

(8/26/90 WSJ)

EPILOGUE: *Tim and Bonnie are still living in Pinnacle, with their two dogs, Willie, a miniature dachshund, and Harley, an apple-head Chihuahua, who have replaced their beloved Cricket, who died. Bonnie remains in Product Development at Sara Lee, and Tim, self-employed, is working toward a computer-information degree at High Point University.*

Any additional advice after 15 years of marriage? They stand by their original comments. Bonnie said, "We still put it ['Let God be the head of the household'] first. Sometimes you have to put it way out first." *(1/25/01 Interview)*

Sometimes Life Will Fall into Place

Happy Thanksgiving?

It couldn't be much happier for Ray Wigley, a local salesman who finished putting a large part of his life back together last week.

"I'm going to tell you," a still-emotional Wigley said after returning from a trip to Sacramento, Calif., for a reunion with a son he hadn't seen for 31 years, "you can't rehearse it. There's no way."

Wigley's son, David, was 3 months old when his mother took him out of state during a not-very-cordial divorce proceeding. The boy was told that his father was dead, and by the time he discovered otherwise—when he was 18—there was no way to get in touch.

But this year David Wigley, a Vietnam veteran and nurse in a Sacramento hospital, came into contact with a Wigley who had been injured in a motorcycle accident. The patient had a relative who kept track of the family, and David was able to get in touch.

So on Nov. 11, Ray Wigley boarded an airplane, bound for California.

By then, Wigley—who seems normally reserved—was so happy that he was telling his story to strangers.

"When I got off the plane in Chicago," Wigley said in a conversation after his return, "this stewardess handed me her name and address and asked me to let her know how it came out in Sacramento.

"In Chicago, we had an hour to wait…I shared [the story] again with the stewardess on the plane. And shortly thereafter the captain came over the P. A. [public address] system and asked passenger Wigley to come to the front. The stewardess instructed me to go into the cockpit. The captain wanted to hear the story himself.…We had a real nice flight into Sacramento, and as I was deplaning the stewardess handed me a bottle of champagne so that my son and I could celebrate.

"You don't think that people are interested in such as this…Really, this has amazed me. They say, 'This is something you read about, and when you know something about it firsthand, it has a different meaning.'"

Still, despite the poignancy of the situation, both the elder and the younger Wigley had concerns about the reunion: Would it be comfortable, would it really be happy, would they feel as if they knew each other.

All reservations quickly resolved, however.

"I promise you," Wigley said in a telephone chat while he was in California, "I wouldn't swap it for anything that's ever happened. I got off the plane going up the ramp into the terminal. Butterflies could have flown out of my stomach, but as I neared the door I said, 'I've got to be stable here.'…

"It was a mountain of joy. That's the best way to explain it to you....We've been talking about the past and really just visiting like you would with your own people that you've been with all your life...and there's a lot to talk about."

For David Wigley, whose life by then was wrapped up in his wife, Johanna, and their three sons, there were also doubts.

"That morning before Dad came in here was a tense one," said David.

"That was when reality finally set in. After 31 years of knowing nothing and then two weeks of intensive communications on the telephone, I was thinking, 'This is it.' It was quite a moment when he stepped off there. The only thought that was in my mind at that moment was, 'Here is my father. This is my father.'

"At that moment, the wondering stopped and the knowing began."

The five-day reunion consisted largely of sharing stories and pictures and just becoming easy and comfortable with one another.

"Really," Wigley said on his return, "you just have to take it one step at a time, and it's hard to find words to describe the feeling that I had. But it is one that I now know that I'll never have in my life anymore, and I fully realize that this could be the answer to a lot of prayers on both sides...

"The whole visit was used up talking about what happened in the past and what we hoped the future would bring. The plans are right now that in August...we're going to Georgia [where David was born] to a Wigley reunion, and, hopefully, there he'll get to meet the rest of my family and meet all of his first cousins that he's never seen."

And how does Ray Wigley feel today?

It was summed up, he said, when the woman across the street asked him if he was proud that he had found his son.

"Yes," he replied. "I could get up on the housetop and shout it, if it would do any good."

(11/25/82 The Sentinel)

"Really Christmas"
Seamstress Takes Time to Sew for Psychiatric Patients

KERNERSVILLE—Every year about this time, Hester Laffoon quits sewing for her customers and gives herself the gift of giving to people who have nothing to give in return.

Nothing but gratitude, that is.

For Mrs. Laffoon, that's more than enough.

She learned early, growing up on a farm in Surry County with five sisters, that helping out is part of life.

"Our parents taught us to never be too busy that we couldn't go help someone," she said during a visit in her home on Main Street here. "They'd send us to help if someone needed help."

The "someones" Mrs. Laffoon helps now, at Christmastime, are elderly psychiatric patients at John Umstead Hospital in Butner. Each year, she makes them robes, gowns or other clothing items. Always, she makes the sturdy apron-like bags that patients can use to organize their toiletry and other personal items.

The bags are treasured items because they give the patients a precious commodity: their own special place to put personal belongings.

"You can imagine how happy people are to have something to put their toilet articles and pencils and papers in—a way to keep them all together," Mrs. Laffoon said.

"The first time I did it was, I'd say, 12 to 15 years ago. My husband's sister was at Butner. I made one for her. She said she couldn't have made it very good without that…

"Several years ago, I talked to the lady in charge of clothing, and she said there's a lot of people down there who are forgotten. They carry 'em there and leave 'em there and don't come back to see them or send them anything."

On Friday, when a dozen or more volunteers for the local Mental Health Association take Santa Claus to Umstead to give the elderly patients a Christmas party, Mrs. Laffoon's handiwork will be among the gifts donated for patients during the association's annual Operation Santa Claus drive.

She thinks it's a great way to observe Christmas. "I just stop other work for a few days," she said. "Everybody knows that. They [customers] don't bother me much then…

"It's mostly what I do for Christmas. I don't go out and buy gifts, even for family.

"And it does me more good than anything else I could do."

For Mrs. Charlie Laffoon (she still uses her husband's name almost five years after his death), doing for others has been a way of life. She's been a seamstress for 55 of her 78 years, and for much of that time her work supplemented the income her husband made as a printer, first at the *Elkin Tribune* and then at the *Kernersville News.*

She does for herself too, of course. She makes all her own clothing—"I've never bought a ready-made coat or dress"—and she still raises much of her own food. Because she has no children and her closest relatives live in Elkin and Wilkesboro, she shares the food mostly with friends and neighbors.

"I grow my own garden," she said. "I plant my garden every year just like I had a family. It's so much better when you pick it out of the garden or off the brier. I give it away."

She enjoys that, just as she enjoys making and giving away the clothing and toiletry bags.

Both, of course, are fruits of her own labor, and that makes them special.

"Our parents taught us to work, and we enjoyed it," she said.

"Not many people my age are able to get up and go to work."

But perhaps her most special pleasure comes as Christmas approaches each year and she goes to work on her gifts for the hospital patients.

"I do enjoy it," she said. "It helps me to know I'm doing for somebody. To me, that is really Christmas."

(12/11/86 WSJ)

EPILOGUE: *Hester Laffoon is still sewing for patients at Umstead Hospital in Butner at Christmas, and she is still in business, doing alterations for customers.*

For her 93rd birthday, friends and customers gave her a trip on a hot-air balloon over Kernersville. Beforehand, she said, "Upstairs is the highest I've ever been." She said, afterward, "I'm a tough old bird. It was fun. I think I could do that again."

(6/26/01 WSJ)

CHAPTER 4

Stars 'N Such

In his job, Sieg occasionally met celebrities or those who had rubbed elbows with them. These stars vary from those who made it to the top in their work or those whose voices told of momentous events or famous people. These include: Winston-Salem's own Ernie Shore, who won fame by pitching a perfect game for the Boston Red Sox and later returned home to serve as Forsyth County sheriff for 34 years; A.R. Ammons, a gifted poet who emerged from the business world; Jesse Owens, who became America's hero at the Olympic Games in Germany in 1936; Anita Loos, author of *Gentlemen Prefer Blondes* and other books, movie scripts and Broadway plays; Johnny Crowell, an early daredevil pilot who started out the same year as Charles Lindbergh and who met him, and E. Celia MacKenzie who was a survivor of the sinking of the *Titanic.*

Ball Player, Etc.
Ernie Shore Has Enjoyed His Careers

Ernie Shore doesn't get around much any more.

Since suffering a stroke three and a half years ago, Shore has restricted his activities mainly to riding around town with friends.

But Shore, 87 and white-haired and carrying a large but somewhat hollowed frame, doesn't feel sorry for himself. He said he felt good, and he welcomed the visit and was happy to share some memories of his careers.

Ernest Grady Shore, a fastballing, mule-strong young pitcher, came out of East Bend High School in 1910 and went to Guilford College, where his pitching was to put him in the collegiate Hall of Fame.

"We had the best team in the country," said Shore. "We won all the games but one in 1914. We beat the University of North Carolina and Duke University, and N.C. State beat us one game. The right fielder dropped the ball.

"I won three games in five days against the University of South Carolina, Davidson College and North Carolina. I had 24 wins the last two years, one tie and one loss."

Needless to say, organized baseball's scouts had not been blind to such a performance. When Shore graduated in 1914, he joined the Baltimore Orioles, which were then one step from the big leagues.

He and another young pitcher, George Herman (Babe) Ruth, were impressive, and in July they were bought by the Boston Red Sox. Both of them stuck with the team.

"I won 10 games and lost four the rest of the season," said Shore. The next season, when he was one year out of college, he won 20 and lost seven, and he seemed firmly established.

It was in 1917 that Shore etched his name forever in baseball's record books, and he did it pitching in relief of his roommate, Babe Ruth.

"Ruth walked the first man," said Shore, "and the umpire chased him for protesting too loudly. I guess he called the umpire some names.

"In those days you were allowed only five warm-up pitches on the mound. The manager said to me, 'Go out there and stall around until I get a pitcher warmed up.'

"I threw the five warm-up pitches, and the fellow on first base, he tried to steal on the first pitch and the catcher threw him out at second base. I retired the next 26 batters in order."

It went down as the third perfect game in modern major-league history—and the first in which a runner had reached base.

The 1917 season took its toll, however. He had injured his arm, and he

Ernie Shore—the legend from Yadkin County. –WSJ

missed a full season while serving as an ensign in the Navy—on active duty in the North Atlantic, where the bitter cold did nothing to heal the arm.

In 1919, when he returned, the Red Sox sold him to the New York Yankees. (Ruth was to follow the next year.) He pitched two seasons for the Yanks, then ended his career with one season at San Francisco of the Pacific Coast League.

Rather than sit around and think about what might have been, Shore seems to feel fortunate for what was. The sparkle in his eye becomes more of a glisten when he talks baseball, and there is often emotion in his voice.

"They were wonderful years," he said. "We won two pennants and two

World Series, and I pitched four games in the World Series. I won three of 'em."

And the inevitable question: What about Ruth? Was he really the crude, beer-swilling, hot-dog-gulping guy he's been said to be?

"He was the most gentle-hearted person you could look for. He'd give you the shirt off his back every time.

"I don't know about beer. He didn't drink it much when I was there. He did like hot dogs and hamburgers. And lobsters—you could afford to eat a lobster then. Now you can't afford to eat one."

After Ernie Shore returned to Winston-Salem…he went into the automobile business and did quite well, married Lucille Harrelson and…when the Depression came, he sold insurance for several years…then decided to run for sheriff of Forsyth County in 1936.

"I just went from house to house [campaigning]," he said. "I had a lot of help—Bert Bennett and John Smithdeal. Before the [second] primary, we had a meeting down here and we had about 600 people. That was before I was nominated."

It was the beginning of what was to be a 34-year career as sheriff—the longest ever in Forsyth County. And if those who say that Shore ran for sheriff as a baseball player are right, he certainly didn't run the office as a ball player.

He took a department with six deputies and left it with 70 in 1970. He fought county boards for money and equipment, and won. He not only got the department its first county cars, but became the first North Carolina sheriff to equip cars with two-way radios. Shore chased down rapists and safe-crackers and killers and would-be killers, and his department solved nearly every major crime that came its way.

Yet Shore, who is known throughout his career as a gentle, unassuming person, is not egotistical or boastful about his long years as sheriff.

"It was new to me [at first]," he said simply, "but I stuck with it and tried to benefit by everything I could imagine."

Shore was reminded of the time his department had an armed fugitive surrounded and he stepped out in the open and talked the man into giving himself up.

"He was wanted for shooting at some of the deputies," he said. "He hit one of them, but he didn't hurt him very much. We went up there to arrest him and he was holed up in the barn.

"I said, 'Now, this is Sheriff Shore, and you know I'm going to treat you right if you come out, but otherwise we're going to have to come in after you and maybe kill you.'

"I didn't think he was going to shoot me. I just told him to throw the gun out and come out and I'd treat him right and wouldn't hurt him. He threw the gun out and came out and surrendered…"

Shore is still happy to help when he can. When Mrs. Shore showed a reporter a stack of mail from all over the country, seeking autographs, she explained that he signs the autographs personally, although it is very difficult for him.

And the reason he does it is simple. At 87, handicapped by a stroke and having served baseball in many ways for well over half a century, he still feels he owes something to the fans and to the game.

Why?

"It gave me so much pleasure." *(8/14/78 The Sentinel, newsfeature)*

EPILOGUE: *Ernie Shore died Sept. 24, 1980, at 89. His wife had died a few months earlier. Sieg wrote: "Ernie Shore's friends and contemporaries were saying the same things about him today that they said while he was alive—he was a great guy, a true gentleman and a good person to be around."*

(9/25/80 The Sentinel)

A Poet: Conversations and Musings
A.R. Ammons Has Joined the Elite—But Not the Elitists

Take a TV sports fan, a university professor, a doting parent, a New York sophisticate, a pool player and a man who may rank among the finest American poets of this century.

Put these together, and you'd still have only a slice—though perhaps as large a one as you could handle at once—of Archie Ammons.

Ammons, known to scholars and students as A.R. rather than Archie, is at home with life.

A truck driver would undoubtedly consider him a nice guy, a simple man.

Poetry critic Harold Bloom finds him "a major visionary poet," obviously a very complex man.

For me, it is enough to find him a man for many moods, and an uplifting experience.

In a lounge at Wake Forest University one man hung back, his fingers fumbling either with each other or with something within their grasp. He appeared shy and wore a roundish face tinged red like that of a clown who has worn his makeup overlong.

Surely, this could not be the Great Man.

But yes, it was: A.R. Ammons, winner last week of the Bollingen Prize, much harder for a poet to earn than a Pulitzer for a newsman. He had added his name to a list that includes Robert Frost, Archibald MacLeish, W.H. Auden and Robert Penn Warren. Earlier, he had won a National Book Award for Poetry.

Ammons was hesitant to characterize his own work, unwilling to tread on the rights of critics. Even on the subject of his thematic interest, he said, "I think I just have to give up...I merely do what I can and let it go at that. I do have a feeling and a concern for basic human rights."

There were, however, areas he discussed eagerly.

Is he a disciplined writer, working at set times and places?

"I always write at home...I prefer to write in the midst of goings-on. Whenever the muse is there, I try to pay attention to her visitations...

"Learning to write is like a conscious preparation for an unconscious event....When the poem is there in your eye, then you're hitting the ball, as in baseball. You react automatically. A lot of times you miss, but sometimes you connect so astonishingly well that it amazes you and everyone else."

What is the need for poetry? Why isn't prose sufficient?

"I don't see why it couldn't be sufficient. You would have, first of all, to name the difference...and I don't know what that difference is myself. I think what may be the case is that…not always, but in general, poetry seems to want to make some use of the intense energies of the language itself, in addition to what it is saying." And poetry, because it creates or demands intense feeling and excitement, can't be read well "over a long period."

Is poetry sometimes unnecessarily complex today?

"I would say that most of the poetry of the 20th century is clear," he said, having shunted T.S. Eliot aside. "There is Robert Frost, who writes a very clear language, though the meaning is often complex.

"As for meaning," he said, tossing a button onto a table, "if you ask the meaning of this button, you're into philosophy."

Ammons came to Wake Forest for the academic year by way of his native Columbus County, with many stops and at least one very important new start along the way.

He began writing poetry while in the Navy at the end of and just after World War II. He grew, and he never stopped:

During his college days that brought him a bachelor of science from Wake Forest College in 1949; during a stint in English that produced no degree from the University of California at Berkeley; and during the dozen years he "worked for Friedrich and Dimmock Inc. in Millville, N.J. It was a medical and biological glassware company. I was the salesman."

Some poems were published; he was asked to do a reading at Cornell University in Ithaca, N.Y., and quickly became an instructor there, in 1964.

"They renewed my contract for one year. Then I went to assistant professor, to associate, to full professor. I now have an endowed chair. My friends and colleagues were generous, awfully generous for someone who only had a B.S. degree.

"It was kind of rough to start out at the bottom at age 38, but you have to take chances.

"You know, this is like a homecoming to me. Of course, it's a different campus, but it's like home…

"Those magnolia trees were brought from the old campus, you know. Yesterday when the ice melted, the trees rained…"

He talked of the danger of overteaching, of damaging something within an aspiring poet. And he told of the pleasures of this year's sabbatical from Cornell.

"Young people today are more attuned to poetry, I think.…They are reading and listening to each other. It seems perfectly natural for them.…

"This is one of the finest English departments for a small university I've ever seen.…Poetry is my hobby…and I love to walk; I try to get that in every day. I love to play pool. I watch some games on television…things that everybody likes to do."

As a novitiate, reading Ammons for the first time and having read none of the critics, I was surprised that the world described in *Sphere* was not the egalitarian one I had expected after meeting the author. But that is probably because, while Ammons has a keen eye for hope, the world is simply not egalitarian.

His world is one of striving and longing; of delight and disappointment; of triumph and disillusion; of the real and the real unreal, and of order and disorder, all in progression. Nature or man's experience may heighten other men's experience, but there should be no reckless imposing or impinging. And, perhaps sadly, the rights of humanity may extend to the ultimate right of being dead without knowing it.

Sphere is an appropriate title for Ammons' latest work. His vehicle is the world in all its animal, vegetable and mineral parts, blown fuller with mankind's and his own extensions.

It is complicated, demanding stuff to the rusty or inexperienced poetry reader, who might better start with *Collected Poems 1951–1971*, in which Ammons begins to climb his mountain with simpler works such as "Chaos Staggered Up the Hill."

That particular poem, for me, quickly said much about the man and his thought, pushing aside some not fully understood portions of *Sphere* which should be taken slowly and more than once.

"Hi, honey. This is Mr. Sieg. We thought you might have some coffee."

"I have a cup," Phyllis Ammons said, interrupting her pie-baking and seeming neither offended nor surprised at the intrusion.

"Can I go get some football cards?" asked nine-year-old John.

'We'll try to do that later," said Ammons.

"John is trying to get a complete collection of Redskin cards," he explained.

Then Ammons turned briefly again to poetry.

"It calls your feelings into play....The poem is supposed to be delightful. That's how it teaches you, through its delight, both in reading it and writing it...

"Teaching poetry is likely to sound very important and snooty, when actually it's a perfectly natural thing to do—read and write. Young people write poetry almost spontaneously....I don't see why it can't entertain us all."

Who is his favorite poet?

"Robert Frost and Wallace Stevens. Let's quit now."

"Drop by anytime," he said. And as I drove off, I thought of something else he had said:

"It just seems to me that a poet is right there at the center of life, not off in some [ivory] tower....I don't see how he'd have much to say if he were off somewhere in a tower."

And I had to wonder if the long experience in what is often thought of as the mundane world of business had rounded some of the edges that academe would have left untouched, helping produce the sphere of man and vision that made *Sphere* possible.   *(1/13/75 The Sentinel, newsfeature)*

EPILOGUE: *In addition to the Bollingen Prize, A.R. Ammons also won two National Book Awards, numerous major poetry awards, and in 2000 he was inducted into the North Carolina Literary Hall of Fame, a program of the North Carolina Writers' Network.*

He published nearly 30 books of poetry. His last book was Glare, *published in 1997. He died Feb. 25, 2001. He was 75.*   *(10/15/00 and 2/27/01 WSJ)*

Jesse Owens Showed Them

Jesse Owens took Berlin nine years before the Russian Army did.

It was 1936 and Adolf Hitler, host to the Olympic Games, was hoping to use athletics as a showcase for his theory of Aryan supremacy.

Along came Owens, a black.

"He was talking about Aryan supremacy, about blue-eyed and blond people as the superior race," Owens said during an interview this morning. (He was to speak at Wake Forest University in the evening.) "I certainly wasn't blue-eyed and blond. We were able to destroy that myth athletically."

The "we" was Owens who set Olympic records in the 100-meter dash, the 200-meter and the long jump and won a fourth gold medal as a member of a relay team.

Owens, who has spent much of his life since 1936 helping and setting an example for boys, doesn't boast of his athletic prowess or achievements. His pride in those things comes from what they have meant in his life and can mean to others.

"I was born in a crossroads town called Oakville, Ala.," he said. "My father was a sharecropper. There were four boys and five girls. We grew cotton on one of the largest tracts of this man who owned the land because we had a large family. Cotton was king."

The World War I boom and the availability of steel-mill jobs for his father and two of his older brothers took Owens out of the cotton field and left it up to him to get out of the ghetto of Cleveland, Ohio.

"It started on the playgrounds," he said. "Where was there to go? There was no money.

"I met these two Italians. They ran a shoe-repair shop. They taught me to shine shoes....The money I made shining shoes was my money....

"Every night I'd get home and you'd go to the playground. We used to play baseball, and when it got dark, in order to have something to do, we'd run races.

"As time went on, I was able to beat all the kids in my age group. Later on, we moved up to the larger kids and I was able to beat many of them."

Shortly afterward, one of two very large influences entered Owens' life: Charles Riley, a junior-track coach, the Old Man to his kids, their Bible, a man who insisted that boys learn early to take care of their bodies and minds, accept criticism and follow instructions to the letter.

While Owens was starring for Riley, another idol appeared. He was Charlie Paddock, the World's Fastest Human, who had just returned from the Olympic Games. Paddock spoke at Owens' school, and Owens was impressed.

"Sometime in life, all of us must dream of something," said Owens. "I

Jesse Owens—track superstar. –WSJ

listened…I wanted to be like this man.

"I think everyone should have an idol. I look at people today. I think that we're cheating our young people in many ways. I get a little disappointed with some of our present superstars. I don't think they perpetuate the things they're supposed to represent.

"I guess I'm of the old school. I don't approve of much of the publicity and some of the actions of our present-day stars in some cases….I think today we have so much that young people don't have a chance to choose. I think that today, fortunately or unfortunately, we have a new star on the horizon every day….A child doesn't get an opportunity to really settle on any one thing.

"When I was a kid and I was 13 years old—I remember that day. I remember this man [Paddock] talking to us. I remember being invited into the coach's office.

"I sat in the chair facing this man. And listening to him."

Later, after Paddock left, Riley asked Owens what he thought.

"I said, 'I want to be me, but I want to be like this man, known as the World's Fastest Human Being,'" said Owens. "And he said, 'Well, that's your dream.'

"He said, 'I want you to know that dreams are high, and you climb a ladder to your dream.' And he said, 'The first rung in that ladder is your determination that you're going to reach that dream....The next rung is your dedication to that dream....The third rung in that ladder is the self-discipline and the sacrifices you must make. And the fourth rung is the kind of attitude you must assume in reaching that dream.'"

Owens passed every test. Before he was out of junior high school, he was beating college students in races and the long jump, and while in high school he tied the world record in the 100-yard dash.

When he was a sophomore at Ohio State—where he went on an athletic scholarship—he set three world records and tied a fourth in one afternoon. His mark of that day of 26 feet 8¼ inches in the broad jump (now called the long jump) stood for a quarter of a century.

Then came the Olympics and his political-philosophical-athletic triumph, which reportedly left Hitler in a rage. Since then, Owens has worked in business and industry—and in settlement houses and boys' clubs, and as a sponsor of youth programs.

And he has never forgotten the lessons that his life and his heroes have taught him.

"Life has its ups and downs," he said. "I've had more high spots than I've had valleys, but I think every man should have the valley to appreciate the high spot when it arrives.

"I've listened to people talk—'I did it myself. I raised myself up by my own bootstraps.' But I know that there's always been someone to lend a helping hand.

"I came out of the ghetto of the South and I came out of the ghetto of the North, and I know that there's always been a hand reaching down and bringing me up to the side of the mountain.

"But I also know that you've got to go back. You've got to reach down and lend a helping hand and pull someone up to the side of the mountain where you are now."

(1/24/79 The Sentinel)

Anita Loos: A Blessing

"I grant that short entries in a datebook can sometimes pose a mystery. In Santa Monica, July 4, 1935, I scribbled: Leave for New York. Lend beach house to Joe. And then, six weeks later, a mystery comes to light: Home from vacation. Find house in order except for footprints on the ceiling."

—Anita Loos, in *Kiss Hollywood Good-By* [2]

You ask what ever happened to Anita Loos?

The answer is that she has never stopped happening to us, the American public, and that is a blessing.

The author of *Gentlemen Prefer Blondes* and several other books, as well as more than 200 movie story lines and scripts and Broadway productions and assorted other works, is alive and well and hard at work at her home in New York.

At age 84.

"I'm just finishing a book on the Talmadge sisters," Miss Loos said over the telephone yesterday. "Norma and Constance—you're too young to remember them. There was a third sister who married Buster Keaton. I was with them for six years in the heyday of the silent movies.

"It seems that we in the public never get fed up with stories about Hollywood. So when the Viking Press came after me to write a history of that era, it was an offer I couldn't refuse.

"I've been working on it for two years off and on, and I've been getting two musicals going on the side. What with a few articles in newspapers and magazines, that keeps me busy."

The voice was crisp, the mind obviously quick despite a winding-down bout with flu, and the image that came through the wires was of a woman who, in her own special and older way, must be as lovely as the wide-eyed and sexy-lipped beauty she was in the 1930s.

Perhaps no one rubbed shoulders with more of the greats, or saw more of the glitter, in the glory days of Hollywood than Miss Loos. She sold her first story line at age 12; she was on the writing staff for D.W. Griffith, the giant of silent films; she wrote for Irving Thalberg, the genius who made MGM; she set trends, bringing subtitles, satire and comic sex to the screen.

H.L. Mencken, that lovable—to some—curmudgeon and great writer, once said to her: "Do you realize, young woman, that you're the first American writer ever to poke fun at sex?"

Could I find a better person than Anita Loos, who wrote, perhaps, as many American movies as anybody, to ask for an assessment of Thursday's selection by the American Film Institute of the supposed best 10 American movies of all time? Of all things, "Singin' in the Rain," "2001: A Space Odyssey," "One Flew Over the Cuckoo's Nest" and "Star Wars" had been included along with more obvious choices, such as "Gone With the Wind," "Citizen Kane" and "Wizard of Oz."

"I don't quarrel with any of those," said Miss Loos. "I think they were all great. But I'm not much of a moviegoer, so an awful lot of the important movies, I never saw."

A writer of movies, but not a viewer? That wasn't all.

"I've always preferred foreign films to American, because I lived a great deal in Europe. As soon as I was able to be on my own, I spent half the year in Europe. I suppose I got a little snobbish about American films."

Gentlemen may still prefer blondes and, as the title of a sort-of sequel says, marry brunettes. But, in looking back on her own work and trying to pick her own favorite, Miss Loos prefers something other than *Gentlemen Prefer Blondes.*

"I think it was a film called 'San Francisco,'" she said. "It was a film that Clark Gable did with Jeannette McDonald. It was the film in which Spencer Tracy got his start, and it still runs quite frequently on the late shows. It's one of the old standbys."

In her many years in Hollywood—she left well over 30 years ago to write Helen Hayes' longest-running Broadway play and concentrate on other diversions—Miss Loos met many people she liked and a few she didn't. She found the toothless (without help) Clark Gable straightforward and, at least, without his store-bought teeth, unpretentious.

But she didn't hang around with actors and actresses except while on the job.

"I look on them as people making ego trips," she said, "and very few of them rose above egomania. My idols were always writers—H.L. Mencken, George Santayana, Aldous Huxley…This makes me sound like an awful snob. But in a way I was. I was a cultural snob. I was only impressed by brains. And when you're living in Hollywood and can choose between Aldous Huxley and Stan Laurel, I think the choice is simple."

Anita Loos, at age 84…She has outlived almost everybody. Today, she lives basically alone, spending her time with the widow of playwright Robert Sherwood and others, whose names would not be recognizable, being with them simply because they are her friends.

Anita Loos became wealthy and famous despite having no particular designs on life. She wandered into her fame and fortune with a sense of humor and a saucy attitude toward sex, which she considered at least as satisfying on an intellectual level as on a physical one.

She was a liberated woman, but she didn't know it, and she still considers "liberation"—as today's feminists espouse it—totally unnecessary.

174

"I think they've made women into the biggest boors they have ever been," she said. "They have no sense of humor. Any woman with a sense of humor doesn't have to be liberated...

"I think ambition is a terribly overrated quality. Most people who are ambitious are boors."

✦　✦　✦

Oh, by the way—about those footprints on the ceiling. Johnny Weissmuller, the then-reigning Tarzan, caused them. You figure out how.

(11/19/77 The Sentinel)

This Aerobat Was a Doer
Who Missed Out on Fame

The *Sentinel's* file on Johnny Crowell of Charlotte bears the notation, "Pilot who met Charles Lindbergh."

The casual file-searcher would miss the irony.

Johnny was, by some accounts, a better pilot than Lindbergh, and he continued flying into his 85th year, logging over 25,000 hours at the controls of more than 90 different types of aircraft.

And if Johnny Crowell ranks behind Lindbergh in overall assessments of early aviation pioneers—well, he isn't all that far behind.

Of course, Johnny didn't make the first trans-Atlantic flight, but that isn't the only reason he hasn't been remembered as vividly as Lindbergh.

If the word unassuming hadn't been part of the vocabulary, it might well have been coined by a writer struggling to describe Johnny. Whether the subject was the techniques he developed for aerobatic flying in the 1920s and '30s or his many inventions, used in automobiles as well as aircraft, he answered questions matter-of-factly, without trying to impress people with the significance of what he said.

Oh, he was proud of the fact that he wasn't a quitter, that he kept pushing his mind and spirit forward although many of his major accomplishments benefited others more, financially, than they did him. When I asked him, during a conversation five years ago, how he had managed to plunge cheerfully ahead for so long despite missing his proper share of fame and glory, the snowy-bearded old man said softly:

"You either do or you don't. And I do."

Johnny began building his first airplane at age 19 in 1912, nine years after the Wright Brothers' historic first flights at Kitty Hawk. He helped produce aircraft for World War I, yet he didn't begin flying until 1922—the same year as Lindbergh, and the year the two met at Americus, Ga.

Over half a century later, Johnny said of Lindbergh, "He impressed me.... He had a look about him that showed he had something going."

Still, he worried when Lindbergh decided in 1927, with only five years' experience, to fly across the Atlantic.

"Anything could have happened to him," he said. "They used to call him 'Lucky Lindy,' though. I guess he really was."

Johnny became a well-known and innovative stunt-flying daredevil, but he considered aerobatics a learning lab, particularly useful for experimenting with techniques that might be helpful in combat.

He developed a "hands-off" method of flying, piloting his aircraft with special foot controls he designed himself, with his hands tied to the plane's struts. He could also control the craft with one hand while standing on the airplane's wing.

He thought his controls and demonstrations had applications for crippled and wounded pilots.

"I tried to get the military interested in it," he said. "I tried to get the governing body of the people that were supposed to judge things that might have military value...They replied that if they were interested in such things, they would develop it themselves."

Johnny began his stunt-flying in the Curtiss JN-4D—the famed Jenny— and his first solo, 61 years ago, was spectacular. He did a loop, a roll and a spin before landing.

"The snap roll in a Jenny was sloppy," he said. "I used to regularly enter spins at 500 feet [too low]...I guess I knew I was going to be a stunt pilot one day. I figured I might as well learn or get killed then. If I was going to get killed, it was no use wasting a lot of time."

In the years to come, he was to be close to death from time to time in his career as an aerobatic headliner, but he shrugged off the near-misses and went on.

In one show at Goldsboro, his engine quit while he was flying upside-down. He managed to flip the plane right-side-up just in time to negotiate a not-too-rough crash.

"I could have walked away from it," he said, "but the ambulance attendants wrestled me to the ground."

Another time, he wound up underwater, in a lake at Charlotte.

In 1938, at Kitty Hawk, Johnny went up when the weather was so bad that military pilots, who were to perform to commemorate the 35th anniversary of the Wrights' flights, stayed on the ground. He did loops and tailspins and rolls, performing those maneuvers into and out of the clouds, seeming almost to scrape the ground at times. The crowd responded loudly, and he loved it, as always.

"It feels good when you've got them blowing their automobile horns and such as that," he said.

For Johnny, the stunts were a part of his long study of aeronautics and technical needs. When asked about his risky flying, he replied, "It makes you a better all-around pilot."

His study did more than make him a better pilot, however. It also helped him develop his many inventions, a few of which were: a compass that automatically corrected for an airplane's wind drift; a meter that ensured even tension on all aircraft wires during assembly; the first timing device for a rotary engine; the first thermostatically controlled automatic choke, which was borrowed by Henry Ford for use in the Model T; the first automatic spark-advance system; the Crowell Three-Castle Locknut, which became standard on automobile assembly lines; a single-blade propeller; the Crowell Trainair, which simulated flight conditions; and a pressure plate that gave aerial cameras 55 percent more exposure area and made pictures sharper.

In 1954, when he was 61 years old and had put in 32 years in stunt flying, Johnny decided to call it quits. He wanted it known, however, that age and the law of probability that had long since caught up with other aerobats had nothing to do with his decision.

"I didn't quit for any reason except that I had a regular job with reputable people [Duke Power Co.]...I could see that maybe they wouldn't like this 'foolish' type flying," he said.

So he went on for years doing another type of flying that some would consider foolish: skimming along at about 100 feet, inspecting power lines while taking pictures and making notes on a typewriter.

He was fully in control of the aircraft, however. He piloted it with his feet.

It had become apparent, shortly before that conversation back in 1978, that Crowell's flying and inventing days were over. A series of health set-backs—one a stroke in 1971 while over Mount Airy, after which he flew back to Charlotte—had grounded him first temporarily and finally, seven years later, permanently.

But his spirit still soared as he talked of undreamed-of advancements to come in aviation and other areas of life.

"It's well known," he said, "that anything that's ever been thought of 'couldn't have been possible.' But there's always the possibility of finding something that hasn't been found before. If it's necessary, they'll find a way to do it."

Johnny Crowell, the last of a breed, was to be buried today in Charlotte.

At age 90, his body finally wore out.

Surely his spirit never did.

I would love to have been there, that day in 1922, when Charles Lindbergh met Johnny Crowell. *(10/18/83 The Sentinel)*

There Goes the Weekend
Harry Golden, Renowned Editor, Author, Dies at 79

"**The** first thing the folks will think of when death enters their lives on Friday," Harry Golden once wrote, "is, their weekend has been screwed up."

Golden, the East Side New York Jew who came South 40 years ago and achieved fame as editor of the *Carolina Israelite* and as an author, screwed up a lot of people's weekend today.

He died at age 79 at his Charlotte home, after a long illness.

The essay he did, long years ago, on picking the best time to die—that was Monday, he wrote, when "the folks have a clear field ahead of them"— was just one of hundreds Golden produced, and for which he became internationally known.

Golden had worked for the *Daily Mirror* and the *Post* in New York before making his way to North Carolina, first to work for *The Charlotte Observer*, then to take over the *Israelite.*

He was an Austro-Hungarian Jew who grew up in New York and headed South to tell us about the plight of blacks and other minorities, and he was not always the most popular man around the city or state.

Still, with his twitting wit and his cigar-chomping, arm-around-the-shoulder manner, Golden managed to win a special place in the hearts of North Carolinians and others.

And one of his essays, perhaps more than any other, put Golden into the limelight. Like other of his works, it was a not-too-modest proposal.

"It was the Golden Vertical Integration Plan," the author told *The Sentinel* in an interview three years ago in his home. "I said that the Negro could walk around the bus station, he stands in line to pay his taxes. It's only when he sits down that some of us get nervous. So I said take the chairs out of the classroom and you've got this thing licked."

He was still writing. He wanted people to know that, and he wanted them to know that his work was newspaper work, and if people put it together in collections and made books out of it, that didn't change what it was.

"I'm a newspaperman first," he said, "an American second, a Jew third, a Zionist fourth and a Democrat fifth, in that order."

Golden had done a little bit of everything, including going to prison for mail fraud, in his New York days. But once he settled in at the *Israelite*, his work, if not his humor, seemed to be almost one-dimensional.

"I wanted it to be a personal journal for the black man, for the civil rights movement," Golden said, "although there was no civil rights movement then.

"I thought if I write for the black man, the daily press wouldn't write it,

Harry Golden: "I had zitsfleisch…it means flesh and the ability to sit." –ALLIE BROWN

so I would be left with the whole story by myself. So I was right. They never wrote it."

It was in 1957 that fame sought Golden out, when a publisher who had seen his work decided to put it into what became *Only in America*.

"I said, 'Well, all right,'" Golden told *The Sentinel*. "He said, 'Why don't you pick out 100 stories or so and send them to me.' So I did…I told him, 'Print 5,000 copies and those you don't sell I'll give away to new subscribers.' Instead of that it sold, oh, half a million."

It was a world-record sale of a nonfiction book other than the Bible, and there were more than two million paperback copies to follow.

For a time, Harry Golden soared. He knew the company of presidents and princes, Kennedys and Johnsons and Humphreys.

In recent years, however, the scope of Golden's life had narrowed. Both he and his wife had become ill, and his public appearances became few.

His normal day became one of getting up, eating breakfast and reading. He would go over his mail, dictate answers and write a weekly column that appeared in dozens of newspapers—ironically, none of them in North Carolina.

He didn't do much more, other than go to the post office or what he called the "Xerox place" to get things duplicated, and meet occasionally with such people as fellow members of the Philosophers' Club in Charlotte.

He published a score of books, and he would tell you in a moment that the publishing of those books ranked as his biggest thrills in life. But his greatest accomplishment was something else, he said.

"My struggle for civil rights. My struggle against bigotry, against superstition. I've convinced a lot of people...convinced them for civil rights, convinced them against bigotry, convinced them against superstition."

But he wasn't satisfied with the progress that had been made, and he was convinced that our society was still racist.

"I've met with some great liberals down here," he said. "For Roosevelt, for TVA, for Social Security. But when it comes to the subject, it's still 'nigger.' They drink it in with their mothers' milk."

But Herschel Goldhirsch, who became Harry Golden, didn't drink that in with the milk of his mother, Anna. He drank, instead, chutzpah and zitsfleisch.

The chutzpah, or boldness, got him into trouble in a youthful illegal investment scheme, which he deeply regretted. But the zitsfleisch, as his mother called it, finally got him his permanent niche in American life.

"It means flesh and the ability to sit," he said. "I could sit and write and think and read for hours. Just go to the bathroom once in a while. I still can."

For that and his other contributions, Harry Golden will be fondly remembered—and not "only in America." *(10/2/81 The Sentinel, newsfeature)*

Mary Mayo's Inspiration
Lives on Through Her Songs

The sky is a blue and white marble today
And a tangerine sun wants to stay out and play
Believe it or not, every day looks this way
In the wonderful Land of Oz...[3]

Those words filled a mountaintop and thousands of hearts in 1970, that magical summer when Oz sprang to real life at Beech Mountain.

It was a place that took children over the rainbow and sent adults' spirits back to their farms in Kansas, or wherever life's meaning lay for them.

With design by Jack Pentes and words and music by Alec Wilder and Loonis McGlohon, it is hard to imagine how that tiny park could have failed to capture the imagination of young and old alike.

But more than anything else, it was that voice—that marvelous voice—that sent the spirit soaring and set the stage for a walk down the Yellow Brick Road with Dorothy.

Do you know of another place scarecrows can dance
And where else could you speak to a lion by chance
Or see a man wearing aluminum pants?
In the wonderful Land of Oz...

The voice was Mary Mayo's, but it belonged to all of us that summer, and for many summers to come. Most of all, in the month of May in 1970, it belonged to those of us who were at Beech, working incredibly long days and nights to catch up with the impossible dream of a May 15 opening. The Ozzies, those high-school and college kids who were to run the show and star in it, were bone-tired, discouraged, questioning whether there was magic in Oz after all.

When Jack Pentes, the designer, made an emotional speech to them, they were moved, but they still had doubts. And then Mary took center stage at the Beech Tree Inn and sang for them.

The Yellow Brick Road winds through hills and through dells
In a world full of pink and blue Easter-egg shells
And if you are quiet, the trees will ring bells
In the wonderful Land of Oz...

The show went on.

Mary had come to the mountain with her husband, Al Ham, a top music arranger—and the producer for the Oz music; they had brought their teen-age daughter, Lorri Marsters Ham. Later, she and her mother would "teach the world to sing" on a hit record, but back then Lorri was everybody's favorite munchkin.

There was a beauty about Mary that went beyond the blonde hair and at-tractive, wide-smiling face. It sprang, I think, from those curious, probing eyes, mirroring the reality of her interest in everything and everyone around her. She was as warm in person as her voice was on the Oz recording.

Where, oh, where could you find
Mountains that touch the sky?
Look there, up on the top
There is a tree hanging clouds out to dry.

If the mountains touched the sky, so did Mary's voice, soaring to the top of a four-octave range like a violin in the hands of a master, then dipping down, husky and rich, to brush the trees in the valleys below. She was a suc-cessful singer and recording artist, having sung with Frankie Carle, Tex Beneke, Ray Conniff and other name groups. When the great Duke Ellington gave a command birthday performance in the White House, he took along only one female vocalist: Mary Mayo.

It was part of her beauty that she could move from opera to jazz to the childlike fantasy of Oz and make us believe in its magic because she sang with such style and force that she herself seemed to believe in it.

Now, mushrooms are purple and
bluebells are white
And the moon paints the rivers
with silver at night
Wherever you look, there's a
magical sight
In the wonderful Land of Oz.

It broke my heart when I heard early this week of Mary Mayo's death from cancer at age 61. I suspect it broke a lot of hearts.

Recently, I gave away copies of the music of Oz as Christmas gifts, along with her most recent recording, "North Carolina Is My Home." And just Sun-day evening, unaware she was gone, I had played her "Wonderful Land of Oz" for friends, telling them about this lovely woman who came out of Statesville by way of New York City to become a special part of a happy time of my life.

A sadness remains, but there is a comforting difference between this and other such losses. Much of Mary's spirit lives in her music, and I can hear her whenever I choose.

(12/19/85 WSJ)

Frankie Laine
Idol and Nice Guy

What will you do with this old song,
When it has been sung?
And what will you do when your hair is gray
And you are no longer young?
You'd better keep this song, don't throw it away;
You're gonna want to hear it again someday...

—"What Do You Do with an Old Old Song?"[4]

What are Prince and Michael Jackson doing for today's young people?

They're entertaining them, of course, exciting them and, perhaps, uplifting them. But more important, I think, they are—to borrow a title from one of their counterparts of the past—making memories. And the memories will be around for long years to come, no matter how briefly the stars may shine.

I have thought much, lately, about the Prince of my youth, Frankie Laine, who recently underwent quadruple-bypass heart surgery in San Diego's Mercy Hospital. There are many memories, for me, of the Frankie Laine of the 1940s through the '60s.

Whether he was whispering low with "That's My Desire" or reaching new crescendos in "That Lucky Old Sun" or "Rockin' Chair," Laine was not only making our memories but paving the way for the age of rock with his swinging blues style. When I think of "Desire" or "Shine" or "Moonlight Gambler," I think of the people I was with in those long-past times, and the experiences we shared. Occasionally, thinking of the songs, or listening to them, brings back temporarily forgotten names of high-school classmates and others.

And there is more reason for my thinking of Frankie Laine and wishing him a full recovery: He is a nice guy, a decent human being. We often wonder whether that is true of our heroes, but few are lucky enough, as I was, to find out.

My first real indication, although it was not my first personal contact with him, came about 15 years ago when I was doing a SAM-type column at *The Charlotte News*. I wrote to Laine, asking him if he or someone in his publishing company could review the work of an aspiring local song writer. He agreed; in fact, he was very much interested in at least one of the songs.

Laine's quick response, and the fact that he had taken the time to listen to demonstration tapes personally, emboldened me further. We were promoting the column through the week with radio spots, and Ed Linsmeier, our promotion director and the man who usually handled promos, asked me if

I could produce one spot in his absence.

"Sure," I told Ed. "I think I can handle that." I wanted to handle it in dramatic fashion. I called Laine at his San Diego apartment.

"This may sound a bit presumptuous, Mr. Laine," I said.

"Frank," he replied. "Call me Frank."

It was difficult, but I did. "Frank," I said, "we've got this column, a real high-readership feature…"

I went on, explaining the nature of the column and telling him I wanted him to tape one of our promos—gratis, of course.

"With 'Mountain' ['You Gave Me a Mountain'] on the charts right now," I said, "I thought we could lead in with the beginning of that. Then we could go to you, talking about the column and what we're up to and sort of teasing the readers into looking at the column to get the full story. Then we could lead out with that big 'Mountain' ending."

It was a lot to ask. "Fine," he said, without hesitation. "Tell you what. I'm going to be playing Vegas starting in a couple of days. You send me a script there and call me, say, Thursday, and we'll tape it then. Can you handle the tape by phone?"

"Sure," I said. "We can do it at Jefferson Productions."

"Okay," he said.

It went beautifully. He made the tape, in which he talked as if he and *The Charlotte News* were old buddies, and we had a powerful promotion for the column. He also stayed on the telephone after the recording was done, sending his hellos to local disc jockeys and beginning to sound like an old friend.

Linsmeier was flabbergasted. So, I suppose, was I. The fears—that Frankie Laine might turn out to be a bit too high-hat and important to take the time even to talk to an old fan—had been dispelled in a warm, human way.

In later years, after coming to Winston-Salem, I became acquainted with an old friend of Laine's, a woman who used to sing with the Jack Teagarden orchestra. She told me how Laine had taken his aging and ailing mother from Chicago to the West Coast to keep her close, to support her in her latter years and assure that she was comfortable and happy. She told me about his devotion to his long-time wife, Nan Grey, and much more. Through it all, she was describing someone most of us would like to know.

I have talked to Laine only once since then, over three years ago, but again he was friendly and warm, and willing to take as much time as needed.

With luck, there will be another conversation, though not before he is feeling well enough. Meanwhile, I'll send him this column, with a personal note.

I want to thank him for being real. Perhaps, young readers will understand one day, if they are lucky enough to make similar discoveries about their idols of today.

(2/6/85 The Sentinel)

Where There's Hope...There's Laughter

You know why Southern Baptists don't make love standing up?

They're afraid somebody might think they're dancing.

Who, you might ask, could get by with that hoary joke in front of thousands of students, alumni and fans of Wake Forest University, a Southern Baptist institution?

Why, Bob Hope, of course.

And he didn't just get by with it—he wowed the crowd of 21,000.

Hope put on such a super show Saturday night that he even woke up a crowd that had been anesthetized for almost three hours by the Wake Forest-Western Carolina football game.

Hope was, simply, the grand master. He strode out and took control of the crowd and kept it until he was ready to relinquish it, and everyone seemed to love him for it.

For far the better part of an hour, he sang and danced and told jokes in the rapid-fire style that has become one of his trademarks. And if at times he had gone on to tell a couple of more stories by the time most of his audience began laughing at a previous one—well, that, too, is the Hope style.

One case in point came during a discussion of face-lifting in which he commented that Phyllis Diller had had that job done so many times that she has lint in her dimple. Hope had left the subject far behind by the time some people in the audience began saying such things as "Lint in her dimple—oh yeah!"—and laughing out loud.

At times, Hope was a bit racy. He asked Debbie Worley, the singing ex-Miss Virginia, if she knew the difference between sex and chicken hash, and Miss Worley said no, she didn't.

"How about having lunch with me tomorrow?" said Hope.

He also poked fun at various religions although he said he doesn't do that very often because "I fly a lot." He told some ethnic jokes, too, but in doing so he went out of his way to make a point many people don't or won't understand about that form of humor. You can use it to make good fun of anyone, or any kind of group, that you choose.

A "Polack" joke thus became a Texas Aggie joke: An Aggie (from Texas A&M) was arrested one evening when he wandered into downtown Dallas stark naked. The police asked him why he was there and why he had no clothes on. "I was at this party," he explained, "and the hostess turned out the lights and said, 'Now, everybody go to town.' I guess I'm the first one here."

Much of the humor, though, was simply about aspects of life that most of us can relate to, such as the tale about the man who took three pieces of luggage to the airport and said he wanted them to go to three different cities that weren't particularly close to one another. When he was told, "We can't do that," he said indignantly, "Why not? You did it last time."

Even where he laid an egg, Hope was usually able to incubate it and hatch a few laughs. One story he told—one, it was widely suspected, that was intended to elicit groans and not laughs—concerned a talking grasshopper in a bar. In the course of the conversation, the bartender told the grasshopper, "We even have a drink named after you."

The grasshopper looked up, obviously puzzled.

"Thorndike?" he said.

With that, Hope launched into a new series of jokes—motivated by revenge for the audience's reaction, he said—pausing between them to explain that the Grasshopper's name was Thorndike and to tell why the story was funnier than the reaction indicated. By the time he was finished, the "bad" Thorndike joke had become a conversation piece among people who had seen the show.

There was no need for Hope to get really low-down and dirty, the way some comedians must in order to hold an audience. (How would George Carlen or Richard Pryor have fared in that stadium, with that audience?)

And through it all, Hope shared the limelight, trying to be sure that others, not just he, got some of the glory.

If other members of the audience were like me, they sat, totally captive, marvelling at finally being in the presence of an American institution—and finding him warmer and funnier in person than in movies or on television.

Here was Bob Hope, 80 years old, holding us all in the palm of his hand with his humor and timing and style and grace, making us understand why he has been a big show-business name for over 50 years.

Much of the reason, we learned, is that there is no pretense or pretentiousness; this is a man who loves people and can sing unabashedly and proudly about his love for his country and catch all of us—from the youngest students to others almost his own age—up in his moods.

He also thanked us, warmly and at length, for his success and his continuing stardom on television after more than 30 years. "You're the reason," he said, sounding as if he believed it deeply.

Personally, I appreciate Bob Hope's taking time out to happen to Winston-Salem. To be sure, he was paid more than generously, by our standards. But instead of going through the motions, as some stars do under similar circumstances, he gave us a legitimate event—not just a show, but something many will be talking about 30 years from now.

What can we say to express our gratitude?

"Thanks for the memories" should do nicely. *(9/22/83 The Sentinel)*

Oh, Perry, Oh, Perry

You have to watch little old widows like Katie Burns.

She was happily married for 38 years and says she'd like to live every moment of that marriage over again.

But for quite a bit of that time, there was a second man in her life.

His name was Perry Como, and he visited her once a week.

"I'd just sit there watching him on television and hearing him sing," she said in a recent chat, "and I could just imagine he was singing to me—'Don't Let the Stars Get in Your Eyes,' 'Miss You.'

"I always, every time he sang, would look at him, and I'd say, 'Oh, I wish I could touch him.'"

That was impossible, of course, and she had to settle for playing his records just about every day on the hi-fi.

Then a funny thing started happening.

It was announced that Perry Como was coming to the Greensboro Coliseum—one week ago today—to do a benefit performance.

And then, in a WTOB radio drawing for members of the "Music of Your Life Club," the station came up with No. 503—which belonged to Katie Burns.

"I had 30 minutes to call in," she said, "and everybody kept knocking on my door and telling me to call WTOB, that I had two tickets [to the concert].

"All my friends and relatives knew that he was my—well, how would I word it?—the No. 2 man in my life."

It happened that the senior citizens of First Baptist Church were going to the show in a group, and Mrs. Burns had planned to be with that group.

But she didn't intend to be just another silent admirer.

"I went to the florist," she said, "and got him [Como] a red rosebud so I could walk on the stage and present it. They [church members] said I might be able to present it to him as he came off the stage, but I never would be able to get on the stage."

They didn't know Katie Burns as well as they thought.

"I went down to see where the steps were, before the program started," she said.

"And I waited there with my rosebud. They were having electrical trouble—the speaker—and I knew that was the time.

"I stepped up the steps and I heard this voice; this gentleman said, 'Wait a minute.' They didn't want me to go up.

"So when he said that I got faster, and I got to Perry. When I presented him the red rosebud, he said, 'Thank you,' and put his arm around me and started dancing. I had so much to tell him and all I could say was, 'Oh, Perry, Oh, Perry.'

"In the coliseum, everybody applauded."

The two danced for a time, but Mrs. Burns was off on a cloud and has no idea how long.

"He turned me around to whirl a bit," she said, "the end of the dance. Several people said, 'Well, that's just part of the show.' I said, 'You think Perry Como invited me up there? I went to him…'

"The happiest day of my life was when I married my husband, Lyndon P. Burns. But Perry Como is my second-happiest moment."

And the stir she created, with one little rosebud and a whole lot of nerve, hasn't ended yet.

"My friends and people I haven't seen for years, they've called. People who were at the show said they'd always liked me until they'd seen me dancing, and they were just envious. I ate their heart out."

And people, some of them envious and some just happy for her, have told her she's such a celebrity that they'd just like to touch her.

So Katie Burns is going to do the natural, accommodating thing:

"I'm going to have a touch-me party."   *(9/9/80 The Sentinel)*

Nyaahh, What's Up, Mel? Eh?

How do you get 400 voices on the telephone at one time?

One way is to call Mel Blanc.

He'll talk to you in Bugs Bunny, Porky Pig, Yosemite Sam, Barney Rubble or any number of the other seemingly countless voices he has created in the past 41 years. But he's at his most interesting talking in Mel Blanc, cheerfully answering questions he's probably been asked hundreds of times.

"I was in radio prior to the time I went into cartoons," he said in an interview from his home in Pacific Palisades, Calif. "I went to the man at Schlesinger Cartoons [Looney Tunes] who was in charge of voices, and he said, 'I'm sorry, we have all the voices we need.'

"I said, 'Won't you at least listen to me?' He said, 'No, we have all the voices we need.' I went back in two weeks and he said, 'No, we have all the voices we need.' This went on for a year and a half. I'd go back every two weeks and ask him to listen to me and he'd say, 'No, we have all the voices we need.'"

Finally, Blanc got his big break. The man died.

"I went to the next man in charge," said Blanc, "and he said, 'Sure, let's hear what you have.' I auditioned for him and he liked it and said, 'Would you do it again for the directors?' I said I'd be glad to.

"They got a big kick out of it, and one of the directors said, 'I have a picture coming up with a drunken bull in it. Do you think you could do the voice of a drunken bull?' I said, 'Yeah, I think so.'"

That small part launched the career of the most listened-to man in America. (A survey found that 100 million people hear Blanc's voice every day.)

"Leon Schlesinger heard me do this drunken bull, and he said, 'I've got a little pig here we're going to have in a picture,'" said Blanc. "'His name is Porky. Do you think you can give him a voice?'"

Immediately, Blanc almost literally threw himself into his work.

"I went out to a pig farm," he said.

"I wanted to be real authentic about it. After a couple of weeks I went back to the studio and they kicked me out and said go home and take a bath, which I did. And when I went back to the studio, I told them that if a pig could talk, he'd talk with a grunt."

That was in 1937, and Blanc's voices have been in great demand ever since. Even he didn't know how many he could do until 17 years ago when a near-fatal wreck gave him time to find out.

"The fire department had to cut me out of the car," he said. "It took them half an hour. Then they put me in a sack and carried me over to the hospital.

"Almost every bone in my body was broken, along with a triple skull fracture. In fact, I was so far gone that they had me in the obituary column in Honolulu. But I fooled 'em; I wrote and told them that they were wrong.

"I was in a full body cast. One morning I decided to see how many voices I could do. I started early in the morning and fell asleep at midnight, and I passed the 400 mark."

He's kept busy these days doing voices for television cartoons (he's Captain Caveman on ABC and Bugs Bunny on CBS at the same time Saturday mornings), producing TV and radio commercials (with his son Noel, he's done 8,000), entertaining at children's hospitals and speaking on the college lecture tour.

Blanc enjoys speaking to and meeting young people, but he doesn't get to do quite as much as he might like to.

"My son won't let me do more than three a week," he said. "He said to me, 'What's more important, dad, money or your life?' I wanted to use the Jack Benny phrase—you know, 'Let me think about it.'"

Blanc and his wife, Estelle, have been married 45 years ("and in Hollywood, too—can you imagine?") and she has tried on occasion to prod him toward retirement. But he won't think about that.

"I say, 'No, I'll just keep going until I drop.' I love my work, and I love to meet people. And it's such a thrill to entertain kids, especially. Just to see them get away from their pain, just to see them laugh for half an hour, is a marvelous satisfaction."

When the interview had ended, I thanked Blanc and asked him if there was anything else he thought he needed to tell me.

"Th-th-th-th—that's all, folks," he said.   *(1/17/78 The Sentinel)*

He Looked Around; There Was Dennis

About 30 years and nine months ago, Hank Ketcham's mind became pregnant.

Ketcham, who had dropped quickly into and out of college because he "wanted to march in the parade, not watch it," worked his way up from the bottom of the art world through Disney studios and was a successful freelance cartoonist for the myriad of magazines that existed back then.

And he had a little boy named Dennis.

"My studio is in my home," Ketcham said in a telephone conversation from California the other day. "One morning Dennis' mother stormed into my studio and, between clenched teeth, said, 'Your son is a menace. Did you know that?' And she stormed out.

"I thought about what she said, and 'Dennis' came through so boldly. I thought, 'Dennis the Menace'? That just seemed to ring the bell, that it would be a good handle for a newspaper feature."

The cartoonist, whose proper name is Henry King Ketcham, went to work on the idea, and in March 1951 *Dennis the Menace* was "born" in 18 newspapers. Today he's in 850, and he hasn't grown an inch or a full year since.

Of course, the one thing that the public "knows" for sure about the strip is that it was based on real life.

Not so, said Ketcham.

"There were no prototypes, actually," he said. "The chemistry demanded that you have a little girl like Margaret, a little fella like Joey. Dennis is kind of a man of the world in Joey's eyes.

"You had to have a big, hairy dog…and naturally you had to have a grouchy old man living on the corner with a beautiful garden that's a terrific shortcut to someplace. I think all of us have known older couples who children have kind of come to relate to either as a grandparent symbol or, like Mr. Wilson, fights [a child] off sometimes, becomes grumpy.

"I think all of these characters represent something in people's memories.

"But the only one, really, is Dennis. His name is Dennis and he looked like [the cartoon] Dennis at the time. But he didn't contribute any of the material at all. I didn't use any of his antics."

Ketcham quickly found that Dennis Mitchell, his parents and others in the strip had to evolve over the years.

"In the early days, I was just telling jokes about a little kid," he said. "I called him Dennis. I didn't get to know the lad until after we'd been producing him for about a year, and then I had to answer a lot of questions: How does his father react, how does his mother react, how is he punished, does he go to Sunday school, does his father travel…"

The real Dennis grew up, served in the Marine Corps, worked in prison security, then joined a "Federal Express-type operation" in Columbus, Ohio, about a year ago.

And over the 30 years, Ketcham's own perspective changed.

"I used to identify with Mr. Mitchell," he said. "Now I'm definitely in Mr. Wilson's corner."

The obvious answer to the question of how a person keeps such a comic strip fresh over all these years is, of course, that kids never change.

Again, said Ketcham, it's not necessarily so—or at least that's not all there is to it.

"I work with gag writers," he said. "I have half a dozen talented young people who contribute ideas. We work by mail and by telephone. One man can't possibly keep turning out material without duplicating. I'm very fortunate to have had these talented young people passing through my life over the years."

Also his remarriage during the years he lived in Switzerland, after being widowed, may have helped. "I have a son who will be 4 on my [61st] birthday this Saturday [today]," he said. "My son will be 4 and my daughter is just turning 8, so I've got a 'prototype' of Dennis and Margaret still living under my roof.

"Dennis has to remain 5½. Every birthday is his 6th, and he immediately becomes 5 again."

Dennis, of course, is not a gloom-and-Doonesbury type of strip, and Ketchum says it continues to be enjoyable for him and he'll stay with it as long as he's able.

"There's nothing negative about this," he said, "and there's nothing political, so I'm not bogged down in all the tragedies and the changing economy and politics.

"I've just gotta keep pushing away. I don't know whether I'll go another 30 years, but it's a lot of fun."

And suppose—just suppose—his son's name had not been Dennis and had not rhymed with menace; what might he be doing today?

"I might be working for Disney," he said. "It's an interesting thought. When the opportunity knocked, I was sitting there with a pencil and paper.

"You don't think I'd do a thing like Henry the Horrible, do you?"

(3/14/81 *The Sentinel*)

EPILOGUE: *"Five-ana-half" Dennis the Menace (the comic strip) turned 50 in March 2001. By then, Hank Ketchum, 81, was supervising the artists Marcus*

Hamilton and Ronald Ferdinand, who took over the drawing. In 1994, when Ketcham stopped creating the weekday panels, the comic strip ran in 1,800 newspapers. Today it's published in 68 countries and 19 languages. The cartoon also inspired a musical, a TV series, a 1993 movie and a playground in Monterey, where Ketchum had his studio. Ketchum died June 1, 2001, in Pebble Beach, CA.

(3/4/01, 6/1/01 WSJ)

"We Just Grazed an Iceberg"

On the night of April 14–15, 1912, the ocean liner *Titanic* sank on her maiden voyage, taking somewhere between 1,503 and 1,517 lives. (Nobody is exactly sure—even yet.)

Recently, to mark the 63rd anniversary of the tragedy, WSJS radio's Randy Gibson and Tom Booth did the kind of thing that makes a boss want to kiss you before killing you. They called a survivor in California and chatted—and chatted and chatted and chatted, all during daytime high-rate long-distance hours.

All of this started at about 10:30 a.m., when the radio audience consists largely of folks at home during the day, so it wasn't exactly heard by a peak audience. But Dick Barron, the station's general manager, generously shared the tape with me, and much of it is well worth passing on.

"There are about 28 or 30 of us [survivors]," said 90-year-old Edwina Mac-Kenzie, still spry and feisty-sounding.

"I think these tragedies do something to us…when I was a little girl, they never thought they'd raise me. My father was a coffin maker, and he had the wood for my coffin for years—and here I am, I'll be 91 in July."

Mrs. MacKenzie had booked passage on the *Oceanic*, but a coal strike prevented some departures and she got "lucky."

"They offered me the transfer [to the *Titanic*] at the same price," she said, "and being as Scotch as I am, I said oh, yes, I'd come on that."

Mrs. MacKenzie—listed as E. Celia Trout on the manifest—told this story:

"We'd had a wonderful trip….And Sunday evening we were all having a nice sing-along…I had to go to bed because I got a cold. And when I got to my stateroom, my [roommate] said, 'This boat will never reach New York.' I said…'Say your prayers or do something; don't tell me that anymore…'

"I was awakened by the ceasing of the vibration of the boat."

She set out to see why the ship had stopped.

"When I got up to a lounge, there were some men playing cards, and they said to me, 'Hello, what's the matter with you?' 'Me?' I said. I wanted to know what was the matter with the ship. 'Oh,' they said, 'it isn't anything. We just grazed an iceberg.'"

Mrs. MacKenzie woke her cabinmate, and they both made it to the lifeboats.

"I never saw any panic," she said. "I just saw one woman screaming when they first had the accident…I saw three priests giving absolution to a crowd all kneeling down, and all those people were drowned, practically."

Women and children were put in the lifeboats first, but "you had to take men also because of the rowing," she said.

"When I got in the lifeboat, there was a light in the distance, and I heard the captain say, 'Now, men, row for that light, empty your boats and come back.' And the more—the further—they rowed, the less they could see of this light.

"Then as they sailed away from the *Titanic*, you could see her gradually sinking, slowly and slowly, and the lights were all burning. And every row of light would disappear, and finally she foundered, and then the scream of death was worse than any siren.

"I couldn't take my eyes off it. To me it looked like it went down very gently, smoothly...It was 10 blocks long and four blocks wide, something like that...Too luxurious to live...

"As she made her final plunge, the master of our boat had us scream as loudly as we could. And I think that was to counteract that terrible scream [from the *Titanic*]. And then he got us all to sing, 'Pull for the shore, sailors, pull for the shore.'"

Mrs. MacKenzie's relatives had been worried because she was to sail on the unlucky 13th. But she was among the 700-plus who lived—rescued in Lifeboat No. 13, among the last to be picked up by the ship *Carpathia*.

Mrs. MacKenzie has read the book *A Night to Remember* and finds it "very authentic...very." But she draws the line at stark visual reminder. "I've tried to see the movie," she said. "But I can't."

Still, she has not let the experience deprive her of enjoying the 63 extra years she was given that tragic night, and she does not fear the water.

"I've crossed the Atlantic in all 10 times since," she said. "And then I took a cruise to Australia...and I went to Bermuda [and back] a couple of times..."

(4/29/75 The Sentinel)

CHAPTER 5

"Mock" History

Read here for revelations of "historical" events not found in your textbooks. Have you ever heard of the story of the "Mock" Indian tribe, or the planting of salt bushes or mining of pepper? Whatever you've heard, I'm sure it hasn't been this version...

Indians Crept Out of Forsyth on Their "Mockasins"

"**D**ear Sir," said the letter signed by a girl named Janet, "Before I go any further, there are two things you should know:

"1. If you don't like letters of request, then throw this away because that is what this is.

"2. If you don't like kids my age (15)…throw it away…because self-destructing letters cost too much….

"One day in my North Carolina/United States history class…I came up with a few good questions my teachers couldn't answer. I'm known for that…

"Question one, during 1776, what Indian tribes were in Forsyth County? Two, during this time, what were they doing?"

The letter went on to explain the many sources, including the Bureau of Indian Affairs, that had been consulted without success.

Well, Janet, it may be fun to be "known for" coming up with questions that can't be answered, but it's even better to come up with answers that can't be questioned. To wit:

We must go back to the 1600s, when the Mock Indians were living in Davie County. They fled to Forsyth—the exact date is not known—after being attacked by a settler, his wife, three children and a beagle.

The incident has been named the Great Mock Massacre. One of the Indians was said to have suffered a torn toenail, another a painful muscle pull. (The Mocks were a very peaceful tribe.)

After the massacre, the settlers took over the Indians' village and fields of mocks, for which the Indians had been named and which they used extensively in cooking. The white men named the town Mocksville.

In Forsyth County, the Mocks fell on hard times. The soil, while only slightly different in composition, grew inferior mocks. In addition, the only efficient way the tribe had been able to harvest the grain had been with a specially trained flock of birds. Without the birds, which to this day are known as Mockingbirds, the harvesting became very difficult.

Still, the tribe continued to depend upon the grain. Its members threw kernels at each other in a monthly ritual that has since become known as Mock Battle, but the ceremony no longer brought them luck.

The Indians also continued to use mocks in their cooking, and this was the reason that they were among the healthiest human beings known to exist at that time. (Unfortunately, they had settled along the Yadkin River, and their clumsiness resulted in a 92.5 percent death rate from drowning.)

In 1776, the Mocks were still living along the Yadkin, but their number had dwindled from 5,741 to 142.

It was that year, in fact, that they opened a restaurant and tried to sell the white man on eating mocks.

One of the specialty items on the menu was Mock Pound Cake. Actually, the mock grain, while extremely nutritious, changed the taste very little and gave more cake per pound.

Another item, which the tribe had invented hundreds of years earlier, was Mock Turtle Soup. This had the same pleasant flavor as regular turtle soup, but adding mocks cut down on the tedious job of killing the turtles and extracting the meat. It also assured a continued supply of turtles since they would not be hunted to extinction.

The restaurant could well have made the Mocks thrive once again, but the settlers knew a good thing when they saw it. Once again, in 1784, the Mocks were attacked, and once again they fled—this time to South Dakota.

The settlers who took over the restaurant began using mocks in many different foods, such as Mock Chicken Legs. Their leader, Gen. Horatio Hereticus Foods, passed his recipes and money down from generation to generation, and this is how the General Foods Corp. eventually came into being.

As for the Mocks, their grain would not grow at all in South Dakota, and the last remaining member of the tribe slipped off Mount Rushmore in 1789 and fell to his death.

Now, Janet, there does exist the possibility that I didn't get all the precise details, or that there may be some fuller answer. So the people at the Bicentennial Commission on Coliseum Drive are scouring their research files, which include information on Indians, to see what they can add. I'll be happy to pass it along.

(3/27/75 The Sentinel)

And Next Week the Lesson's on Pepper

Where does salt come from, and when did man start using it?

—Randy Mudley, Ardmore

Imagine, if you would, a large boxwood shrub that has been allowed to grow out of control; then it has been squared off and trimmed so that it is six feet tall at the front and three and a half to four feet tall at the rear.

This is a salt bush.

Among certain peoples, including our native Indians, the use of salt goes back many centuries. Growth of the bush in this part of the world is thought to have originated around Saltillo, the capital of Coahuila, Mexico.

The seeds of the bush are windborne, and they soon spread to the Salt River area of Arizona, which also had soil that was hospitable to the plant. Later, the bush spread northward, and today it still grows in its greatest profusion in the Great Salt Flats area of Utah.

Contrary to popular belief, the use of salt among Caucasians wasn't widespread until the 19th century. These people knew only that the plant, which was rare in their part of the world, was prickly and could cause salt rheum, which later came to be known as eczema, and they were afraid of it.

Because they were getting salt only from foods and beverages that contained it naturally, in some climates and under certain conditions, these white people did not get enough in their systems. This led to the stereotype, among other races, of the white man as slothful and lazy.

As white settlers moved westward in America, however, they noticed two things: first, the Indians seemed to have much more stamina in running, hunting and battle than the whites; second, there were more and more salt bushes all around. Still, the bushes frightened them.

During a period of peace, they asked the great Apache chief Cochise why his people were so quick and alert.

Cochise explained the use of salt. He also pointed out that, since salt grains were so small, they were very difficult to pick. He said, in fact, that in his particular tribe it was necessary to assign half the women to pick salt as their tribal duty.

Cochise added that, while using one-fourth of his people to pick salt seemed excessive to the white man, the salt itself made the remaining three-fourths able to do twice as much, so there was a 50 percent net gain in productivity.

Soon the white man began using salt on his food, and he found that it gave him a great deal more stamina in his daily battle with the plains and mountains. In fact, it is said, the salt made him feel like jumping and dancing, and thus was born the tradition of the Saturday night dance.

(It should be noted that when the usage spread to Italy, the Italians renamed a lively native dance the saltarello. And, to this date, Webster's defines the word saltation as "the act of leaping, jumping or dancing.")

The settlers discovered that, like the Indians, they needed to assign a certain number of people to pick salt. This is why, in those early days, there were usually at least eight people in each family: one to keep house, five to do the chores and farming, and two to pick salt.

This was fine for the settlers, but for the commercial salt grower who shipped his product back East, it meant a great deal of investment in labor, since one good worker could pick no more than two pounds of salt per day.

By the time the salt got back East, it cost almost $2 a pound. Nevertheless, people bought all they could: They ate it at salt parties and jumped and danced and did all sorts of odd things.

One Easterner, while under the influence, even designed a structure shaped like the salt bush and named it the "saltbox" house.

Finally, however, in 1882, Alexander Alva Columbus invented the saltpicker, a machine that shook the salt off the bush and brought its price down so that almost everyone could afford it.

The significance of the machine remains such that each year we observe the inventor's birthday. In fact, we celebrated it just yesterday.

(10/14/80 The Sentinel)

Hold the Mustard!

How did the custom of using pepper come about?

—*Marsha Malaise, Old Town*

Pepper, of course, is a mineral known to science students by the chemical symbol Achu. Because we use it in and on our food, many people still mistakenly believe that it is a vegetable product of some sort.

For centuries, the rock we now call pepper was considered a nuisance. For one thing, wind and water easily eroded it, creating caves that seemed perfect for overnight stays by early pioneers such as Daniel Boone. Once they had pitched camp, however, they found that they could not sleep for sneezing, and their animals would become sick from grazing nearby. (Only later would the term "pepper-grass" be coined.)

In those early years, perhaps, the natives of the West Indies were the only people utilizing the material in a practical way. The rock was the only one both soft and durable enough to use to make the large pots needed to cook their traditional meal of vegetables, fish and boiled cassava sap for large gatherings. To their surprise, the pots seemed to add zest to the stew, which some of the finest restaurants in the nation now call "pepper-pot stew."

It was not until the Revolutionary War, when the Mountain Men of the southern Appalachians rose up and marched to the battle of Kings Mountain (S.C.), that the real discovery of pepper as a good additive was made. One night during the march, rain poured so hard that it was impossible to keep a fire burning. Arthur McCormick, the cook, had to do his work in the cave, where he took to sneezing almost uncontrollably.

The men said the meal was the best McCormick had made, and he began to think. He had been to the West Indies and watched the preparation of the fish stew, and he had noticed that the rock in the cave looked much like that used for the islanders' pots.

Before breaking camp, McCormick pulverized a large piece of the rock and stored it in his wagon. He continued to use it in his cooking, and the men's spirits seemed to improve. Later, may of them credited their stunning and significant victory at Kings Mountain to McCormick's cooking.

After the war, McCormick began mining the mineral on his family property. He set up a mill that broke the material down into what looked like small kernels of corn. He used a second mill for the fine grinding, but he also sold the larger pieces for others to grind as they wished. These are sold in supermarkets and elsewhere today as peppercorns.

McCormick's business was doing all right, but it was only regional, and he felt that he needed some public-relations help to expand into other areas. So he sent a packet of his product to President George Washington, who, fearing that it would discolor his new elk-teeth dentures, passed it along to Thomas Jefferson.

Jefferson used it at a cabinet luncheon and remarked that it was a real "pepper-upper."

Alexander Hamilton, Jefferson's sometimes-bitter rival, leaked his version of the remark, and the result was a *Washington Post* headline that said: "TJ Using Uppers?" Jefferson immediately issued a clarification saying that he had merely said that he liked the stuff and that it would be a real "pepper for supper."

The *Post* did another story, with a headline that read, "No Uppers, Says TJ; It Was McCormick's Pepper."

This story went nationwide on the *Washington Post-Los Angeles Times* news service, and the term "pepper" was quickly adopted.

McCormick and his family became millionaires overnight. In fact, their descendants branched out and are still selling pepper and various herbs and spices, and the original pepper mine is still in use.

I believe the only table seasoning the McCormicks do not sell is salt, and I am told that this is because it does not grow well on the farms they own in this and other countries.

(10/21/80 The Sentinel)

"Sam, The Sentinel Answer Man" Column

I read an article in The Sentinel *some months ago about the mining of black pepper in the United States. I told this to some friends and they said I was "bananas." I talked to another friend and he said he had read the same article. We looked up black pepper in the dictionary and it said it comes from a plant from the East Indian countries. We would like some clarification regarding the black pepper issue.* —L. M.

Fair enough, especially since you are not the only reader asking about this "issue." The article you refer to on pepper-mining was a satire in the "Ask Andy" format by columnist Tom Sieg. A week earlier he had written a similar tall tale on how difficult it was to hand-pick salt until the development of special salt-harvesting machines. He said he is now working on the germination of doughnut seeds and expects a little later to share with his readers an easy solution for the energy crisis.

(1/23/81 The Sentinel)

Two Ways to Make Money Off Kudzu

I don't know why, but even my best friends don't understand me.

Take Urban Walls, my good buddy from way back. Urb was through town again the other day, and as usual we went to talking over a glass of sarsaparilla.

"How's the old newspaper game coming?" asked Urb.

"Well, frankly," I said, "I'm thinking of getting out."

"Getting out?" said Urb. "How in the world could you be considering getting out of something as glamorous and exciting as the old newspaper game? Why, you must meet the most *interesting* people."

"Sure," I said, "but I'd like to go for the big bucks for a change."

"You mean, like go into business?"

"That's right."

"What business?"

"Giving away kudzu."

Now, Urb is from the North and unaccustomed to people giving away anything at all, and he just couldn't understand how I could expect to make money that way. He carried on for about 10 minutes about what a dumb idea it was, and then I proceeded to reconstruct his thinking.

"Look, Urb," I said, "the idea hit me last year. I had these two friends, one of them from the North and the other a native Southerner, who had gotten into decorative landscaping.

"I stopped by to see the Southerner first.

"'What's that in your hand?' he asked, his voice quavering.

"'It's kudzu,' I said. 'I've come to plant it along that brick wall you just put in.'

"Well, he began trembling, shaking like a bowl of lutefisk. 'Tom,' he said, 'don't give me any kudzu. *Please* don't give me any kudzu.'

"'Nonsense,' I said. 'You spent all that money putting in that wall, and it just needs a touch of greenery to set it off. I'll just go out there and put a little bit along the base.'

"My friend was on his knees by then.

"'Tom,' he said, 'you've got to remember that I have some very bad personal memories involving kudzu. You see, I lost a 300-year-old oak tree, a farmhouse, a barn and several other outbuildings to kudzu. And that's not even mentioning my grandmother.'

"'I know, I know,' I said. 'But it's just like flying. When you've had one bad experience, you've got to get up there in the air again. Now, I'm going to go out there and plant this stuff, and I know you'll thank me for it later.'

"My friend was sobbing now. 'Tom,' he said, 'I'll give you $300 not to give me any kudzu.'

Kudzu jungle threatens Southerners and transplanted Yankees alike. —WSJ

"'Make it five and you're on,' I said.

"'Five it is,' he said."

Urb was impressed. "Wow," he said, "$500 for an hour's work. That's not bad. But what about the Northerner?"

"Oh, he accepted the kudzu."

"So you didn't make any money off him?"

"Not right away. But about a week later he called to ask how to get the stuff out of the basement—and the street, too; it was beginning to chase cars.

"So I explained that kudzu has to be trimmed three to four times a week with chain saws and flamethrowers, and he asked if I knew anybody who did that kind of work. Well, it so happened that I had just established Kudzu

Control Inc., and I've been providing the service ever since. The ultimate goal is extermination, but my friend understands that this could take 10 years or more.

"The beauty of the whole thing is that with the extermination service, I get an automatic inexhaustible supply to give away to other people. So with the two sides of the business, I make money by not giving kudzu away and by getting rid of it after giving it away."

"Gee," said Urb. "You can't lose that way, can you? You know, you've given me a great idea. I believe I'm going to go into business myself."

"Doing what?" I asked.

"Giving away beagle puppies," he said.

"Golly," I said, "why didn't *I* think of that?"   *(4/21/79 The Sentinel)*

Kudzuphobia

Pernicious Vine Is Wending Its Way Through the Soil in the Dead of Night

This is another of Tom Sieg's occasional updates on kudzu. He swears—"Trust me," he said—that it is every bit as true as his last such report. —The editors

Everyone who knows kudzu knew it had to happen.

Who among us, after all, has not seen this insidious vine do its grim work?

It begins slowly, sneaking into the yard from behind a tree and making off with an azalea in the dead of night.

Then, unless we take flame throwers, backhoes, bulldozers and TNT to it immediately, it flexes its muscle and raises its sights. It takes down your trellis, shreds sheds and outhouses, terrorizes tulip trees and offers cover for copperheads.

You've seen it. So have I.

I shudder at the memory of the night in 1962 when poor, forgetful Aunt Maude left her bedroom window open while kudzu was known to be marauding the neighborhood.

The vines took Maude away; that's all we ever knew for sure, because we never saw her again. It was the same night it took the roof off the lean-to kitchen.

Historians know, now, that the Japanese sent kudzu to the U.S.A. in 1876 in early preparation for the Pearl Harbor attack. Fortunately, kudzu grew poorly on the West Coast, where we were most vulnerable; sadly, it grew superbly in the South.

As recently as 14 years ago, with the publication of *The Book of Kudzu*, people still spoke as if kudzu were some harmless little house plant, perhaps even beneficial to mankind.

"Kudzu," the authors wrote, "is an ancient genie that delights in the endless, shape-shifting play of transformation—it is at times a prankster, at times a selfless servant."

Prankster? Servant?

Who, pray tell, thought it funny or helpful when the vile vine began pulling down power poles, fences, transmission towers and entire forests?

But enough. On to my point.

Now we have the spectre of SKUM, or the Sudden Kudzu Underground Migration.

SKUM was the cause of this week's closing of Interstate 40 near Hickory: Kudzu, migrating from Rutherfordton, undermined a quarter-mile section of the highway and then burst through to the surface.

On Monday, when I visited the scene, it was like doing so in a dream, totally detached from reality, in a world of grim make-believe. But that couldn't be, could it? Besides, I took a picture of the stuff while it was pulling down a highway marker. Pictures don't lie.

As I gazed at the forest of kudzu, I saw slabs of pavement thrust upward, snapped like matchsticks. Flashes of metal were visible between the leaves—cars whose drivers didn't take the kudzu onslaught seriously enough at the outset.

The direction marker above an I-40 sign near Hickory is slowly swallowed. –TOM SIEG

"Just look at that!" a sheriff's deputy said disgustedly. "Yankees, every one of 'em. Musta been 15, 20 people in them cars, all told."

You know, we should probably warn tourists from the North about kudzu. But I digress.

This was the kudzu mass that had begun migrating from Rutherfordton on Thursday. State officials had been encouraged when it had advanced only to Casar, about halfway to Hickory, by Sunday. Then, however, it shot all the way to Hickory overnight.

"This stuff doesn't just *grow* anymore," said John Xmond, a plant-growth specialist from North Carolina State University. "Heck, we're used to growth. What's happened now is that it *metastasizes*. Kudzu cells move through the soil the way cancer cells move through the bloodstream, only much faster, and then the stuff springs up as if out of nowhere."

I was aghast. Utilizing all my investigative-reporting skills, I pressed Xmond on what this development could mean to the South as a whole. He shook his head.

"It might mean the end of civilization as we know it," he said. "On the other hand, it might not. It depends on a lot of things."

Sensing that he was getting too technical for my readers, I moved on.

Doing so, I noticed that the vines had not yet enveloped the I-40 highway marker—that four-foot-high shield-shaped thing painted red, white and blue, with a rectangular "EAST" or "WEST" sign above it. It would have made a perfect memorial marker now, except that it too was about to be consumed.

I backed my car out of the immediate range of the kudzu and snatched my camera out of the trunk.

When I turned back to take the picture, I saw a woman not 10 feet away from the highway marker, struggling to rid herself of the vines that were tugging and pulling her toward the earth.

"Help me!" she shouted. "This stuff is about to kill me."

What a dilemma. With the kudzu moving at near-record speed, I had two choices. I could rescue the woman or record this momentous SKUM event for history.

"Where are you from?" I shouted to the woman.

"I'm from the North," she said.

I snapped the picture.

I don't know what I would have done if she had been from North Carolina.

Anyway, as you may know, the kudzu went into remission minutes later and the highway was to reopen at 6 a.m. today.

The only permanent loss was that of 17 tourists from the North, and the governor's office said that this would have no significant effect on state tourist revenues.

(8/14/91 WSJ)

CHAPTER 6

Potpourri (Mixture)

Potpourri—a mixture of fun and odd characters—tells of George, the safecracker; and reveals ALL on how real Americans eat corn on the cob. It tells how President Harry Truman's visit left behind a bit of folklore. The fall of the Union Suit and an interview with a possible future Lady President are recorded here. This chapter is a must for transplanted Yankees who need to know how to cook greens.

For Best Southern Greens: Launder Well

One of the hardest things about being a Southerner is retraining Yankees who have learned that there are places to live without freezing their knitzes off six months a year.

Therefore, so that hundreds of individuals won't have to perform each educational task, I am starting a Retraining by Newspaper program. Today's installment deals with greens—collard, mustard, turnip, creasy, kale and so on.

Every good Southern cookbook tells how to cook greens. Most, however, do not adequately describe the process of preparing them for cooking.

First, cut out the stem. (When you become adequately reconstructed, you may want to skip this step.)

Now, we come to a very important part: washing the greens. When you have enough greens to fill a two-gallon container, put them in a bathtub and run water over them until the tub is two-thirds full. Stir vigorously with a canoe paddle for 20 minutes. Drain tub.

Repeat above step.

Repeat again.

Now, remove the greens to your kitchen sink. Run water over front and back of each leaf while scrubbing it with a greens brush, which is available in most Southern hardware or department stores.

Dry the greens in your clothes dryer for 20 to 30 minutes on warm setting. This is very important because it has somewhat of a vacuum effect that removes particles that water can somehow miss.

Next, if at all possible, find a fast-running unpolluted stream. Put your greens in a greens net and tie it to a rock or tree limb, with the greens net in the fast-running water. Leave for eight hours or overnight.

Now, hang your greens on a clothesline and dry them with an air hose. If you do not have an air hose, most Southern vacuum cleaners are equipped with an airflow-reverse feature to serve this purpose. Borrow your neighbor's. She will be delighted to know that you are cooking greens, and she will be happy to help you.

The next step is very important. Without it, you just won't enjoy your greens after they are cooked.

Wash the greens in your clothes washer, including spin-dry cycle. Most Southerners do this only once or twice, but being a beginner, you may want to repeat the step several times.

Next, many people like to repeat the clothes-dryer treatment, but I feel that this is optional. In any case, it is certainly unnecessary to use any heat in the dryer this time. Just let the greens spin in cool air for 30 minutes or so.

Next, put your greens in the net again and take them down to your local fire department. There, they will be hung on a greens rack and hosed down. This is a free service that all Southern fire departments provide.

Keep in mind, however, that there may be others ahead of you, and greens require two hours of hosing on each side. For this reason, many Southerners prefer to buy their own fire hoses, although this can be costly because the city charges $340 to put in a special valve to increase your water pressure.

Your greens are now ready for cooking. Just follow any Southern cookbook recipe. When your two gallons of greens are done, they will have cooked down somewhat. You should, however, have at least four servings.

There will be a little sand and grit in them, but you will get used to this.

Our next installment will deal with okra. If you have no pets or livestock, you may want to skip this one. *(11/12/77 The Sentinel)*

Survey Is Way Off on How to Eat Corn

Well, people, the statisticians have been at it again.

This time, they're not messing around or up with anything as trivial as an election.

This time, they're hitting close to home.

Maybe you already saw what they said in that news report last week—the one about the book *The First Really Important Survey of American Habits* by Mel Poertz and Barry Sinrod.

I don't mean the part saying that only one of three Americans wash their belly buttons daily. That was no surprise.

What bothered me was this:

"Eighty percent eat corn on the cob by going around the ear in a circle; 20 percent nibble from side to side."

Can you believe that?

Of course, you can't!

You know, and I know, that the majority of red-blooded Americans eat their corn on the cob from side to side, three or four rows at a time, then go back and repeat the process until the ear is stripped.

Convinced that the authors were subversives out to mess up our minds, if not our behavior, I rushed off to the K&W on Coliseum Drive to gather a refute with another of my totally impartial scientific surveys.

To be truthful, however, a few respondents didn't treat me or my questions with a great deal of respect or dignity.

"This is crazy!" said Thelma Cavin, a visiting Charlottean. "You mean they're *paying* you for this? This is vital statistics—a little bit corny."

Then, adding injury to insult, she continued:

"I think I eat mine *around* the ear. Yes, I do. I'm sure."

I was wounded, but not mortally. Mrs. Cavin' s husband, Miller, an octogenarian who seemed a level-headed sort, said:

"I take about three rows and come *across*. When I finish that, I go back to the left-hand side and eat another three rows. The city folk, they use these little handles. But I just pick the ear up with my hands, butter and all."

Now, it was 50-50. And elsewhere in the cafeteria, things started turning the way of truth, beauty and justice. Which is to say, my way.

Except, oddly, at another table full of Charlotteans. There, Mary Maxwell and Pearl Maxwell reported eating their corn from side to side, but Herbert N. Maxwell and Jackie Miller said that they go around the corn in a full circle before moving laterally.

I thought of dropping Charlotte residents from my sample, since it's a kind of weird place. On the other hand, I knew it's no weirder than New York City, which was probably included in the national sample.

I decided to go ahead and leave everyone in, although I must say that it was refreshing to run into a bunch of simple, normal RJR employees from Winston-Salem.

Among them, sharing a table, were Steve Tucker, Tom Cleary and John Powell.

"I eat mine left to right—whatever you call that," said Tucker. "Why? Who knows? Why do you read a newspaper from left to right?"

Cleary broke in: "Why do funeral homes put all the expensive caskets on the left side of the room? Because that's where people look…I'm a four-row man. I eat it left to right. Don't know why. My wife does the same thing."

Tucker broke back in, eyeing me suspiciously: "Was this survey financed by the federal government?"

I assured him it wasn't.

He proceeded, saying he used to just slather the butter on the corn with a knife, until his wife instructed him that the proper way was to score the corn with a sharp knife first so it would absorb the butter. "She's from up North," he explained.

Tucker shook his head. "I put the butter on the dish and roll the corn around," he said.

Finally, Powell joined in, looking intense, as if I had hit on a subject of some importance to him.

"I eat my corn from right to left, about four rows [at a time], very system-atically," he said. "When I get through with an ear of corn, it's stripped com-pletely. I usually complete a row before I'll take a bite of some other food….

"It irritates me a lot to see someone eat corn and just bite it anywhere and then roll it over and take another bite. When they're finished, about 15 per-cent of the corn is still left on the cob. It's a mess. My ex-wife ate her corn that way."

It struck me that his tone and emphasis may have implied some connec-tion between the eating habits and the ex. I couldn't be sure, however, and didn't want to be rude enough to ask.

Nearby was another unanimous table. This time, James Gobble and Ronnie Long were actually *eating* corn on the cob—from side to side—while table partner, Wayne Hester, lunched on other vegetables.

"It's a whole lot neater that way," said Gobble.

Added Long: "It just seems the natural thing to do."

And Hester: "I go from one end to the other and then I go back again. I start on the left side."

In the end, only five of 20 respondents admitted to eating corn on the cob by going around the ear in a circle. (Three of those were from Charlotte. Draw your own conclusions.)

The rest, 75 percent, nibbled from side to side.

Why?

"I thought everybody did it that way," said Sylvia Davis.

Not quite, Ms. Davis. But close enough.

And thanks for helping me shoot down those ridiculous findings by the authors of *American Habits.*

I can't imagine what possessed them to publish such a ridiculous set of findings.

Unless they're from Charlotte. That would explain a lot.   *(10/15/89 WSJ)*

Safe Jobs Paid Well, But...

George retired some years ago after a 40-year career as both a tradesman and a businessman.

His trade was safecracking.

His business was bootlegging.

He did well at both, really, and his chief regret today seems to be those four prison stretches he did.

"I went into the safecrackin' business in the 1920s," he said. "I opened my first safe in Toledo...."

"I was workin' for 75 cents a hour and got to gamblin' with some friends and won $1,100, but I used it up gamblin' some more. This fella says, 'I know where we can get some money.'"

It was a safe job. The friend told him where to set his punch and how to hit it; he followed instructions, and a safe with $1,800 in it just flopped open.

At that point, George told me this week, "I says, 'Oh-eh, I done learned me a trade.'"

As far as money went, it was a good trade.

"We used to leave from here, go up through Virginia, West Virginia, Ohio, Tennessee, Kentucky, sometimes Georgia, and then back. We never did come back in here with under $5,000 each in our pockets. And in the 1930s, things was tough."

His best safe job was $200,000, "countin' everything that ever came out of it," and his fastest was three minutes. "We was drinkin' pretty heavy that night, and this fella told me, 'If you open the S.O.B. in three minutes, I'll give you my cut.' Of course, it also worked vice versa, but I opened it. He was a good 'un."

The bootlegging, hauling out of Virginia and Tennessee, came a bit later, but it was no less lucrative.

"Back then, you could get all the liquor you wanted for $1 a gallon.... Today, you'll pay up to $26 for a case of six gallons.

"They made good liquor then. You don't find that kind of liquor anymore."

And back then, it was possible to ditch the law at Mount Airy and get back into Winston-Salem safely, even if it meant back roads and 60 miles out of your way. After all, you had such things as smokescreens tied into your exhaust, and "you get behind me, your — has had it."

And, too, "Now they can radio ahead and get you."

But it wasn't a radio that got George. It was a trip through the Great Smoky Mountains National Park, carrying "132 gallons and a pint." Seems George had a faulty light on his car, and he explained to the officer that he was going to get it fixed, but the officer decided to shake the car down.

That cost George three years. "The judge was passin' out suspended sentences left and right," he said, "and when he got to me, he run out."

That might have been because the judge developed a sudden case of acid indigestion, or because George had jumped bond, but it didn't matter. He went straight to the federal penitentiary in Atlanta, without passing go.

It was George's last stretch, and he's now working at a regular job, though he's at an age when most people would be collecting Social Security.

"I got through with that," he said simply of his life of crime, but he did have some fascinating thoughts based on those years. Among them:

—On safecracking: "Today, a fella will try to rip [peel the back off] one. You can start up in the corner and try to rip it. You can get into the combination box, but…it takes longer." George feels that even blowing a safe, as opposed to drilling or punching, is better than ripping, though he gave up that practice long ago.

—On prisons: "I wouldn't go through any of it again, but I'll take Atlanta [federal] before I would a state. It's damn nice. You can watch TV, listen to the radio.…I worked in the kitchen three months.…On industrial, you make money and can spend $15 a month. I got out with a satchel and $500 that was sent to a parole officer in North Carolina. You take a state prison, it's rough."

—On Summerfield Martin, celebrated local safecracker and frequent prison escapee: "You got to watch him. He's…one of the biggest cowards I've ever known. I seen someone slap him around and threaten him, and he did nothing. He couldn't kick his way out of a paper bag until he teamed up with me.…He come out of the pen and was workin', and then he tied up with me. He didn't know what a safe was until then. He couldn't open a can of pork and beans."

(11/17/73 The Sentinel)

"The Last Democratic Seats in the House"

So often, we fail to give proper credit. Here we are in a very preservation-minded city, where even a gasoline station has been placed on the National Register of Historic Sites, or whatever you call it.

At this moment we have people engaged in the lofty battle to preserve everything from factory buildings to rundown houses.

Yet who's given Grover McNair the credit he so obviously deserves? No one.

To rectify that oversight, I must go back to 1951, when Harry Truman came to town to turn over the first spadeful of earth for the new Wake Forest University.

An outhouse had been put up on the site, mostly in case someone in the presidential party had need for it. Sure enough, said a gentleman who was close to the scene, the president himself had a call just as he arrived, and he asked something like, "Where in goodness' sake could a fellow find a bathroom around here?" (Those may not have been Truman's exact words.) Whereupon, the president and Secret Service were led or pointed toward the "facility."

The outhouse—a two-seater—was to be demolished after the ceremony.

Enter McNair, then a young architect and now in the contracting business here—and always public-spirited. McNair was aided in his public service by another architect. Or, as he put it, the two of them were "just some young fellows who wanted to have a piece of history. And they [the seats] were available at no cost."

So McNair and the friend removed the board and the two seats. "We did not remove the outhouse," McNair said in a recent chat, "which does distract from the glamour of the [original] story. We placed these two seats in a rustic outhouse at my cabin at High Rock Lake."

Outside the structure was a pine post. "We hung a Confederate flag from the pole outside the outhouse," said McNair.

He did not say anything about having a premonition that the next year was going to be a big one for Republicans, but apparently he had some idea of what was to come.

"We put a plaque up on the wall which read, 'The Last Democratic Seats in the House,'" said McNair. "And those toilet seats still exist today."

Please note that all this was done without a federal grant, or even a committee, let alone a broad-based organization.

I cannot speak for *The Sentinel*, but I, for one, salute Grover McNair. And I hereby nominate his outhouse for inclusion in the National Register of Historic Seats.

(10/9/80 The Sentinel)

The Union Suit Must Not Fall

Time was, when Mother Nature called in the middle of a cold winter's night, you cursed the inconvenience but were ever so grateful for your Union Suit.

That suit, with its flap of varying shape and dimension, made it possible to negotiate the hazards of the outdoor privy without freezing a very sensitive part of the anatomy.

Why did you stop making Union Suits? —ALLIE BROWN

Quite naturally, I was shocked to learn recently that Washington Mills—the next-to-last major producer—had stopped making the Union Suit, consigning it to the ever-growing list of endangered species.

There seemed nothing to do but go out to Washington Group headquarters on Trenwest Drive and protest.

"Why did you stop making Union Suits?" I demanded of Mary Jane Beavers, the receptionist.

She gaped, gasped, giggled and guffawed, acting as if she had never seen a newsman before. "I didn't know we did," she said, finally.

Rosann Clark's response was no more satisfactory.

"I beg your pardon," said Mrs. Clark, between giggles. "I'm with Convenient Systems. Ask me about the Mayberry stores."

Nearby, Ed Allman, a lawyer for the company, stood smirking. Being a long-time newsman, however, I am accustomed to the occasional expression of contempt from the public. I persevered.

Raymond Lamb, the company controller, said little more than, "You do look cute in that. I'll have to admit it." (Aha, I thought. It's the casual clothing; these people are so used to suit and tie that anything else looks odd to them. I wondered if they realized that they were laughing at their own product.)

Even Joyce Stone, with whom I have been acquainted for years, was of little help.

"You're Tom Sieg, aren't you?" she asked.

"Of course," I replied. "Didn't you recognize me?"

"Not without your clothes on, I didn't," she said.

It was obvious by this time that if I was going to get anywhere I would have to go straight to the top—to Robert Vaughn, the company's chief executive officer.

Vaughn walked out, started to extend his hand, then said, "Oh, no," and ducked back into his office. Unrelenting, I ignored the snub and followed him.

After he warmed to the subject, Vaughn reminisced about the old, old days.

"Many, many years ago," he said, "Washington Mills started out making just yarn. Hanes used to buy the yarn from us. We used to kid about the fact that when Hanes started making their own yarn, they forced us into the underwear business."

For many years, underwear was the company's only product, with Union Suits selling by the pound. The basic line consisted of a white, an off-white and a gray that was popular in the coal fields because it didn't show dirt and grime.

Production hit a peak of 6 million Union Suits a year shortly after World War II. But in that war, the U.S. Navy had developed thermal underwear, and for the Union Suit that meant that, sooner or later, the bottom was going to drop out.

This year, only about 240,000 Union Suits came off the one sewing line that was left producing them. Then the company quietly quit making them.

"You know," said Vaughn, "it really was kind of a traumatic thing for those old ladies up there [at the Mayodan plant]. I guess the Union Suit was kind of their security blanket."

The explanations did not totally satisfy me, but there seemed little further that could be done about the demise of the Union Suit. I left, having decided that I had raised enough of a flap.

So to speak.

(12/2/78 The Sentinel)

You Can't Call a Man First Lady

Joy Davis isn't sure she'll be able to attend the inauguration of Jimmy Carter as President of the United States.

"I think I should," she said yesterday. "I think I should, at least, go to somebody's inaugural because when you like a person and he wants you to come…you should go."

Friday, Joy received her official invitation to "view and take part in" the Jan. 20 inaugural ceremony and parade. Her parents, Mr. and Mrs. Harding Davis of 2824 Shorefair Drive, were not included because the 1977 Inaugural Committee doesn't know about them.

It all began when Joy, who is 7 years old, wrote Carter a letter last spring, while he was running in the primaries.

To Joy, whose bearing and speech are like a thoughtful and sophisticated young adult's, it was natural that she should support Carter.

"He's a great man," she said, "and I really think I should help a person as good as he is. He is one of the greatest Americans in the whole world.

"I really wanted him to know how much I wanted him to win. And I liked him more than any other person who was running, because of the things he said he would change and, otherwise, because of how nice he was.

"I said, 'I would like to help you get elected, and I would like it because you have the best heart of the people who are running.'

"I wrote some of my friends' names and said that they wanted him to win. And I told him he would make the best president so far.

"I asked some of my friends, and I had more than 17 people—and that's a lot in second grade—I had them to do little things and go around to some of the kids and get *them* to want Carter, too."

Joy feels very special because of the invitation, and she doesn't intend to forget. If Carter lives long enough, she intends to invite him to *her* inauguration when she becomes president, which because of age restrictions will be at least 28 years from now.

She has no doubts that she will reach that lofty position.

"I think I *should* be president," she said matter-of-factly, "because I have all the right interests in politics and because I'm really quite honest. And I think the people would appreciate my leadership."

Joy's platform isn't complete yet, but if kids could vote and run for office, she'd probably be a threat right now.

"I would change kids' allowances," she said. "I want the nation to be able to afford to give the kids $10 a *week*.

"I would also make it so that everyone could buy the necessary things for their kids. If people can't afford to buy the necessary things, then what *can* they afford?

"I'd make it so grown-ups *and* adults don't have to pay so much of their money in taxes.

"I would also change the noise on the school buses if I could. That *might* be possible. I mean the noises like they're yelling ignorant things at people when they get off the bus. I ought to know. It happens to me all the time....

"I'd make it so that every store would give out a lollipop to every parent with a kid. I'd rather have lollipops because I don't like chocolate that much."

Joy plans to get a law degree, but she's not sure where. She doesn't know how she plans to kill time between her graduation and her own inauguration, either, but she has some ideas.

"I'm going to try to think of some other ways to help people," she said.

In the meantime, will she go to Congress, or perhaps to the statehouse?

"I'd rather be governor first."

And when she does become president, what is her husband going to be known as?

"You can't call a man a First Lady," said Joy. "I'll call him the First Man, because he might not be a gentleman." *(1/5/77 The Sentinel)*

CHAPTER 7

Newshounds at Bay

Newspaper people face many obstacles during their workday. Here, we mention only a few: the difficulties in combatting and dealing with editors (not to mention, the law); the tyranny of the deadline; the struggles faced in carrying out the daily assignments; the frustration of diligently digging out information only to find out it will not be used.

Nevertheless, newspapering, according to Tom Sieg, "was indeed the maddest, gladdest work."

The Final Stories by "an Occult Hand"

It was in 1967, I believe, that I resigned in the morning, changed my mind during lunch, was fired at 1 p.m., got my job back at 2 and quit again by 4.

The next morning, of course, I reported to work as usual.

That was life on *The Charlotte News*, where a columnist once got so upset at being unable to meet his deadline that he pitched his typewriter out a third-story window, not bothering to check to see if there were people on the pavement below.

It was a wild and crazy crew.

Oh, I know: All old newsmen say that about the old days and old papers. But this is gospel.

I well remember the night that the police were summoned to pursue the newspaper's associate editor, city editor, editor-to-be and police reporter, a-mong others. They had illegally entered their own newspaper's premises, stolen a ladder and other equipment and materials, and brazenly—with much work and planning aforethought—converted the company's billboard into an advertisement for *The New York Times*. Then they successfully eluded the police. The next morning, of course, they reported to work as usual.

That all occurred during an initiation into the Order of the Occult Hand, which was born at *The News* during my years there and spread across the continent. One earned eligibility for membership by slipping the words "It was as though an occult hand had reached out and..." into the paper.

We even had our own logo, painted in oil: a bloody stump of a hand coming out of a purple cloud. One of our distinguished members once sneaked the painting into a position of honor among works in a traveling exhibit at the Mint Museum. More impressively, when the exhibit was about to move on, he sneaked it back down and out.

Then there was the annual Gold-Plated Beep-Beep Award, given to the staffer judged to have the nastiest temperament and fewest redeeming social qualities. I won it the instant I became eligible. I'll never forget the words of Jim Banbury, now a Presbyterian minister but then a veteran newsman, at the awards banquet. Jim wishes I would, but I won't.

I suppose that kind of craziness came to an end a long time ago. Now, as of Nov. 1, *The Charlotte News* is coming to its end, joining *The Sentinel* and other members of the endangered species we call p.m. newspapers.

Readers will miss *The Charlotte News*. It was, for 97 years, a good newspaper.

It was fashionable, in the Charlotte of the 1960s, for staff members of *The Observer* to revile those who worked for *The News*, and vice versa. If you worked for one newspaper, the other lacked professionalism and integrity. It made no sense, but it didn't have to.

I was fortunate. I worked for *The Observer* first and then for *The News*. Thus, I came to know the strengths of fine journalists on both sides: Kays Gary on *The Observer*, for example, and John Kilgo on *The News*.

It was during my tenure as city editor that the nation's "most-wanted" fugitive was arrested in Charlotte. He had been pursued from the scene of a bank robbery by Gary, of all people. It was later learned that the robber had been living with a church-choir member, but her identity was so closely guarded that the media's best and most exhaustive efforts had failed to break the curtain of secrecy.

I turned to Kilgo.

"Killer," I said, "I know the cops and the FBI have said we're never going to get close to that woman. But it's too damn big a story. I want you to find her and interview her. Promise her anything, but get the story."

Later that day, he got back to me.

"Sieg-O," he said oh-so-casually, "I've found her. I'm going to interview her tonight. Is there anything else I can do for you?"

It was, indeed, the maddest, gladdest work.

Other workhorses, wheelhorses and thoroughbreds helped make the memories of those years, of course. A few remain in Charlotte, but most are scattered across the land. To name one or several would be to cheat others. I hope that they have some of the same feelings when they think of me that I have when thinking of them.

Losing *The Charlotte News* is regrettable, but I have learned that there is life after p.m. newspapering.

Besides, all is not lost.

Just Tuesday, on page 3B of *The Charlotte Observer*, the following appeared as a bold-faced lead-in on an item about Australia's cult-like devotion to the movie "The Blues Brothers":

"It Was As If A Cult Hand…"

It's not perfect, but the spirit lives.

And that counts for a lot.   *(10/18/85 WSJ)*

A Question Often Put to a Lot of Journalists

Why do people get into the newspaper business?

That question always takes me back to my first "job" in the so-called game. I was a student at the University of Missouri School of Journalism, in Columbia, and that meant I had to report for the daily city newspaper, the *Missourian*.

One night at about 11, a photographer walked into the Campus Snack, where I was having a beer with a fellow student who has since become a respected North Carolina journalist.

"I just heard over my police radio that three local people have been kidnapped by an escaped mental patient," said the photographer. "They've got the guy pinned down in Kirkwood, and they're in the middle of a shootout."

Kirkwood was 120 miles away, which, of course, meant that the victims would have had to have been taken that distance by force—gunpoint, as it turned out—before the shootout.

"Well," I said, "let's get the hell out of here."

We almost immediately began telephoning law-enforcement authorities, only to discover that they knew absolutely nothing about the case. We tried the highway patrol, the sheriff's department in St. Louis County and even the St. Louis police, although St. Louis is independent and totally separate from the county that bears the same name.

We called Jefferson City, the capital of Missouri, and learned nothing.

We even called other newspapers, as well as radio and television stations, to find out if they had heard anything. They hadn't.

Finally, at about 4 in the morning, I decided to wake up Pearlie Lukeheart, a Boone County deputy sheriff who I had long believed was the closest thing to a law-enforcement officer in the area.

"I haven't heard a thing," said Pearlie.

"Bill," I said to the photographer, "I think you got hold of some bad information or some bad beer, one."

"No," he said. "We've just got to keep trying."

I made another call to the suburban St. Louis highway patrol station, and sure enough, a report had come in. It turned out that Pearlie had also gotten the information by then, and he told us that the kidnap victims had been returned to Columbia. He gave us their address and told us that the house was in back of another, and very hard to find.

We found it.

We also found three people who had just had a very harrowing experience, and who had been home for just a short time. There was a husband and a wife, and her brother.

The wife was ready to pour out her soul, which is a situation we newspaper people love. She told of her fears for her life and the mental patient's attempts to reassure her with such great quotes as, "I'm not going to hurt you. Women weren't meant to be hurt; they were meant to be loved."

Her husband filled in the nuts-and-bolts details, such as his figuring out a way to short out the car's electrical system as he was driving on the highway—a move that ultimately allowed the highway patrol to come in and capture the kidnapper.

By the time we were ready to leave the house, our interviews and calls to the patrol had produced enough information for a main story and two others. Just as I was about to reach for the door, there was a knock.

It was my competitor from the *Columbia Tribune*, with his photographer.

The competitor introduced himself to the lady I had just interviewed for over two hours, and she collapsed, sobbing, "I just don't want to talk about it anymore," she said. "I can't."

That suited me just fine. It also suited me when I walked into the newsroom and found a very nervous city editor who had been looking for an available reporter.

"Sieg," said the editor, "I just got a call saying that three people have been kidnapped."

Before he could say much more, I held out my notebook, patted it and said, "It's all in here. Bill is processing the pictures right now."

It was not to come as a surprise, later that day, when Bill and I got the entire front page except for one brief story. But, at that point, there was work to be done.

I wrote my stories, waited around while the city editor scanned them and then, already having worked about 12 consecutive hours, ran off to do my daily duty of covering the sheriff's department and the courts, despite the fact that I was feeling a bit ill. Just as I got to the court clerk's office, the telephone rang, and it was for me.

"Tom, this is Bill Bickley," said my news editor. For a brief moment, I was sort of thrilled, because I assumed he had called to tell me what a great job I had done.

"Yes, sir," I said.

"In this kidnapping story," he said, "you refer to this guy's shorting out the car's battery and having to stop at a service station. But you don't say whether he had to get a new battery or just have the old one recharged. Can you clear that up for me?"

"No, sir," I said. "I don't know." There was a pause.

"Dammit, Sieg," said Bickley. "You've got to learn to ask these questions."

He hung up. It was the only comment any editor on the paper made on the stories.

Couple Got Help from Savvy Source

Periodically, when a young reporter complains about a news-gathering failure or frustration, I offer a standard bit of advice.

"Think of it this way," I say. "Anyone who can learn to report effectively in Winston-Salem can report *anywhere!*"

Why do I say that? Because ours is a stick-together town, a circle-the-wagons town, a place where business, funny or otherwise, is done behind closed doors and mouths. Public exposure is viewed as cancer-causing and every leak as a thinning of the ozone layer.

To illustrate my point, I have been known to tell a story or two about Charlotte, that city on the make where only a tetanus epidemic could keep a significant number of mouths closed for long.

A favorite among those tales, and one I can't conceive of unfolding here, concerns Pat Hall, the Mecklenburg County industrialist and developer once considered a potential governor of the state, and Ben Douglas the elder, the owner of Douglas Furs and other enterprises and a beloved former mayor of Charlotte.

It began, for me, when an aging couple came to my office at the old *Charlotte News* to ask for my help. I remember their tears, not their exact words, but their plea went something like this:

"We just finished building our dream retirement home down on the Catawba River and moved into it last month. This is a home we built with our own hands, over the past several years, just hoping to live out our lives peacefully there.

"But the other day a man came to our door and said a company he represented was buying up property in the area. He said they were willing to pay us $18,000 for our house, take it or leave it. He said if we didn't take it, we'd be mighty unhappy living among the stuff that would go up around us."

It was a standard tactic. While $18,000 wasn't a terribly low price for a small, three-bedroom home in those days, the offer itself said that it must be worth more to the developer.

I told the man and woman to go home, sit tight, and do nothing until they heard further from me. Then I called Douglas, who seemed to know everything that was going on in Mecklenburg County, and told him I'd like to drop by and drink a cup of coffee with him. He said to come on, so I did.

First, I told him the story of the aging couple, dwelling at some length on their dashed hopes and dreams, and the tears they had shed at seeing their future so callously threatened.

"Mr. Douglas," I said, "what the devil is going on down there at the river? Is Pat Hall up to something?"

It was a good guess. The old man, a truly delightful person whose heart-strings often opened his purse to those in need, nearly choked up at hearing of the couple's plight. Then a smile broke over his face, and he excused himself to go to an inner office. When he returned, he was carrying a set of maps and plats detailing *exactly* what Pat Hall was up to down on the river.

For the next two hours, I went over the documents as Douglas explained and interpreted. Before leaving his office, I called the couple and asked them to meet me at my office. When they arrived, I greeted them with a genuine smile and asked them to be seated.

"You will probably end up wanting to sell your property," I said. "But you will *not* want to sell it for $18,000. You see, your house is in the very heart of a new development that is absolutely crucial to Pat Hall.

"The project is going to be called Carowinds. Let me tell you about it…"

A year later, after I had left *The News* to go to work as promoter of Beech Mountain and its Land of Oz theme park, Pat Hall dropped by the mountaintop for a visit.

I took him down to the then-illegal open bar in the Beech Tree Inn and bought him—us—a drink. Then, not having heard from the couple about their house since our last talk, I succumbed to curiosity. "Tell me, Pat," I said. "How did things work out with all the land you needed to acquire for Carowinds?"

"Oh, great," he said. "We did well—except in a couple of cases. You know, there was this one old couple, we offered them $18,000 for their land, and I thought for sure we had them. Then something happened, and they wouldn't sell. You know, we wound up paying them *$92,000* for their little old house."

I shook my head, as if in disbelief. *"No!"* I said. *"Really?"*

Should I, or Ben Douglas, have felt guilty about causing Pat Hall such extra expense? I think not. Had the situations been reversed, and had Hall's emotions been played upon as I played upon Douglas', he would probably have done the same thing.

Douglas and Hall have long since died, and I have not known news sources like them in years—and never in Winston-Salem.

On the other hand, maybe it's not the difference in towns. Maybe it's the difference in times. Maybe they just don't make 'em that way anymore.

(5/24/91 WSJ)

This Proves That It Is Possible to Tell a Reporter's Notes from Garbage

The trouble with you readers is that you have no appreciation of the agony reporters and editors endure to bring you the stories in your daily newspaper.

In my time, to get a story or column, I have had to do things that would appall or sicken the average person: drinking four-hour-old Ashe County white liquor, placing myself between the law and a wanted man, even walking behind the elephants in a circus parade.

And did you appreciate my pain? No. And Monday, when you read the *Business Journal* coverage of the recent conference of the United States-Japan Association, you won't appreciate what Richard M. Barron went through to bring you that, either.

Well, let me tell you something. If not for a lucky twist of fate, Barron might have spent last week in therapy rather than here, writing.

His story is worth telling—and reading—not only because of the drama and trauma, but because it proves once and for all that it is possible to tell a newspaper reporter's notes from garbage. But I am getting ahead of the tale.

It began with one of those business-type meetings at The Homestead resort at Hot Springs, Va. Barron's job was to interview Gov. James G. Martin and other dignitaries, and to cover some of the talks.

Like most such meetings, this one didn't know when to end, and Barron found himself at one of those dull, wind-it-down sessions.

"It was an especially boring program," he said.

"I'd gotten all the interviews I needed and was just serving my time."

Finally, he picked up his briefcase and came home to write his stories. And then, when he opened his briefcase the next day to get his notes out, it happened: that chilling moment we all wait for in horror movies, only to cover our eyes or ears when it comes.

The notebook wasn't there!

Being a highly trained professional journalist, Barron went to pieces very quietly.

"Fearing the recriminations of editors," he said, "I made a call to the Homestead from the privacy of my apartment at lunchtime, without telling anybody. I called lost and found. A nice woman named Lynn Lockridge said she would be glad to look down in the convention hall, but they probably had cleaned it out already.

"I wasn't even positive I'd left it up there."

Barron couldn't know it at the time, but Ms. Lockridge was about to go

Journal *reporter Richard M. Barron studies his rescued notes.* –COOKIE SNYDER

far beyond the extra mile for him.

"We knew that it was an important conference," she said when reached by telephone. "And when he called, he seemed like it was life or death that he find those notes. I'm sure it was."

Then began a drama that should have been captured for a sales brochure: Ms. Lockridge getting in touch with the convention setup crew and having its members search the hall and then go through the convention garbage. Luckily, it had not yet been Dumpsterized.

"About an hour later," said Barron, "she called me back and said the convention staff had found it....They had gone through the trash for the whole day's conference....It was waterlogged, but never fear:

"She was ironing the pages one by one and stacking them up to dry!"

Barron, being young in the newspaper business and relatively unjaded, believed her. It was good that he did, because it was true. "Two days later," he said, "I received a manila envelope with a nice 1-inch pile of ironed notebook paper."

He had the notebook pages at his desk to prove what he was saying. And in a cover letter, Ms. Lockridge—who had spent 90 minutes ironing the pages to dry them and make them legible—said: "It was a pleasure being of service to you, and I hope you enjoyed visiting Hot Springs and The Homestead."

Later, by telephone, she said that, although this was something more than a routine case, "We do a lot of little extra things for our guests."

Meanwhile, Barron pored over his salvaged notes, some of them ink-smeared but all at least minimally legible. From them, he wrote the copy that appears in Monday's *Business Journal*.

And after all that, you'd better read it.

If you don't, we may have to consider canceling your subscription.

(10/26/86 WSJ)

News Folks "Slip a Cog"

A newsroom operates like a well oiled machine; every part, every cog, must serve its purpose smoothly and efficiently, or deadlines simply will not be met.

For example, let us look at an assignment that was carried out this week. It didn't just come about; The Boss started planning it almost a week ahead of time.

"We want to do an expanded man-in-the-street interview about the census forms and people's reaction to them," said The Boss. "I figure maybe you and Janet [Fox] can do the interviews, and you can put the story together."

Sure, I said. No sweat.

The Boss coordinated the effort with The Boss of the photography department, so that the possibility of foul-ups would be minimized.

Finally, assignment day arrived, and I decided to check with Allie Brown, the photographer I was to go with.

"Who's the other photographer?" I asked.

"What other photographer?" said Allie. "I'm it, and we'd better get it done quick, because I've got another assignment right after it."

"But one photographer can't go out with two reporters," I protested weakly.

To which Allie replied something like, "No kidding? Golly gee, I believe you're right." But things were quickly straightened out; the Assistant Boss lined up another photographer.

At about 12:30, Allie came to me and said, "Let's go."

"But it's not time yet," I said. "I've got some things I have to do."

"It's 12:30," said Allie, "and my assignment is from 12:30 to 2:30."

"Gosh," I said, "the assignment I got said 1:30 to 3:30. We can't work an assignment together at different times."

"Golly gee," said Allie, "I believe you're right." I rushed through my other work, but it was still about 1:15 before we were able to leave.

"Nerslatz bunch of slobborians!" Allie said as we left. "I'm supposed to be back here by 2:30."

"Well," I said, to the best of my recollection at this point in time, "let's not complain. Let's just do the very best we can. How about stopping by Dunkin' Donuts. There's usually a pretty good cross-section of people there, and that should give us a good start."

We got off to a flying start with a couple of good short interviews.

"I'm going to try next door at Baskin-Robbins," I said.

"Okay," said Allie. "I'll just bring the pickup over there."

At the ice cream shop, I got more interviews, one of which was to be among the best of the day. But there was no Allie, and I wondered where he was.

I found him standing beside his partly backed-out pickup, still at Dunkin' Donuts. Behind his vehicle was a car with a brand-new crease in its left-rear quarter.

"Don't tell me," I said.

"Yep," said Allie.

While he waited for and dealt with the police, I dashed up and down the street, popping into service stations, banks, whatever. When he was finally ready to go again, time had already run out, but we were determined to get the story. Besides, I was assigned to get 20 interviews, and I had only 11.

"Before we go back," I told Allie, "let's just hit Hardee's and see what we find."

"Please," he said. "Let's don't be saying 'hit.'"

Three more interviews and we had to call it quits.

"Oh, well," I said, "let's just hope Janet got her 20"—which, of course, she had done.

All that was left was the writing.

This is just one small example of how your newspaper is put together each day. To be fair, I must admit that things sometimes don't go so smoothly.

(4/3/80 The Sentinel)

"Pulling Leg" Is Old Game That Newsmen Play Too

The devil made me love it when a young ABC-Television reporter made a national fool of himself last week while covering Hurricane Gloria.

He told the world that the Bonner Bridge over Oregon Inlet was built in a straight line, but had been twisted into its present sweeping S-shape by years of winds and tides.

Obviously, some coastal salty dog had netted a real trophy this time: a 170-pound inland sucker. I could visualize a weather-wizened Outer Banks fisherman cupping his chin, slapping his knee and shouting, "Did you hear that, Ma? The little whippersnapper fell for it!"

Pulling the reporter's leg is as old a game as pinning the tail on the donkey. It arose, I suppose, because news-gathering is a know-it-all business whose practitioners seldom seem to appreciate the value of humility.

It was, in fact, a game much played by newsmen themselves, until it began to dawn on publishers and other serious-minded people why those embarrassing little ridiculosities kept getting into the paper, or on the air. We who have played it, in recent years, have had to keep very low profiles and feign much innocence.

My only recent targets, in fact, were the youth-page correspondents who used to trek past my desk on their way to and from the office of their guru, Larry Queen. Being young, they were gullible. And being gullible, they were a lot of fun.

"Mr. Sieg," one of them once asked, "did they have color movies when you were young?"

"Oh, yes," I replied. "They'd had color for a long time, but it wasn't until the late 1930s that the big Technicolor extravaganzas like 'Gone With the Wind' came along. They were great, but I never got to see them in color."

The young man, puzzled, said something like, "Huh?"

"The theaters in my neighborhood didn't have color screens," I said. "Only the expensive downtown theaters like the Century had color, and we couldn't afford them."

He looked like a light bulb had gone off in his head.

"You know," he said, "I never thought about that."

There were other lies, of course, told mostly to young men. The women were more skeptical, harder to fool.

Once an aspiring young poet, college-bound, engaged me in a discussion of the language.

"The derivation of words is fascinating," I told him. "We grow up with words and assume they have always existed, but some of them are actually quite new. Flip through a good dictionary some time. Some of it will surprise you."

Like an unsuspecting fly, he stepped into my parlor, asking for examples.

"We were talking about poetry," I said. "Did you know that the term 'poet' was itself coined only in the late 19th century? Earlier, rhymers were called odists or versifiers, even bards. In his time, Shakespeare was a 'sonnetist.'"

Pausing only for oohs and ahhs, I proceeded.

"What happened was, young writers started to copy Edgar Allan Poe. Critics hated the trend. One, who wrote for the *New York Herald*, started referring to them sarcastically as 'Poe-Ettes,' or 'little Poes.' It caught on, and a word was born."

Lord, that young man was *impressed.*

"How do you find time to learn so much?" he asked.

It is our duty, I replied, to read voraciously.

As noted earlier, the young women were more of a challenge. Some, for no reason I could think of, didn't trust me at all. With them, I often resorted to grains of truth that they might be unfamiliar with, couching my story in a way that might make them refuse to believe it. The effect—fooling them—was the same.

Once, during a discussion of rubber products, I told a world-wise high-school senior that if it hadn't been for World War II, we might not have been able to produce the tires and other products that were so necessary to our prosperity.

She asked what I meant. Although my reverse-lie was so outrageous it seemed doomed to failure, I ventured forth.

"When I was young," I said, "about all we had was real rubber, the kind that comes from trees. We had to learn to mass-produce synthetic rubber because some of our supplies were being cut off. Besides, there weren't enough rubber trees in the world to meet wartime demand."

She was rolling her eyes by this time.

"Rubber trees?" she said. "Mr. Sieg, you're too much. How dumb do you think I am?"

I did not respond. Actually, she wasn't dumb at all; she was quite bright. But she was young, and she had to learn about grown-up deviousness and deception from someone.

I looked upon it as a solemn duty.

You don't think I'd do something like that just for fun, do you?

(10/2/85 WSJ)

Columnists Can't Know Everything

Poor George Will.

He's being bashed by everybody these days, from the critics to satirists to comic-strip cartoonists. As a highly popular newspaper and magazine columnist, he is, of course, a public figure. Thus he becomes what is known in the trade as a safe target.

So Will is being attacked in the *Doonesbury* strip, not to mention elsewhere, and accused of having assistants do all the research for references and allusions that make his work sound wise and profound.

In Tuesday's *Doonesbury*, a young man reported to work as the new "quote boy." His job was to consist of looking up quotes that would bolster the columnist's arguments and make him look—well, literary, perhaps, and extremely well-educated.

In short, George Will is being presented as a phony, a man whose work is contrived and produced partly by the labor of others to project and strengthen a carefully preconceived image.

Well, pooh. The truth is that newspaper columnists have *always* had to rely on such assistance. Even the intellectual giants such as Russell Baker and Art Buchwald, when switching almost daily from philosophical dissertation to penetrating historical analysis, cannot have every minuscule bit of needed information on the tips of their brain cells at all times.

If we went around attacking everybody who relies on the specialized knowledge of others, even I would be a target. Just the other day, while attempting to delve deeply into a national issue that had local implications, I found it necessary to call on my government girl, Betsi Robinson, for a bit of obscure information.

I simply asked Betsi for the information. Within minutes, the answer came flying back through my computer: "There are *eight* members of the Board of Aldermen."

Now, wasn't that efficient? Suppose I'd had to spend an hour looking that stuff up? There goes seven or eight bucks of the company's money. It wasn't just a matter of making myself look good. And I'll bet that's really all that Will is doing.

For example, he *must* have a verb boy—or girl. You can't do without that sort of thing these days. Take Monday, for example. I was puzzling over a verb usage: Should I say, "Joe Jones, along with others in his organization, has—or have—libeled me in a newsletter"? Sure I could go to the grammar books. But again, looking up something that tough would consume a lot of valuable time.

So I did what any columnist would do. I sent a message to my verb boy,

Richard Creed. He came back at me, zap: "'Has' is correct. Joe Jones, a singular noun, is the subject....The plural element provides additional information, and the commas surrounding it serve much as parentheses would, setting it off from the subject." Now, does that sound like I was trying to make myself look better than other people? Of course not. I just wanted the sentence to be grammatical. And what the heck, when you've got somebody like Creed around, why not use him?

Similarly, yesterday, I relied on my entertainment boy, Tom Travin. I wanted to cast a Civil War allusion—to the effect of the war on Southern planters, the upper crust—in a framework that the reader would identify with easily. I racked my brain with no success, and then I asked Travin if there wasn't a movie or something I could use.

He replied quickly: "'Gone With the Wind,' produced by David O. Selznick and directed by Victor Fleming, was released in film version in 1939." There followed a very thorough discussion of the movie, its story and stars. I was, quite frankly, very grateful. In fact, it sounded a lot like a movie I'd like to see, and I wondered how I'd missed it.

But I begin to ramble. Also in the past couple of days, I found out some other fascinating things in just the same way. For example, David Watson, my research boy, informed me that the place to go for a couple of bits of information was the *World Almanac*, which he said could be found under the rubble on top of my desk. Jim Laughrun, whom I'd best not call any kind of boy, explained that Pilot Mountain is called Pilot Mountain because it served for many years "as a guidepost by which travelers could steer, or pilot, themselves."

There is no substitute for this kind of thing, if our columns are to be— well, you know, depthy. In fact, it never ends. Each day when I report to work, my computer's message field is filled with so many responses to questions I have asked that I sometimes forget what my questions were. Yesterday's batch included "1921," "Humphrey Bogart" and "You'd better hope your wife doesn't find out you asked me that."

But enough. My point is simple: We columnists, like presidents of corporations, cannot compile all our own data and information. I mean, if we're going to have to do all that menial stuff, we might as well quit writing columns and go back to work.

I don't want that.

I'm sure George Will, who makes thousands of dollars a crack speaking to conventions and meetings, doesn't want it. After all, that's a pretty cushy deal, when you figure how little money you have to pay a speech boy.

Come to think of it, I don't have a speech boy. Maybe that's why I'm not rich.

(7/10/86 WSJ)

Editors Wrangle Cows in Quest for Truth

As a former city editor, I sometimes miss the front lines of the news business, where editors come to grips with the finer points and nuances that give a newspaper its special character and flavor.

Most readers would find it hard to believe the lengths to which some of those editors go, mostly unseen and unappreciated, to bring you the best and most polished product possible.

Hard to believe, that is, unless someone showed them. That's what I hope to do today: to demonstrate to readers the sensitivity and thoughtfulness of some of these unsung heroes.

What follows are actual messages exchanged by editors last Thursday, by way of the *Journal* computer. Don't be bothered if some of the content goes over your head. That happens to me, too. These are our intellectuals, our deep thinkers, our probers.

Here are those messages, with just a few comments.

Senior Editor 1 to Senior Editor 2: "I noticed that you fetched [called up] the story on the uses and origins of the word 'cowabunga,' as it is used in 'Teenage Mutant Ninja Turtles' and picked up by kids. The story quotes a dictionary as saying that the word originated with 1960s surfers.

"I may be wrong, and I don't know how it could be checked, but I would bet that the word goes back much further than that, and that it is of African origin, or at least a Western parody of African speech. I am fairly sure that I used to hear it in jungle movies ('Tarzan'?) of the 1940s and '50s, and that it was being used among the general populace even then."

Is that something? No inaccuracy or careless usage, no matter how small, is safe around these people. And they're quick. Before I could interject that "bunga" is a Transkeian native council in South Africa, the exchange continued.

Senior Editor 2: "Well, I'm glad to hear that, so I won't think I'm crazy. When I saw that story, I thought it was incorrect. I could have sworn they said 'cowabunga' on the 'Howdy Doody' show when I was a child. Didn't Clarabelle or somebody say 'cowabunga' on that show?"

Senior Editor 1: "Heavy, dude. I don't know about that. Ed [a reporter] suggests that I may be confusing 'cowabunga' with 'umgawa,' but I don't think so. Could it be 'umgawa' that Clarabelle or somebody was saying?"

Senior Editor 2: "Ha! Nah, 'umgawa' is more pure African, or rather pure Tarzan. 'Cowabunga' is an Americanized form. Clarabelle would have had to swing into the set on a vine if she (he?) had said 'umgawa.' Now we get to the question of Clarabelle. The person portraying Clarabelle was a man, but was the character a woman?"

Shazam! That's how it works in this business. An editor asks one question and it leads to another: Was Clarabelle the cow a man or a woman? No sooner had it been asked than this pithy response flashed back:

Senior Editor 1:
"I've never seen a transvestite cow.
"I never hope to see one.
"But I can tell you anyhow,
"I'd rather see than be one."

Boy, who wouldn't? But I digress. By this time, the exchange was drawing broader attention, with the entry first of Bossman Editor and then of SAM Editor.

Bossman Editor: "Anybody who doesn't remember 'Cowabunga, Buffalo Bob!' had a culturally deprived childhood."

SAM Editor: "'Umgawa' or 'ungawa' is of Tarzan fame. It may or may not be a real word. 'Umgawa, pacee pacee' is a famous command used in Tarzan movies to get people and animals moving. Other noted words: 'bwana' and 'juju.' Usually put together as 'Juju, Bwana,' when a porter saw signs of evil natives....I will check the word books on 'cowabunga.'"

Ah, the curious minds. Is this a great business or what? It was at 2:44 p.m., five hours and 41 minutes after the first message flashed, that the following ensued. (There was confusion when SAM Editor typed a "g" where a "b" should have been, but it was short-lived.)

SAM Editor: "'Kawagunga' (with a k-a, not c-o) was said by Chief Thunderthud, a character played by Bill Lecornec on 'Howdy Doody.'"

Senior Editor 1: "Well now, let me see if I have this straight: Are you trying to tell us that Clarabelle the cow yelled 'cowabunga' while Chief Thunderbird [sic] ran around shouting 'kawagunga!' Are you sure you haven't been to one too many Easter Sunrise Services and heard a little too much of that antiphonal playing by the Moravian band?"

SAM Editor: "No, only Thunderthud used 'kawabunga.'"

At last, the mystery was solved: "Cowabunga" was a minor corruption of "kawabunga," a word those 1960s surfers had grown up with as "Howdy Doody" kids.

Did I tell you these people were quick? They did all that in less than six hours! Oh, to be sure, they didn't get around to figuring out whether Clarabelle the cow(abunga!) was male or female, but that's a whole udder question. And as it turns out, we don't plan to use the story anyway.

But hey, that's what it's all about: truth, beauty, justice.

Lord, how I love this business! *(4/24/90 WSJ)*

Take My Cubicle—Please

The *Sentinel* news staff is once again in new quarters.

If others' friends are like mine, they have been eagerly awaiting this moment since it was announced that we were going to erect a new building.

There appears to be some confusion, however. That's why I am considering having an open house in my new office, which I am told is more than large enough for a gathering of my regular readers.

I think I'll start with some of the people I see regularly at prayer meeting, some of whom are among the curious.

"Oh," one of them said recently with a sad-sounding sigh, "I really did think you'd be in the new building."

"Well," I said, "actually, I like the old building. You know, it's a replica of Freedom Hall, and it's got real character. It would certainly be a shame and a disgrace to let such a fine old historic structure stand idle. Besides, they remodeled a whole floor for us."

"Gosh," she replied, "as important as you are, it must really be nice and plush."

"Rest assured," said I, "my new quarters are commensurate with the stature I enjoy within the company."

"Oh, good," she said, probably believing in all her innocence that my office was going to be something like that used by President Reagan or our company's production manager, Gene Carter.

Among the inquiries that have been hardest to deal with have been those about the carpet and draperies.

"No," I told a woman, "I wouldn't call the carpet real plush. That is, you don't sink down into it and stick. But it is quite lovely, sort of soft and velvety."

Unfortunately, she pressed further on the drapes.

"Frankly," I said, "I did not personally select drapes. I've been quite busy working on a series of articles about the Smoky Mountains, and I've just had to leave some things up to other people."

There have been other questions, of course, including a couple about the view—you know, how panoramic is it?

"It's a little hard to describe," I have said. "Being right downtown, it's not exactly a scenic vista, but as urban views go, it's not bad."

One friend, a doctor, inquired about the size and configuration of my office, and the furniture. It seems that in most businesses you can pinpoint your spot in the hunt-and-pecking order by such things. You know—real hardwood furniture, lots of it and a good bit of space mean you're in good shape.

"Actually," I said, "I don't think there's a single reporter on the newspaper more satisfied with his space and furnishings than I am. As for the furniture, my credenza is the same as the managing editor's, I think." (The word "credenza," as defined by Webster, leaves room for much interpretation.)

Sadly, I have also had to admit that there is no original art on my walls. I had thought of contacting Bob Timberlake or Larry Barton to see if one of those gentlemen would consider accepting a commission to do an original mural, but I doubt that either would have time for such a monumental undertaking. I haven't calculated the square footage that would have to be painted, but you simply wouldn't believe how much there is.

For now, the only thing I shall put on my wall will be a small poster that says, "Thank You for Holding Your Breath While I Smoke." This is a gentle dig at friends who have signs in their offices and waiting rooms smugly saying, "Thank You for Not Smoking."

Speaking of waiting rooms, I don't have one. Nor do I have a secretary. In fact, I have no filing cabinet of my own, and my visitor's chair is missing.

Which brings us to truth-telling time.

A few of us get private offices—people who deal with high-powered businessmen or ministers or very young people, any of whom might take offense at bizarre behavior or language.

The rest of us get cubicles.

Why do we get cubicles?

"Rest assured, my new quarters are commensurate with the stature I enjoy within the company." –DAVID ROLFE

We get cubicles because study after study has shown that when reporters are allowed to hide away behind walls and closed doors, they work crossword puzzles, indulge in sexual harassment, drink whiskey and charge long-distance telephone calls to the company.

When they are in cubicles, within the managing editor's line of vision, they spend fully 50 percent of their time working. This represents a 400 percent increase in productivity.

So there you have it, doctors, businessmen, junior executives: We don't get the drapes, picture windows, fancy furniture and furnishings and decorated walls that you people get.

Before you rub it in, however, pause a moment to reflect.

Do you get paid to spend five days in a glorious place such as the Smoky Mountains and, then, to come home and tell people about it?

Keep your status symbols and perks. I'll take my cubicle.

(6/11/84 The Sentinel)

Notes Throughout the Book

CHAPTER 1

Ruby Days: Oz Magic Gone
1. Loonis McGlohon, Alec Wilder (original music), "The Wonderful Land of Oz," (Navona Music Company, Charlotte, N.C., 1970).

CHAPTER 4

Anita Loos: A Blessing
2. Anita Loos, *Kiss Hollywood Good-By*, (The Viking Press, Inc., New York, N.Y., 1974).

Mary Mayo's Inspiration Lives on Through Her Songs
3. Loonis McGlohon, Alec Wilder (original music), "The Wonderful Land of Oz," (Navona Music Company, Charlotte, N.C., 1970).

Frankie Laine: Idol and Nice Guy
4. John Herring, "What Do You Do with an Old Old Song?," (Cannon Music, Golden Beach, Fl., 1969).

MG 10/08

ML

3/08